"To understand God we look to his Word, and to understand his Word we are dependent on the Old and New Testaments. What we discover is that amid the many stories is an underlying Story, which leads us to Jesus, Immanuel. Michael Williams ably goes book by book, offering suggestive and stimulating ways for us to see Christ as the climax of the Story; from this vantage point he then offers contemporary implications that should inform our lives. Let Williams begin to shape the way you read the whole Bible, seeing it all in light of Jesus the Messiah."

> — Kelly M. Kapic, Professor of Theological
> Studies, Covenant College; author of
> *God So Loved, He Gave*

"Michael Williams has written a book that is badly needed: a survey of all the books of the Bible that shows how they work together to point toward Jesus Christ. While reflecting solid research, the book is readable and attractively packaged, making it accessible to almost any reader."

> — Douglas J. Moo, Wessner Chair of Biblical
> Studies, Wheaton College; Chair, Committee
> on Bible Translation (NIV)

"Average Bible readers—like me—want to answer three overarching questions when they read God's Word: What's the big idea in each book? How does each book point to Jesus? How does each book speak to contemporary life? In this concise and well-written book, Michael Williams deftly guides us to the right answers. Few books do a better job of giving us an overview of Genesis to Revelation in such a compact way. This is the sort of book I'd love to have in the hands of every member of my church!"

> — Justin Taylor, Managing Editor, *ESV Study
> Bible*; author of the popular blog Between
> Two Worlds

"The basic intention underlying this succinct treatment of every book in the Bible is to examine each of them in order to expound for modern pilgrims what Jesus had already explained to two distraught followers on the road to Emmaus two millennia ago: "what was said in all the Scriptures concerning himself" (Luke 24:27). In that effort, author Michael Williams succeeds admirably. Using crisp, contemporary, and often humorous language, he invites us to focus our attention on the major theme of each of the sixty-six books of the Old and New Testaments in a mere four or five pages apiece. The middle section of each of these brief chapters is entitled "The Jesus Lens," in which Williams zeros in on how every biblical book contributes to the centrality of Christ as the unquestionably dominant and infinitely most important figure in Holy Scripture. To be sure, *How to Read the Bible through the Jesus Lens* is a captivating and challenging read in its own right. But I am delighted as well to recommend it without reservation not only because of its impeccable scholarship but also because it is both solidly evangelical and stunningly evangelistic."

— Ronald Youngblood, Professor Emeritus of
Old Testament and Hebrew, Bethel Seminary
San Diego

How to Read
the Bible
through the Jesus Lens

How to Read
the Bible
through the Jesus Lens

A Guide to Christ-Focused
Reading of Scripture

Michael Williams

ZONDERVAN

How to Read the Bible through the Jesus Lens
Copyright © 2012 by Michael Williams

This title is also available as a Zondervan ebook.
Visit www.zondervan.com/ebooks.

Requests for information should be addressed to:
Zondervan, 3900 Sparks Dr. SE, Grand Rapids, Michigan 49546

Library of Congress Cataloging-in-Publication Data

Williams, Michael James, 1956-
    How to read the Bible through the Jesus lens : a guide to Christ-focused reading of
Scripture / Michael Williams.
       p. cm.
    ISBN 978-0-310-33165-0 (softcover)
      1. BiblexCriticism, interpretation, etc. 2. Jesus Christ—Person and offices. I. Title.
BS511.3.W56 2011
    220.6'1—dc23   2011049791

Cover Design: Tobias' Outerwear for Books
Cover photo: Andy Terzes / Terzes Photograph
Interior design: Matthew Van Zomeren

Printed in the United States of America

HB 01.30.2024

Contents

The Beginning Matters

*"These are the very Scriptures that
testify about me." (John 5:39)*

The simple truth that all of the Scriptures—Old Testament and New
Testament—testify about Jesus seems to be often overlooked. For modern readers, the picture of Christ in the Old Testament can be obscured
by veritable whiteout conditions of chronological, sacrificial, architectural,
geographical, and genealogical details, so that all that can be made out
after spending some time in the snowstorm is a mound of white where the
car used to be. To an admittedly lesser degree, the problem exists for the
New Testament as well. Names of apostles and disciples, travelogues, letters
to forgotten churches in obscure locales regarding confusing theological
issues—all of this can seem like so many differently shaped jigsaw pieces
without a picture on the box to help us to put it all together. This book
is intended to help believers make out the picture on the box. And it is a
picture of Jesus.

Reading the Bible through the Jesus lens is reading it the way it was
intended. It keeps our reading, understanding, teaching, and preaching
properly focused on God's grand redemptive program that centers on his
own Son. Seeing how each biblical book makes its own unique contribution
to that redemptive focus enables us to use these diverse materials with much
more confidence and accuracy. The Jesus lens ensures that our exegetical
bowling balls stay within the lane and don't go crashing over into areas
where they can cause a lot of damage to the faith of believers and to our
ability to use the Bible fruitfully in our service to God.

I hope I have avoided the usual dry, data-intensive introduction to the
Bible in which dusty details of disparate documents are examined in an aca-
demically detached fashion apart from any apparent relatedness to Christ or

contemporary life. Rather, the goal of this book is parallel to that of Christ for the disciples he joined up with on the road to Emmaus: "Beginning with Moses and all the Prophets, he explained to them what was said in all the Scriptures concerning himself" (Luke 24:27).

To accomplish this purpose in a book that one doesn't need a wheelbarrow to carry around, the chapters are brief and similarly structured. In each one, I present the overarching theme of each biblical book along with a discussion of how that theme ultimately finds its focus in Jesus Christ. I then explore how this focus in Christ is subsequently elaborated upon in the New Testament. Finally, I consider what that fulfillment in Christ must necessarily entail for believers, who are being conformed to his likeness, along with ways to communicate those entailments to others effectively. By means of these considerations I hope to help brothers and sisters in the faith grow in their awareness of how all of Scripture finds its focus in Jesus Christ and so help them to root their Christian life, theological discussions, and evangelical witness in the one who is our life (Colossians 3:4).

Below are some resources that have influenced my own thinking along these lines. I recommend these books to those who wish to explore the details of the biblical books more deeply.

Arnold, Bill T., and Bryan E. Beyer. *Encountering the Old Testament*. Second edition. Grand Rapids: Baker Academic, 2008.

Elwell, Walter A., and Robert W. Yarbrough. *Encountering the New Testament*. Second edition. Grand Rapids: Baker Academic, 2005.

Fee, Gordon D., and Douglas Stuart. *How to Read the Bible Book by Book*. Grand Rapids: Zondervan, 2002.

Fee, Gordon D., and Douglas Stuart. *How to Read the Bible for All Its Worth*. Second edition. Grand Rapids: Zondervan, 2003.

The NIV Student Bible. Grand Rapids: Zondervan, 2002.

TNIV Study Bible. Grand Rapids: Zondervan, 2006.

Walton, John, et al. *The Essential Bible Companion*. Grand Rapids: Zondervan, 2006.

Available spring of 2012! The course from which this book arose will be available online to visitors at https://www.calvinseminary.edu/continuingEd/openCourses.php. Enjoy a video presentation of the details of each biblical book with music, images, author narration, and in-depth analysis.

I must thank several people who enabled me to complete this project before the events recounted in the book of Revelation transpired. John

Rottman gave me many practical insights from his homiletical perspective. Ronald Feenstra ensured that my theology was well within the pale. Barbara Blackmore parted the sea of papers on her desk to give this book a priority read and to keep me from drifting into academic-speak. Nielsen Tomazini provided wonderful technical assistance and is largely responsible for the electronic flashcards that accompany this book. My students at Calvin Theological Seminary gave me a lot of feedback, much of it proving useful. Paul DeVries, my pastor, audited the course in which this material was presented and shared his ideas over several lunches with me while also leading our congregation through the book. Katya Covrett, my editor at Zondervan, made the mechanics painless.

The greatest thanks goes to Dawn, my amazing wife, who encouraged, supported, gently corrected, and participated in the process at every point. Although the last sentence applies most pertinently to my efforts with this book, it applies as well to my life in general. Of course, should anyone take issue with the book or my life at any point, it is precisely there, no doubt, that I have departed from my wife's advice.

Michael Williams

GENESIS

Separation for Blessing

The Bible begins with a book that takes us all the way from the murky recesses of the distant past to a populated world whose future revolves around the fate of one family group. How are we supposed to get our minds around all of this information? Why did God bother to communicate these details to us? What are we supposed to take away from all this that has anything to do with our lives today? We can begin to answer these questions by looking through the Jesus lens at this book whose very name means "beginning" or "origin." This is an appropriate name because the book of Genesis describes the genesis of life, and the genesis of a long divine program to restore that life to its fullness in Christ following the genesis of sin.

Theme of the Book

God separates out one through whom he would bless all nations.

From the beginning of creation in the opening chapters through the millennia of conflict and struggle after the fall, God's activity in Genesis can be summarized by the word *separating*. God separates:

- light from darkness (1:4)
- the waters in the heavens from the waters on the earth (1:6)
- dry ground from seas (1:9–10)
- animate life in the sea and on land from inanimate vegetable life (1:11–12, 20–25)
- human beings from animals (1:26–28)

- the line of Seth from Adam and Eve's other children (5:3–32)
- the line of Noah from other people (6:9–14)
- the line of Noah's son Shem from Noah's other children (9:25–27)
- the line of Abraham from all other people (12:1–3)

❤ Memory Passage: Genesis 12:2–3

I will make you into a great nation,
  and *I will* bless you;
I will make your name great,
  and you will be a blessing.
I will bless those who bless you,
  and whoever curses you *I will* curse;
and all peoples on earth
  will be blessed through you. (italics added)

The repetition of "I will" in the "Abrahamic blessing" above clearly emphasizes the fact that God is relentlessly committed to a purpose in all of this separating. God's good creation, and especially his human creations, had been mortally damaged by sin (3:1–19). But it is through the line of Abraham, the one whom God had separated out, that God would provide the avenue through which human beings could once again experience divine blessing. From Abraham, to his son Isaac, to Isaac's son Jacob, to Jacob's children, God himself maintains this channel of blessing against all external and internal threats so that his human creations can experience the fullness of life he always intended for them. Through accounts of human failures, wars, family intrigues, deceptions, international slave trade, famines, and miraculous births, Genesis presents to us God's relentless and gracious separation and preservation of the human line he had chosen to bring his salvation to the world.

🔍 The Jesus Lens

Millennia pass, and God's separating for the purpose of blessing finally comes to focus in Jesus Christ. In the first verse of his gospel, the apostle Matthew reminds us that this Messiah, Jesus, is from the line of Abraham and is the focus of the promise God made to Abraham so long ago. The apostle Paul further explains this connection by calling God's promise to bring blessing to all nations through the line of Abraham "the gospel" (Galatians 3:7–8). Jesus is the one to whom all God's separating was always meant to lead, and Jesus is separate from all others in his ability to bring the promised divine blessing to the nations:

> Salvation is found in no one else, for there is no other name under heaven given to mankind by which we must be saved. (Acts 4:12)

The ultimate focus of all God's redemptive activity is Jesus Christ. Anything or anyone else that is held up as a legitimate alternative is only snow on the satellite dish, distorting the clear picture of salvation that God is sending us in his Son.

Contemporary Implications

God's past work of separation for blessing comes into focus when it is viewed through the lens of Jesus Christ, but God is not done working. He continues his work of separation today, and for the same reason — so that his blessing is realized by all nations. To accomplish his divine purpose, he separates out his people, you and me. The apostle Paul puts it this way:

> All this is from God, who reconciled us to himself through Christ and gave us the ministry of reconciliation: that God was reconciling the world to himself in Christ, not counting people's sins against them. And he has committed to us the message of reconciliation. We are therefore Christ's ambassadors, as though God were making his appeal through us. (2 Corinthians 5:18–20)

As Christ's ambassadors, we have been "separated out" by God not just to *receive* the blessing of reconciliation with God and the life that flows from that divine, saving act, but also to *pass on* that blessing to others by making the good news of God's salvation in Jesus Christ clear to them with every aspect of our lives. This is not an option. It is what we have been separated out by God to do. It is the reason for our Christian existence.

Hook Questions

- In what ways has God equipped you to be a blessing to other people? Do people avoid you, or do they find in you some evidence of Christ's life, which has a character and quality they desire for themselves? Are you able to tell them about the source of this life in a clear way? Do your words and life communicate something good and attractive to unbelievers, or something no one would want?
- Are Christians a blessing to you? Many of us seem to struggle with communicating the blessing of God in Jesus Christ as good news. Is there anything about the *way* this communication sometimes takes place that puts you off? How can you avoid these problems yourself?
- What can you do to make yourself a clearer (and more relentless) message of the good news of Jesus Christ to those around you? Are you tapping into the resources God has made available to every believer? Are you aware of how you come across to others? Can you identify areas in your life that hinder your service as Christ's ambassador? Are you willing to tackle these areas with the strength God provides you?

When we grasp what God is doing in Genesis by separating out his avenue of blessing to the nations, we will be able to recognize how that blessing finds its focus in Christ. We will also recognize the responsibility of those of us who have been separated out by God through faith in Christ to live out that communication of divine blessing to those around us who need to realize it themselves. There is no doubt that God may, and often does, call us, as he called on so many of the characters in Genesis, to communicate something of that blessing even through tough circumstances — sometimes *really* tough circumstances. But we can be confident that when we seek God's help in carrying out this task, we will indeed be praying for his will to be done because we will be doing exactly what he has separated us out to do. And when we do it, we will begin to appropriate the fullness of life that God wants us to enjoy. We will be blessed and will be a blessing to others as well.

EXODUS

Deliverance into Presence

Things were not supposed to be this way. Abraham's descendants were supposed to thrive. They were supposed to be a living testimony to the blessing of God. These people who had been separated out by God to be a channel of blessing to the nations had indeed grown in number. But through time and circumstance they had ended up in Egypt, where their situation had taken a terrible turn for the worse. Pharaoh was oppressing them and using them mercilessly as slave labor for his massive building projects. Does the ruler of Egypt have the power to frustrate God's promise? What does this major obstacle to the promised blessing of Abraham's descendants mean for those of us who are to experience God's blessing through them? The book of Exodus, whose name means "departure" or "exit," keeps our confidence in God's faithfulness from "exiting" and prompts us to keep our focus on Jesus Christ.

Theme of the Book

God delivers his people from slavery into his presence.

God uses Moses—and his two siblings, Aaron and Miriam—to teach Pharaoh, and us, that no person or thing can thwart the divine deliverance God intends for his people. Just as God delivered Moses through unusual events when he was a baby, so God will deliver his people through unusual events while they are in their national infancy. Through a series of ever-worsening plagues (chaps. 7–12) that culminate in the death of all the firstborn sons of Egypt, God demonstrates his superiority over the gods in which the Egyptians trusted. God "passed over" the firstborn sons of his own people and so, once again, established that he had separated them out for his special favor. God's powerful demonstration broke Pharaoh's resolve, and he sent the Israelites packing. With one more decisive victory over Pharaoh's pursuing army at the Red Sea, God's deliverance of his people from their Egyptian bondage was complete. But this deliverance was not an end in itself; there was a larger divine purpose in view.

> ## Memory Passage: *Exodus 29:46*
>
> They will know that I am the LORD their God, who brought them out of Egypt so that I might dwell among them. I am the LORD their God.

The words "so that" in the memory passage clue us into an often overlooked dimension of this biblical book—and one that millennia later would find its ultimate fulfillment in Jesus Christ. God doesn't just deliver *from*; he also delivers *into* (6:6–8). In Exodus, God delivers his people *from* their slavery (chaps. 1–18) and *into* his life-giving presence (chaps. 19–40). He makes that presence frightfully clear at Mount Sinai, where he presents his people, through Moses, ten commandments. These commandments provide the parameters for realizing the fullness of life God intends for his people, a fullness that flows from his life-generating presence among them.

Yet, even before the dust had settled from chiseling out these life-directives, God's people choose to exchange the presence of their deliverer for a golden calf substitute (chaps. 32–34). This event reveals that although they had been delivered from external bondage, there was another bondage, internal and tenacious, that would require even more powerful divine measures to break. With breathtaking mercy and love, God not only spares his ungrateful people for preferring an idol over him, but gives them instructions for constructing the tabernacle (chaps. 25–31, 35–40), a visible reminder of his presence with them. The details of this tent-like structure and its furnishings also point to the future, to the one through whom God would bring about a greater deliverance into an even greater presence.

The Jesus Lens

The tabernacle included an altar for sacrifice (27:1–7), pointing toward the ultimate sacrifice that Christ would make to deliver his people from sin. This cleansing from sin is indicated by the basin for washing (30:17–21). The table of the bread of the Presence (25:23–30) anticipates Christ as the bread of life and the visible presence of God, who gives and sustains life. The lampstand (25:31–40) signifies the one who would come as the light of the world. And the altar of incense, where incense was burned daily and atonement was made annually for the sins of the people (30:1–10), is fulfilled in the atoning sacrifice of Christ, who always intercedes for his people. In fact, it is difficult to read the details of God's deliverance of his people from bondage and into his presence without seeing the ultimate fulfillment of those details in Christ.

> So I find this law at work: Although I want to do good, evil is right there with me.... What a wretched man I am! Who will rescue me from this body that is subject to death? Thanks be to God, who delivers me through Jesus Christ our Lord! (Romans 7:21–25)

Through Jesus Christ, God accomplishes our deliverance *from* sin, and also our deliverance *into* a rich life of meaning, purpose, and significance in his presence. By his almighty and unfailing power, God delivers us from the penalty of sin as well as from the power of sin that seeks to reclaim us after we have escaped its menacing clutches.

Contemporary Implications

Not even one of the most powerful nations on earth could hold on to God's people when he had determined to deliver them. And that deliverance had as its goal being brought into God's presence — a presence that God takes pains to preserve, despite the wrenches of human sin that we keep throwing into the gears. If God was willing to deliver us from the infectious clutches of sin by means of the immense cost of the death of his own Son, he will certainly safeguard his precious purchases by the exercise of that same divine mercy and power.

> Since we have now been justified by his [Jesus'] blood, how much
> more shall we be saved from God's wrath through him! For if,
> while we were God's enemies, we were reconciled to him through
> the death of his Son, how much more, having been reconciled,
> shall we be saved through his life! (Romans 5:9–10)

Not Egyptian pharaohs, pursuing armies, mobs crying out for crucifixion, our own sinfulness, or even nagging self-doubt are stronger
than God's love or his power to deliver us and to keep us in his life-
giving, life-sustaining, and life-enriching presence that comes to us
through our relationship with Christ Jesus our Lord.

 Hook Questions

- Does the fact that you are a Christian feel like a burden (something to be delivered from) or deliverance? Are your eyes open
  to the wonders of the presence of God into which you have been
  brought, or are you still focused on the features of your life in
  captivity? What could you do to change your perspective? What
  could you do to help others to change their perspective?
- Do you feel as if you're in the grip of God, or of sin? On whose
  strength are you relying to free yourself from sin's power?
- What can you do to make others aware of the freedom from
  their captivity to sin and its horrible effects that is available to
  them in Christ? Can they see evidence of that freedom in you?
  What can you do to make others aware of the rich life of fellowship with God himself that is available to them in Christ? Can
  they see evidence of that rich life of fellowship with God in you?

Like the Israelites, we often forget the powerful divine deliverance
we have experienced through faith in Christ. We, too, often forget that
the whole purpose of that deliverance is that we might enjoy the rich,
full life that God wants for us as we live in his presence. As a result, we
are prone to look for that life in other things — things that promise a
lot but only end up enslaving us again. But God has ensured that nothing can snatch us out of his hand. When we put away our golden calves
and turn to God, he is ready to lead us on our journey through life with
assurance, security, and confidence in a celebration of his bountiful
presence from which nothing can ever separate us.

3 | LEVITICUS

Life in God's Presence

The name of this book is Latin for "concerning the Levites" — admittedly not a captivating title. The Levites were descendants from the tribe of Levi, and they assisted Aaron's sons, the priests, in the service of the tabernacle. The tabernacle was the visible place of God's dwelling among his people during their wilderness wanderings. God had delivered his people from their slavery in Egypt so that they could enjoy fellowship with him, fellowship that centered around the tabernacle. But fellowship with God is not a casual matter, like the weekly gatherings of the Saturday afternoon book club. God is holy. He is pure and perfect. For impure and imperfect people to enjoy a close relationship with him, specific measures would have to be taken.

Theme of the Book

God instructs his people how to live in his presence.

In this book, God instructs his people how to set themselves apart for him and the purposes he has for them—in other words, how to be holy. God had set his people apart for his special purpose of bringing blessing to the nations. He had delivered them from their slave-labor existence and into his life-giving presence so that they were free to carry out his purposes and experience the fullness of life that such freedom brings. Now they had to acknowledge and live in the reality of God's purpose for them and his presence with them. They had to be holy.

> ### 🙂 **Memory Passage:** *Leviticus 20:26*
>
> You are to be holy to me because I, the LORD, am holy,
> and I have set you apart from the nations to be my own.

God lays out procedures for the Israelites to follow that would remind them of his presence with them and of their dependence on him to accomplish the purposes for which he had set them apart. These procedures included five main sacrifices, each one communicating an important aspect of the holiness that was to characterize their lives as individuals and as a community. The burnt offering (chap. 1) had to be totally burned, indicating the total surrender to God on the part of the offerer. The grain offering (chap. 2) was a physical acknowledgment of the Lord's gracious provision for life. The fellowship offering (chap. 3) expressed the desire for the perpetuation and deepening of their special relationship with God. The sin offering and guilt offering (4:1 – 6:7) were acknowledgments of departing from the relational requirement of holiness and were divinely provided ways to atone for sin's damages and to mend the breaks in their relationship with God. All of these sacrifices, with their emphases on acknowledging, celebrating, deepening, and restoring our relationship with God, reveal aspects of a coming ultimate sacrifice when we view them through the lens of Christ.

🔍 The Jesus Lens

The sacrifices that the Israelites offered to God were a means of acknowledging both his holiness and the requirement for those in special relationship with him to keep themselves holy. The things sacrificed to God had to be without any imperfection, and even those designated to offer the sacrifices on the part of the people — the priests — had special rules and procedures to follow when doing so. This demand for holiness in our relationship with God has not been removed or minimized. Not only do we need a perfect sacrifice, we need a perfect priest to offer it for us. Jesus, because he is both the flawless sacrifice and the sinless priest, fulfills both roles.

> Unlike the other high priests, he [Christ] does not need to offer
> sacrifices day after day, first for his own sins, and then for the sins

of the people. He sacrificed for their sins once for all when he offered himself. (Hebrews 7:27)

When we acknowledge our unholiness and put our trust in Jesus
and what he has done, his self-sacrifice is credited to us and achieves for
us everything the many sacrifices of Leviticus could only point toward.
It secures our unimpeded and uninterrupted fellowship with God as we
live out his sacred purpose for us. Christ's holiness admits us into God's
holy presence. There we find abundant stores of mercy and grace to help
us as we seek to carry out our divine mandate to bring his blessing to
all people (Hebrews 4:16).

Contemporary Implications

Christ is our holiness. He is our spotless offering. He is our blameless
priest. He is the one who secures our fellowship with God and peace in
his presence. He has also shown us most clearly what life — real life — in
God's presence looks like. This is the life he wants for us, and it is the
life that is available to us to the degree that we become like him. It is
the life that God has enabled us to realize by sending us his life-giving
Spirit (Romans 8:10 – 11).

> Make every effort to be found spotless, blameless and at peace
> with him. (2 Peter 3:14)

This effort will take more resources than we have. Thankfully, God
has all the resources we lack, and he graciously provides those resources
to us through Jesus Christ — the one who secures for us life in God's
holy presence, preserves us in that life, and by his Spirit transforms us
into those who experience that life more fully every day.

Hook Questions

• Are you cultivating a life of holiness? What practices in your life
remind you of your special relationship with God and his special
purpose for you? How are the purposes of the various sacrifices

in Leviticus realized in your own experience? How are they realized in the life of your faith community?
- What does such a life look like today? How would anyone recognize that you are set apart to God and his purposes for you? Do *you* recognize those things?

Most of us, if asked to pick an adjective to describe ourselves, probably would not choose the word "holy." But, amazingly, through our faith in Jesus Christ, that is exactly what we are in God's sight. High Priest Jesus, the Lamb of God, has offered himself as a perfect sacrifice so that the goal of all biblical sacrifices is now realized forever for all who put their faith in him: fellowship with God. The holiness that God has graciously achieved *for* us he is at work making more clearly recognizable *in* our everyday experience by his holy change agent, the Holy Spirit.

So, by the sacrifice of Jesus Christ, God "has made perfect forever those who are being made holy" (Hebrews 10:14). Why should we cooperate in this holy metamorphosis? Because "holiness" is another way of describing the kind of life God wants and intends for his human creations. It describes a life in relationship with God himself, a life whose potential is not held back by sin, a life that is vibrant, pure, and powerful. This kind of life that is possible through faith in Jesus Christ is good news—news that people need to see more of in our own experience as well as hear about.

NUMBERS

Promised Rest

In fulfillment of God's promise to Abraham (Genesis 15:4–5), the Israelites had grown dramatically in numbers—the specific numbers are provided in chapters 1 and 26 of this book and provide the rationale for the book's name. Unfortunately, the Israelites' faith in and obedience to the God who had delivered them from their horrible life of slavery in Egypt had not grown proportionately. Instead, they rebelled against God again and again as he led them through the wilderness to the place of rest he had promised them. Finally, when they even refused to trust him to give them the ability to take possession of that Promised Land, God was forced to take action. Even though he loved his chosen people, God's holiness and justice compelled him to judge their sin.

📖 Theme of the Book

God chastens his disobedient people but reaffirms his intent to bring them into the Promised Land.

The Israelites had been delivered from Egypt with mighty displays of divine power. Before their very eyes they had witnessed incredible demonstrations of God's sovereignty. They had heard God thunder from Mount Sinai and had been reminded of his holy presence in their midst. Throughout their trek through the wilderness, God had lovingly provided for their material needs. He protected them and guided them to the doorstep of the Land of Promise. But in the Israelites' eyes, the visible, physical challenges they saw lying ahead of them in that land seemed greater than the invisible, un-physical God who was with them. Their trust gave way to doubt and rebellion. God's patience, love, and forgiveness had to make room for his discipline.

> ### 🐟 Memory Passage: *Numbers 14:18*
>
> The LORD is slow to anger, abounding in love and forgiving sin and rebellion. Yet he does not leave the guilty unpunished; he punishes the children for the sin of the parents to the third and fourth generation.

The spies sent by Moses all reported the same thing: the Promised Land was rich and fruitful (13:27). However, this confirmation of God's promise to them was quickly followed by some buzz-killing news. The good, fertile land was already inhabited by gigantic people and seemingly impregnable cities (13:28). God's people quickly forgot how he had dealt with Egypt and supposed that he was not up to the task of dealing with these new challenges. Their faith dried up like the desert through which they had traveled so long and far. They were even ready to return to Egypt, the land of their slavery.

This situation raises a theological problem that will ultimately find its resolution only through the Jesus lens: How can God punish the rebellion and faithlessness of his people and still bless them? Make no mistake, God's intention to bless his people remains unshaken. Even after their sin, he puts words of blessing into the mouth of the foreign prophet Balaam, who had been hired to curse them (chaps. 22–24). But how could God's holiness and justice allow him to bless his people whose faith always wavers and whose obedience always falters?

◯ The Jesus Lens

Obedience is difficult at the best of times. When the road of obedience is full of potholes of apprehension, struggle, and sweat, it is awfully tempting to pull over into a rest area, or even pull a U-turn and head back the way we came — just as the Israelites wanted to do. And this is where the problem lies. Disobedience demands judgment, and everyone disobeys—except one. There is one person, the God-man Jesus Christ, who did not sin and yet paid the price for the disobedience and rebellion of all the rest of us schlubs. Jesus had a hard road ahead of him, yet unlike the Israelites in the wilderness, he did not rebel. Instead, "he entrusted himself to him who judges justly" (1 Peter 2:23). In fact, the taunts of the mockers while Jesus hung on the cross unintentionally include his greatest commendation: "He trusts in God" (Matthew 27:43). When we believe in our trusting, obedient Lord and what he has done for us, the way is clear for us to enter into God's promised rest.

> We who have believed enter that rest. (Hebrews 4:3)

It is through Jesus Christ that God's holiness and justice are satisfied and his unshakeable promise of blessing can be realized. All that remains for us is to believe in the gracious provision God has made for us and to enter into the rest he has promised and prepared for us.

🏙 Contemporary Implications

We, as God's people today, also have a Promised Land before us. It is a place of fellowship with God that characterizes our salvation in Jesus Christ. When we, like the Israelites, allow the big challenges of life to cause us to forget the even bigger power of God, he disciplines us so that we don't stray far from the real peace, security, and fulfillment that are found only in our relationship with him.

> [Our fathers] disciplined us for a little while as they thought best; but God disciplines us for our good, in order that we may share in his holiness. No discipline seems pleasant at the time, but painful. Later on, however, it produces a harvest of righteousness and peace for those who have been trained by it. (Hebrews 12:10–11)

God has made our relationship with him possible by allowing his own Son to suffer the penalty for our rebellion. He makes our continued relationship with him continually richer by disciplining us, as only one who cares deeply for us would do. That discipline leads us to the place of rest and peace that God has prepared for his children.

Hook Questions

- In what ways have you already begun to know God's rest? How would you explain this rest to someone else? Can others see in you a peace, security, and fulfillment in life that they don't have? Do you see these things in other believers?
- What is keeping you from knowing God's rest more fully? What are the biggest challenges in your life that threaten to cause you to forget how great God is? Where have you turned for rest and fulfillment in life instead of to God? Are you satisfied with the results of doing that?

It is so easy for us to get distracted. When we focus on the obstacles on our paths, which may in fact be huge and scary, we can get distracted from seeing the rich and fruitful life God intends for us and has made possible through Jesus Christ. When we focus on our own inconsistent faith and sketchy obedience, we can get distracted from seeing the payment that has already been made for us through Jesus Christ. When we look through the Jesus lens, God's past, present, and future blessings for us, his people, gain clarity and we begin to cross over into that Promised Land of new life in fellowship with him.

The Israelites had been trudging through the sand for forty years, about the amount of time it has taken modern society to move from the first handheld calculator to iPhone apps. Those who had left Egypt under Moses have passed from the scene and their children have grown. This new generation stands just across the Jordan River from the Promised Land and are ready to enter. But Moses, their leader for so many years, will not be with them when they do, because of his disobedience at Meribah (Numbers 20:12). So Moses gives this new generation one last charge before he must hand over leadership to Joshua. With these words, Moses passes on those things he considers more important than anything else. He reminds them of who their God is and how they can remain in their special relationship with him by living in the way he has described, the way that leads to the fullest life possible.

Theme of the Book

God gives Moses instructions for the second generation of Israel regarding faithful living in the Promised Land.

In Moses' address to the Israelites at this critical point in their national existence, he lays out for them the formal details of their relationship with God. Moses reminds them of everything God has done for them — things that have proved his love for them, given them confidence in his continued care for them in the future, and motivated their loving response. Moses also encourages God's people to live in a way that nurtures their relationship with him and leads them into a fuller experience of life. Moses further encourages this kind of living by describing to the Israelites what God will do for them in the future, and also what they can expect if they reject God's path to life. God calls heaven and earth as witnesses to his relationship with his people (30:19) — witnesses that are as enduring as he desires his relationship with his people to be, witnesses that testify when that relationship is secured forever by the perfect obedience of his Son (Matthew 27:45 – 54).

> **Memory Passage:** *Deuteronomy 10:12 – 13*
>
> And now, Israel, what does the LORD your God ask of you but to fear the LORD your God, to walk in obedience to him, to love him, to serve the LORD your God with all your heart and with all your soul, and to observe the LORD's commands and decrees that I am giving you today for your own good?

In all this talk of laws and instructions, it is easy to overlook the last four words of the memory passage: "for your own good." God desires his people to have the best life possible, and he should know what that is because he made them. This rich and full human life is only possible in relationship with him. That relationship with God is maintained when his people live in the way he has outlined for them *for their own good*. Moses uses his last opportunity to address God's people and to plead with them to live in just such a way. But God's people throughout the ages have had trouble living as God has instructed. The problem, of course, is not with the divine instruction, but with sin-infected human beings (Romans 7:10 – 12).

The Jesus Lens

For the divine-human relationship to endure and thrive, what is needed is a human being who never fails to live as God has instructed, who can represent all of God's people, and who can thereby ensure that our relationship with the source of life will never be broken. In other words, we need a sinless human being who is perfectly obedient to God's instruction. After we had proven through many years of painful trial and error that we are unable to come up with such a person ourselves, our relentlessly gracious Creator provided one for us—his own Son, born a human being. Jesus Christ came not to do away with God's life-giving instructions, but rather to fulfill them perfectly on our behalf and ensure that their benefits continue to us without interruption.

> Do not think that I have come to abolish the Law or the Prophets; I have not come to abolish them but to fulfill them. (Matthew 5:17)

Christ perfectly fulfills God's life-giving, relationship-sustaining instructions and so secures our relationship with God forever. For those who by faith claim him as their representative, he secures the divine blessings for obedience to God's instructions (Deuteronomy 28:1–14) by experiencing on our behalf the divine judgment for our disobedience (Deuteronomy 28:15–68).

🏛🏢 Contemporary Implications

Because of what our Lord has done on our behalf, our whole perspective on God's law has shifted. Now we do not look to our own obedience as the guarantee of our relationship with God (really no guarantee at all), but rather to the obedience of the perfect law-keeper, Jesus Christ. He sent his Spirit to indwell us, guide us, and empower us to follow God's blueprint for the full human life that God wants for us.

> Now, by dying to what once bound us, we have been released from the law so that we serve in the new way of the Spirit, and not in the old way of the written code. (Romans 7:6)

Our Creator himself has brought about for us, the people he loves, a new and unbreakable relationship with him. He has done this by means of his own Son, who has perfectly fulfilled the law on our behalf. And we have the Spirit of this perfect law-keeper dwelling within each one of us so that we may now serve God gratefully and confidently, without fearing any longer the penalty of the law. We now have diplomatic immunity from prosecution because our brother is the King.

Hook Questions

- What drives your relationship with God, fear or gratitude? Do you want to know your Creator better, or are you just trying to avoid his anger?
- Do you view God's instructions as restrictive or freeing? How does your view of God affect your answer to the question? Who would know best how a human being should live in order to experience life most fully?
- Whose effort secures your relationship with God? Where does the Spirit of Christ dwell?

Our relationship with the Father is now every bit as secure as the obedience of the Son is perfect. When we view our relational bond with God through the lens of his Son, our life-depleting fears and doubts will decrease and our life-enhancing gratitude and responsiveness will grow. We will read God's instructions not as a collection of confining rules that inhibit the enjoyment of our lives or keep us from experiencing their full potential, but rather as divine trail markers that lead us to the fullest life imaginable. Of course, living according to God's instructions does not and cannot establish or maintain our relationship with God (that is accomplished only by his Son), but living that way will keep us on the path toward making that relationship everything it could be.

Moses had died, and God has raised up his aide, Joshua, as his successor. Joshua's job description is clear: he must lead the Israelites into the land God had promised their ancestors. This would not be a simple task. The job would be at times filled with fear and doubt. There would be disheartening losses and setbacks. There would be many battles with fierce enemies who vigorously opposed them. But God reassures Joshua that he will be with him and will never forsake him. God promises that he will ultimately give the Israelites victory under the leadership of this man whose name literally means, "the LORD gives victory" (cf. 1:5–6). There will, in fact, be rest for the people of God on the other side of their battles—a victorious rest promised and ensured by God himself.

Theme of the Book

God uses Joshua to lead his people to victorious rest in the Promised Land.

Long ago God had promised Abraham that his descendants would possess the land of Canaan (Genesis 17:1–8). Over four hundred years have passed (about the same stretch of time as from the publication of the King James Bible until now) until the promise finally begins to be realized in the events described in this book. Under Joshua's leadership, the Israelites cross over the Jordan River into the Promised Land (chaps. 1–4). However, the land was already occupied by others and had to be taken from them by force. There were battles to be fought (chaps.

5–12). The inhabitants of the land opposed God's people physically and spiritually. The Israelites had to be reminded repeatedly that their military victories were integrally tied to the health of their relationship with their God, who brought about those victories. Eventually the battles were won and the land could be divided up (chaps. 13–21) and settled (chaps. 22–24). The promised rest was realized.

Memory Passage: *Joshua 11:23*

So Joshua took the entire land, just as the LORD had directed Moses, and he gave it as an inheritance to Israel according to their tribal divisions. Then the land had rest from war.

The "rest" the land experienced was not the result of fatigue or surrender or idleness on the part of the Israelites. No, it was a *victorious* rest. It was the result of much determination, struggle, and sacrifice. But even these praiseworthy attributes and actions would have been entirely insufficient if they had not been accompanied by an expectant trust and confidence in God's power and faithfulness. When the Israelites finally achieved victorious rest in the Promised Land, they reasserted their commitment to serve this God who had delivered them, guided them, and given them victory (24:1–28). God had indeed done amazing things for Israel. But God had even greater things planned for his people. In the future he would deliver them, guide them, and lead them to victory over sin and its consequences through his own Son.

The Jesus Lens

The name "Jesus" is the Greek form of the Hebrew name "Joshua." Joshua was the man God raised up to lead his people to victorious rest in the Old Testament. This historical reality gives redemptive focus to the actions of Jesus, the new Joshua. Unlike Joshua, however, Jesus is both fighting alongside his people *and* is himself the God who brings them ultimate victory. Just as Joshua encouraged the Israelites in their battles to keep their eyes focused on the source of their victory and not to rely on anyone or anything else, Jesus does the same for us. He reminds us that our peace, our rest, our victory comes from him alone. It is also important to note that just as ultimate rest for the Israelites involved real struggle on their part, so ultimate rest for believers today involves struggle. But there is nothing in the world that can successfully overcome the Creator of the world or his Son:

> I have told you these things, so that in me you may have peace. In this world you will have trouble. But take heart! I have overcome the world. (John 16:33)

Christ brings his people victory over the challenges of this life. He does not necessarily make the challenges go away, but he gives us motivation, strength, and reassurance to fight the battles, and he protects us from being overcome by opposition, no matter how fierce. Until we enter into our ultimate rest, we can rest in the confidence that God has already won the victory.

Contemporary Implications

It was surely a scary prospect for the desert-weary Israelites to go up against experienced troops, fortified cities, and people who greatly outnumbered them. We can well understand their temptation to call in reinforcements (that is, foreign gods) or to abandon their mission entirely. Appropriating their promised inheritance must have seemed impossible at times. Our circumstances may often seem just as impossible to overcome. Thankfully, just as for the Israelites, the accomplishment of our own victorious rest is not in our hands, but in God's. He has secured our eternal inheritance for us through our own Joshua, Jesus Christ.

> Praise be to the God and Father of our Lord Jesus Christ! In his great mercy he has given us new birth into a living hope through the resurrection of Jesus Christ from the dead, and into an inheritance that can never perish, spoil or fade. This inheritance is kept in heaven for you, who through faith are shielded by God's power until the coming of the salvation that is ready to be revealed in the last time. (1 Peter 1:3–5)

We are able to realize victorious rest even now in the face of the challenges of this life through the power of him who loves us. Though the enemy may hit us with trouble, hardship, persecution, or a whole arsenal of other weapons, he cannot make a dent in the love of Christ that shields us through the power of God until our ultimate victorious rest is fully realized (Romans 8:31 – 39).

Hook Questions

- What battles are you fighting today? Are you surprised that you should have them? Did Jesus have battles to fight?
- Where do you look for strength? What other things might you be relying on instead of God? How do you keep your focus on the only one who can bring about victory for you?
- What counts as victory? Is the rest you seek the same as that of those who don't know God? How do you know when you have the rest that God intends for you?

Looking at the book of Joshua through the lens of Christ enables us to see the contours of our own Christian experience. We face many and often imposing obstacles on the way to victorious rest. Along the way we are tempted to rely on other people or things to bring us a rest that can only come from God—and sometimes we give in to those temptations. But if we keep our eyes focused on Jesus, then the meaning of his name will be true for us as well. Because "the LORD gives victory," our relationship with Jesus means that we too will know and experience victorious rest. We will know it fully in the future when we reign with Christ (2 Timothy 2:12; Revelation 20:6), and we will know it even now when we look for it in our Almighty God and Savior.

JUDGES

Rebellion and Rescue

After the Israelites entered the Promised Land and experienced victorious rest under the leadership of Joshua, we expect them to live out their existence in peaceful contentment and in dependence on and trust in their gracious God. But such is not the case. After Joshua died, God's people became distracted by the new people, religions, and ways of thinking to which they had been exposed in this new land. The old ways seemed so last year. Again and again they forgot the amazing things God had done for them and the rich, full life they had enjoyed in healthy relationship with him. So God would remind them of how vulnerable, weak, and empty life is without his protecting and providing presence. He allowed them to be attacked, defeated, and oppressed by some of their new neighbors until they recognized their error and called out to him again for rescue. In relentless grace and mercy, God raised up "judges" — leaders chosen and equipped by him — to deliver his people, at least until the next time they forgot about him.

Theme of the Book

God raises up judges to rescue his errant people from the consequences of their rebellion.

A characteristic of this period of cyclical turning away, oppression, turning back, and deliverance is that "everyone did as they saw fit" (17:6). Instead of following the guidelines God had given to them — instructions from the Creator on how to live the most enriching human life—the Israelites periodically concocted their own life programs. These inevitably ended in disaster. Nevertheless, the everyday attractions and encouragements to try out other, alternative paths regularly won out over the proven path God had shown them. Entertaining the ideas of other religions and other gods seemed to promise a greater degree of sophistication and inclusiveness than the narrow road that leads to life (Matthew 7:14). Amazingly, God did not give up on his people, but rather repeatedly provided for their rescue after they came to realize the emptiness of life apart from him.

> ### ❤ Memory Passage: *Judges 2:16–17*
>
> The LORD raised up judges, who saved them out of the hands of these raiders. Yet they would not listen to their judges but prostituted themselves to other gods and worshiped them.

These judges are a fascinating and diverse group of characters. Among their number are a left-handed assassin (Ehud: 3:12–30), a fighting prophetess (Deborah: 4:1–7), a mighty warrior who ends up offering his own daughter as a human sacrifice (Jephthah: 11:29–40), a busy father with thirty sons and thirty daughters (Ibzan: 12:8–10), and a long-haired, riddle-loving strongman who killed a thousand Philistines with a donkey's jawbone (Samson: 15:11–17). That each of these deliverers has a prominent character flaw only underscores the fact that it was ultimately God who was doing the delivering. And the depressing cycle of rebellion and rescue in the book of Judges only underscores the fact that there needs to be an ultimate divine rescue from the source of that rebellion.

◯ The Jesus Lens

The Israelites repeatedly detoured from the way of life that God had revealed to them. He gave them instructions and laws to guide them safely toward full human life. By comparing how they actually lived with how God desired them to live, we can understand how far they had veered off course and how desperately they needed divine deliverance. As God's people today, we too take detours from the path of life. Yet God has raised up for us the ultimate deliverer, or judge, in Jesus Christ. He delivers us from sin's ultimate consequences, and also picks us up, dusts us off, and sets us back on the right road after our own ill-conceived excursions down the dead-end roads we careen into.

> The sting of death is sin, and the power of sin is the law. But thanks be to God! He gives us the victory through our Lord Jesus Christ. (1 Corinthians 15:56–57)

The Israelites experienced sin's deadly sting when their rebellion against God led to its natural consequences. Even the deliverers God mercifully raised up for them were flawed and temporary. But the ultimate deliverer, Jesus Christ, has no flaws. So his rescue of those who believe in him is complete and everlasting. His deliverance extends beyond the rescue from sin's consequences to the rescue from sin itself.

Contemporary Implications

Even though we have an ultimate deliverer in Jesus Christ, with dismaying regularity, believers reenact the cycle of the book of Judges. Our attention and affection are all too frequently drawn away from God by the everyday attractions and alternative paths presented to us in eye-catching packages that conceal the emptiness hiding inside them. We forget God, experience the negative consequences that always come from doing so, realize our error and turn back to God, and then enjoy renewed life and peace in fellowship with him. In other words, we are delivered from the oppressive reign of sin back into the life-giving reign of God. The apostle Paul encourages us to embrace our deliverance in Jesus Christ and to waste no more time struggling under the oppressive reign of sin, our former cruel master.

> In the same way, count yourselves dead to sin but alive to God in Christ Jesus. Therefore do not let sin reign in your mortal body so that you obey its evil desires. Do not offer any part of yourself to sin as an instrument of wickedness, but rather offer yourselves to

God as those who have been brought from death to life; and offer every part of yourself to him as an instrument of righteousness. For sin shall no longer be your master, because you are not under the law, but under grace. (Romans 6:11–14)

The reign of sin is described as death, and the reign of God is described as life. Jesus Christ delivers us from death to life. He is the only one who has the power to do so. Whenever we realize we have been invaded by the forces of sin, it is time once again to call on the righteous Judge (11:27) to provide us victory and life.

Hook Questions

- Are you overcoming the world, or do you feel as if it is overcoming you? What aspects of life do you believe are richer outside of your relationship to God? What might you be relying on for victory instead of Christ?
- In what areas are you most in need of divine rescue? To what temptations are you particularly drawn? Why do you think this is so? How can you realize God's deliverance over these? What steps can you take to safeguard yourself from relapse?

Our deliverance is Jesus Christ. When we forget about him (3:7) and instead do what seems best to us (17:6; 21:25), we will find ourselves falling victim to those forces and powers that are set against God and his people. When we find ourselves overrun by these oppressive enemies to life, we must call on the righteous and all-powerful Judge, who is always ready to deliver us. In a world seemingly bent on getting us to take our eyes off of God and the path of life he has revealed to us, only by a continued, learned practice of dependence and focus on him will we be able to enjoy a secure and rich life that will bring us peace and contentment, and also draw others to the kingdom.

Empty to Full

The events of the book of Ruth take place during the time of the judges and highlight the main message of that book by means of a specific, and tragic, family situation. Instead of Israelites turning away from God and having to be painfully reminded that fullness of life exists only in fellowship with him, this book presents us with Naomi, an Israelite woman who has experienced the nightmare of losing her husband and sons, but who nevertheless finds fullness in life through the selfless and redeeming love she experiences by means of unexpected characters God brings into her life. The book opens with Naomi suddenly finding herself without any means of support or prospects for relief. The book ends with Naomi having a renewed joy and provision for life. In the chapters between, God uses her daughter-in-law (whose name attaches to the book) and the surprise appearance of a family relative to accomplish this transformation.

Theme of the Book

God uses Ruth and Boaz to fill Naomi's emptiness by providing her with food and a son.

At the start of the narrative, Naomi is not even in her homeland of Israel. In just five short, anguish-filled verses, she moves to a foreign country and loses her husband and two sons. Naomi has nothing left to her except her two daughters-in-law. And even one of them leaves her for better pastures. Naomi and Ruth, already grieving the loss of family, are also facing the frightening reality of no resources or means of supporting themselves. Naomi and Ruth head back to the land of Israel — with Naomi herself acknowledging that she went away full but has returned empty (1:21).

Yet in the midst of this emptiness God is still at work! First, Ruth, who is not even an Israelite, pledges her faithfulness to Naomi and the two of them walk together into an uncertain future. Next, while Ruth is doing what she can to provide food for herself and Naomi, she encounters Boaz, a relative and guardian-redeemer. Such a person had the responsibility to provide for the needs of the extended family. God had providentially led Ruth to the field of Boaz and provided for Naomi and Ruth through him.

♥ Memory Passage: *Ruth 4:14–15*

The women said to Naomi: "Praise be to the LORD, who this day has not left you without a guardian-redeemer. May he become famous throughout Israel! He will renew your life and sustain you in your old age."

Boaz fulfills his responsibility as the guardian-redeemer for Naomi and Ruth. In fact, he goes well beyond what was required. Boaz marries Ruth, ensuring that Naomi will be provided for. The emptiness that characterized Naomi's life at the beginning of the narrative is replaced by a fullness of life brought about by the Lord. Instead of scraps and a dismal future, she will enjoy abundance and a renewed future. Ruth eventually bears a son who will become the forefather of one who brings about an even greater redemption of those who belong to his family.

◎ The Jesus Lens

Naomi was just as powerless to effect her own redemption as we are powerless to effect ours. Until God brought Ruth into contact with Boaz, there was nothing but emptiness ahead of Naomi. But God was working behind the scenes to provide her with wonderful things, a full, secure life, and even a grandson. That grandson, Obed, will grow up to become the grandfather of David. David will become the ancestor of Jesus. So God's providential provision of a redeemer for Naomi will, in time, also become his providential provision of a redeemer for all those whom God adopts into his own family. And the result is the same for Naomi and for us: a reversal of an empty, hopeless life to one of fullness. Jesus himself describes this as his redemptive purpose.

> I have come that they may have life, and have it to the full. (John 10:10)

God became flesh in Jesus Christ in order to become our guardian-redeemer and fill our emptiness with the fullness of life. We no longer have to be satisfied with scraps and an uncertain future; we eat the bread of life now and know our future is secure with God.

Contemporary Implications

God reversed Naomi's situation from emptiness to fullness, and God wants us to experience that fullness too. But the rich life God desires us to know is not necessarily the kind of life that is promoted on store fronts in the mall. That life only offers emptiness on sale in the latest fashion of the season. No, the life God wants for us is one that provides real contentment and has staying power. He has sent his own Son as our guardian-redeemer so that we can experience it.

> I pray that out of his glorious riches he may strengthen you with power through his Spirit in your inner being, so that Christ may dwell in your hearts through faith. And I pray that you, being rooted and established in love, may have power, together with all the Lord's holy people, to grasp how wide and long and high and deep is the love of Christ, and to know this love that surpasses knowledge—that you may be filled to the measure of all the fullness of God. (Ephesians 3:16–19)

We too may have been wandering around in a foreign land a bit too long. Life can get wearying out there. Perhaps we, like Naomi, realize our emptiness and long for something more. Let's come back to the land of promise and embrace the fullness of life in Christ. Our Redeemer, "a man of standing" (2:1), is ready to give you "all the fullness of God."

Hook Questions

- Are the things you are relying on for fulfillment only leaving you empty instead? Do you really believe that other people would know how to meet your deepest needs and desires better than the one who created you? Isn't it time for you to choose fullness over emptiness?
- Is your Christ-card maxed out? Are you cashing in on all the fullness of life in Christ? Do you know the contentment that God wants for you whatever your circumstances may be? How could you raise your credit limit?

Our circumstances change. Sometimes we're on top of the world and other times we feel as if we have to climb up to reach bottom. If we rely on our circumstances for contentment, not only will those circumstances prove unreliable, but even when times are great we will have a hard time enjoying them because we know that things can change in a heartbeat. And there is no way for us to anticipate when those changes are coming. God has sent a guardian-redeemer to bring us out of the empty vacuum of circumstance-dependent existence apart from him into a new world bursting at the seams with a life in relationship with him. Come and experience as much as you can hold.

9 | 1 & 2 SAMUEL
Exalted and Humbled

The two books of Samuel were originally one book that was later separated into 1 Samuel, which describes the period from the birth of Samuel to the death of King Saul, and 2 Samuel, which describes most of the reign of King David. The books are named after Samuel, the judge-prophet whom God used to bring about the transition from the sporadic rule of judges to the continuous rule of kings. But the Israelite kings were not supposed to rule like the kings of other nations. The Israelite king was not to rule by his own authority and strength, but rather by the authority, direction, and power of God. The fact that power and authority are ultimately in God's hands was, and is, a hard truth to learn.

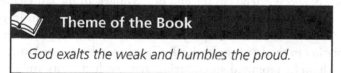

Theme of the Book

God exalts the weak and humbles the proud.

This theme is demonstrated in the lives of the main characters of these books. Hannah, a woman cruelly reminded of her childlessness, had her humiliation turned to celebration when she was blessed by God with Samuel, a son whom God used to direct the course of the nation of Israel (1 Samuel 1:1 – 2:11). Eli, the respected high priest, was humbled by God for letting his own sons run wild (1 Samuel 2:12 – 36). Saul, the first Israelite king and a physically imposing, yet humble, young man, was brought down by God when his humility curdled into pride and self-reliance (1 Samuel 10:9 – 24; 13:1 – 14). In the famous account of young David and the massive Philistine champion Goliath, we see how

God can turn the humble trust of a shepherd boy into victory over a giant ego. Though God would later raise up David from obscurity all the way to the kingship of Israel and would promise him an enduring kingdom (2 Samuel 7), God would still humble him when David forgot who was ultimately in control of people and events.

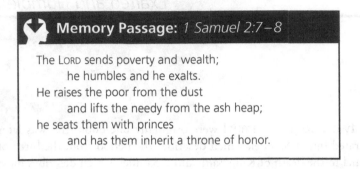

Memory Passage: *1 Samuel 2:7–8*

The LORD sends poverty and wealth;
    he humbles and he exalts.
He raises the poor from the dust
    and lifts the needy from the ash heap;
he seats them with princes
    and has them inherit a throne of honor.

God had promised David amazing things; yet David forgot that he owed his power and position to God and instead misused them to satisfy his personal desire for Bathsheba, another man's wife (2 Samuel 11). As a consequence, David endured the loss of a child and struggled to retain the kingship against rebellions from his own sons and others. The battle within David between humble trust in God (with its positive consequences) and occasional, prideful self-reliance (with its negative consequences) extends to the end of 2 Samuel. In the last chapter, David's pride in the number of his fighting men rather than in the strength of his God results in a plague that only David's repentance and reorientation to the Lord could check. Clearly, God's chosen king, the one to whom he promised an enduring dynasty, had faults and occasionally needed divine humbling. God himself would have to provide a king who would have no faults. The image of this king comes into focus under the Jesus lens.

The Jesus Lens

God fulfilled his promise to David. A distant descendant would indeed occupy his throne forever. But how could any human being avoid the periodic, and (let's be honest) often frequent, outbreaks of pride that require divine humbling? How could any human being occupy the throne of David forever when human nature seems to disqualify us? God solves this problem by means of his own Son. Because Jesus himself is God, all power and authority are already his. Yet Jesus put these divine prerogatives aside to become human. And not just any human, but a human who would both humble himself and be demeaned by others. Unlike David, Jesus perfectly obeyed his Father's will, even when that obedience led to rejection, humiliation, torture, and death. Because Jesus humbled himself in this way, the Father has exalted him to a kingship that makes all past, present, and future rules and rulers pale in significance.

> And being found in appearance as a man,
>   he humbled himself
>   by becoming obedient to death—even death on a cross!
> Therefore God exalted him to the highest place
>   and gave him the name that is above every name. (Philippians 2:8–9)

God has exalted the humbled Christ to an eternal and all-powerful kingship. The one who allowed himself to be overpowered by earthly rulers is now the one who has all authority not only on earth, but also in heaven (Matthew 28:18). He has gone from being the victim of misrule to being the almighty King who exercises a righteous rule.

Contemporary Implications

Because Jesus is on the throne and his Spirit indwells every believer, we, like the Old Testament kings, have the responsibility to exercise his authority with humble trust in him. Whatever our circumstances are now, we can be confident that we will reign with him as kings and queens in due time (2 Timothy 2:12), because *God opposes the proud but shows favor to the humbled and oppressed* (James 4:6). Therefore, though we are, in fact, now coheirs of the kingdom together with Jesus Christ (Romans 8:17), we must serve God in humility as we await our exaltation in Christ:

> Humble yourselves before the Lord, and he will lift you up. (James 4:10)

> Humble yourselves, therefore, under God's mighty hand, that he may lift you up in due time. (1 Peter 5:6)

In doing so, we will be imitating our Lord and showing a power-hungry and self-confident world that true power and authority reside not in sinful human beings, but in the only sinless human being, who has demonstrated his right to sit on the throne forever.

Hook Questions

- What have you bragged about lately? Do you consider humility a weakness or a strength? Do you regard Jesus as weak or powerful? Who are some humble people whom you admire? Is it harder to come up with names for these people than it is for self-promoting people?
- Does the source of your pride focus on God, or on yourself? Where do you turn first when things get tough? To whom do you give credit when things go well?

In the accounts of the characters of 1 and 2 Samuel, we are reminded that God does not regard human appearance or strength the way we so often do. What makes us attractive and strong in God's eyes is our humble trust in him. It is so easy for us to fall into the mind-set of those around us who want us to pin our self-worth on things that do not and cannot last. God lasts forever. Doesn't it make so much more sense to pin our self-worth on him? The irony is that when we give up trying to gain security and significance for ourselves and instead turn to God in humility, obedience, and trust, we achieve a security and significance for our lives that are divinely secured forever by the King of kings.

10 | 1 & 2 KINGS
Turning Away

Like 1 and 2 Samuel, these two books were originally one; only later were they separated into the books we now have. They describe how the twin kingdoms of Israel (in the north) and Judah (in the south) gradually drifted off the road of life until they ended up overturned in the ditch. Of course, things didn't seem to be heading that way in the beginning. We left the people of God in the capable hands of King David at the end of 2 Samuel. After some confusion regarding his successor, David named his son Solomon as the next king. Things started out well with the building of the temple for God and its dedication. But Solomon's son and successor fumbled the ball, and the nation divided in two in 930 BC. Both Israel and Judah — apart from only occasional efforts by godly kings and despite the repeated warnings of the prophets — one after the other experienced the drastic consequences of turning away from God. Only a remnant of Judah would survive in exile. This book explains to the exiled community how things ended up this way.

📖 Theme of the Book

God expels Israel and Judah from his presence in the Promised Land when their kings turn away from Torah.

After Solomon's reign and the subsequent division of the kingdom, both Israel and Judah begin a roller-coaster ride of faithfulness and faithlessness to God, with faithlessness eventually winning out with both kingdoms coming off the rails. The northern kingdom of Israel steps out on the wrong foot under King Jeroboam I, whose first major act is to erect golden calves in his most northern and southern cities to provide alternative worship opportunities for his citizens. Things don't improve by the time King Ahab takes the throne. Swayed by his wife Jezebel, Ahab promotes the worship of the false god Baal. Despite strong warnings by prophets such as Elijah and Elisha, Israel continues its downward spiral. Their rejection of God becomes so complete that he has no choice but to remove them from his presence in 722 BC by means of the invading Assyrian army.

The southern kingdom of Judah holds out longer, but its fate is the same. Good kings, such as Hezekiah and Josiah, try to stem the tide, but it's of no use. With heart-gripping compassion and patience, God uses his prophets to plead with his people to turn back and experience the life he has desired for them, but they refuse to listen. God removes Judah too from the Promised Land in 586 BC, this time by means of the Babylonians.

❤ Memory Passage: *2 Kings 17:20*

The LORD rejected all the people of Israel; he afflicted them and gave them into the hands of plunderers, until he thrust them from his presence.

It's not easy to read these books. They lay out for Israel and Judah the reasons why they had missed out on life and were instead experiencing the crushing emptiness and misery of exile. We wonder how they could have allowed themselves to continue on a path that was so clearly heading in the wrong direction. How could they ignore the divine messages spoken to them so often and with such power? Were they just stupid?

But if we stop to consider our own situation, we realize that we are not so different. We have God's Word available to us in print! We have pastors who preach it and its contemporary significance to us every Sunday—or at least they would like to, if we showed up. God has revealed to us the path of life, but we, too, often choose to head out in our own direction. Are we just stupid? Incredibly, even in judgment God provides a ray of hope. Surely it isn't deserved, but it is there just the same. These books end with King Jehoiachin being released from prison (2 Kings 25:27–30). The exile is not the last word from God. Judgment must be experienced, but God in his grace and mercy has not given up on his people.

The Jesus Lens

Our turning away from God calls for judgment as well. God cannot be just and holy and simply excuse sin. And we have all sinned. All of us, therefore, have merited divine judgment. Incredibly, God in his grace and mercy has provided a way out of this seemingly impossible situation. The only solution to the human problem of faithlessness is a human being who is entirely faithful. Such a person would not merit any divine judgment himself, but he could experience that judgment for all the rest of us who are ready to claim his representation for ourselves. This is the reason—the only reason—why God became a human being. Jesus, both human and divine, is the one person who never turned away from the Father, but was willing to experience the judgment deserved by all the rest of us who have. We turned away from God, and God, in judgment, turned away from his own Son on the cross as he suffered for us:

> Jesus cried out in a loud voice, *"Eli, Eli, lema sabachthani?"* (which means "My God, my God, why have you forsaken me?"). (Matthew 27:46)

We can't imagine the physical pain and mental anguish of the Son as he experienced the exile of the Father on our behalf in order to bring us from exile to life-giving and life-sustaining relationship with him. Jesus paid the price for our turning away so that we could turn back to God.

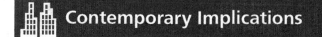

Contemporary Implications

Our relationship with God has been secured at a terrible price. That's how much God wants it. And even though Jesus has paid the price for our turning away, we aren't for that reason immune from the harm that sin can do to us. Sin robs us of life while deceiving us into believing that it is providing a fuller, more exciting life.

> See to it, brothers and sisters, that none of you has a sinful, unbe-
> lieving heart that turns away from the living God. But encourage
> one another daily, as long as it is called "Today," so that none of
> you may be hardened by sin's deceitfulness. (Hebrews 3:12–13)

We need to rely on God's strength and the encouragement of each other to keep from turning away from the path of life. Let's be honest; talking about this topic isn't a popular thing to do in most church communities. The prevailing view is that the less said about sin or temptations, the better. But not talking to each other about our struggles does not protect our lives, but rather endangers them. Too often we wait until sin has accomplished its destructive work before we are willing to talk about it. Jesus talked a lot about the dangers of sin and its threat to life. Let's name the enemy and bring against it the resources God has given to us, so that we can enjoy the fullness of life Christ died to provide us.

Hook Questions

- What is your "rule of life"? What spiritual disciplines can help you know the life God wants for you in relationship with him?
- What are you more likely to do: what you know is right or what you want to do at the time? Have you considered the long-term consequences of your choices?
- What are you doing to guard against turning away from God? Are you trying to stay faithful on your own, or are you drawing on the strength of God and his people?

When we read 1 and 2 Kings through the lens of Christ, we recognize ourselves. Like Israel and Judah, many of us have brief periods of faithfulness and long stretches of faithlessness. Thankfully, Jesus has paid the price for those long stretches and our relationship with God remains secure. By the power of his Spirit, we can now shorten the duration of those dry periods. We also have the community of our brothers and sisters in the faith to help us stay on track and to keep us accountable. There is abundant, rich life to enjoy when we are in fellowship with God. But there is meaninglessness and hurt when we turn away from him. Let's get on the path to life and do everything we can, drawing on the strength of God, to stay there.

Like Samuel and Kings, these two books were originally one and only later separated into the two books we have now. While they cover much of the same history as 1 and 2 Kings (and are therefore often ignored), they view it from a much different perspective. The two books of Kings were directed to the exiled people of God to explain how their actions had brought divine judgment on them; 1 and 2 Chronicles are directed toward the people of God after they had returned from exile. These books are intended to answer the questions that were surely at the front of everyone's mind: Has God rejected us completely? Do we have a future with him? What confidence can we have that God still cares about us?

> ### Theme of the Book
>
> *God encourages postexilic Israel by means of an account of Davidic kings who acknowledge the Lord's rule.*

These books begin to answer these questions by means of genealogies. Beginning with Adam and followed by over eight chapters, 1 Chronicles reminds the returned exiles of how God has preserved the people he has chosen to be a channel of blessing to the nations. And even though the last half of 2 Chronicles describes the reigns of the last kings of Judah who, with significant exceptions, "did evil in the eyes of the LORD" and so brought about the destruction of Jerusalem, the book ends with the decree of their conqueror granting the exiles permission to return to the Promised Land. Israel has survived because of God's faithfulness.

But it is the faithfulness of those kings who followed his instructions and listened to his words spoken through his prophets that served as the basis for God's irrevocable promises of future blessings. The books of Chronicles highlight these kings as the justification for Israel's continued confidence in God. It is no surprise, then, that almost half of these books are devoted to the reigns of David (the last twenty chapters of 1 Chronicles) and Solomon (the first nine chapters of 2 Chronicles). God's promises to them are at the heart of the returned exiles' hope.

Memory Passage: *2 Chronicles 7:17–18*

If you walk before me faithfully as David your father did, and do all I command, and observe my decrees and laws, I will establish your royal throne, as I covenanted with David your father when I said, "You shall never fail to have a successor to rule over Israel."

David, in particular, is held up as an example of a leader who sought to live in accordance with God's instructions and so lead his people into a deeper relationship with God. This relationship is physically signified by the temple David planned and prepared to build and which was successfully completed by his son Solomon. But David and Solomon, as exemplary as they were, were not perfect. If only there were a king in the line of David who would perfectly keep God's instructions and so ensure God's enduring fellowship with his people! Such a king would be a picture of God himself, one who knows what true life is and who leads the people he rules into the enjoyment of that life. The books of Chronicles encourage the returned exiles to trust that God's promise to David would someday lead to just such a king.

The Jesus Lens

Power corrupts. We human beings are unable to resist the temptations that come with power and influence. It seems that every day we read about local and national rulers who have abused their positions for personal gain. It is apparently difficult for many leaders to keep their behavior within the bounds of what is prescribed by the laws of the people they govern. It is impossible for them to keep their behavior within the bounds of what is prescribed by the laws of God. But any hope that God's people may have for an enduring relationship with him is entirely dependent on a king from the line of David who is able to perfectly follow God's instructions. We might be tempted to despair that such a ruler can ever exist. And we would be right, if God had not sent his own Son, Jesus Christ, to be that ruler.

> "Do not weep! See, the Lion of the tribe of Judah, the Root of David, has triumphed." (Revelation 5:5)

Just as 1 and 2 Chronicles encourage the returned exiles by means of an account of Davidic kings who acknowledge the Lord's rule, so God encourages us by means of an account of a Davidic king, Jesus, who has perfectly done all that the Father has commanded. His royal throne is established forever, and he leads his people into deeper relationship with God.

Contemporary Implications

Those who submit to the kingship of this perfect Davidic king have his obedience credited to them. We become citizens of a new kingdom (Philippians 3:20), which is governed and safeguarded by the King of kings. It is important to note that Jesus does not do away with God's law; the law is the guidebook to life. Rather, Jesus perfectly fulfills the law in every way so that he is able to lead his subjects into an appropriation of that life.

> Christ is the culmination of the law so that there may be righteousness for everyone who believes. (Romans 10:4)

Too often we behave as if we had no king. We think and act as though it is our own obedience to God that will earn for us the Good Lawkeeping Seal of Approval. We feel depressed and defeated when we realize how far and how frequently we fall short of carrying out God's relational demands. First and Second Chronicles remind us that it is the obedience or disobedience of the king that determines the fate of God's people. Thankfully, the obedience of our King is perfect; through it he merits life for his people. Our King has secured our relationship with God forever, because he reigns forever. We can direct our energy toward exploring and developing this new life instead of wasting our efforts on worrying whether that life exists.

Hook Questions

- Are you good enough for heaven? Do you behave as though you were? Do you expect other Christians to behave as though they were? If you are relying on your own righteousness (whatever that is) to bring about or maintain your relationship with God, then what do you think Christ's righteousness accomplished?
- How do *you* acknowledge the Lord's rule in your own circumstances? Do you regard yourself as a subject of King Jesus? If someone watched you during the day, who would they say really ruled your life? Jesus? Public opinion? You?

God chose to rule his people through the Davidic kings. The books of Chronicles show that when those kings fulfilled the demands of God's law — the instructions for personal and communal life — God blessed his people with life, with meaning and purpose, with security and significance, and with clear direction. We can be encouraged in the fact that our Davidic king, Jesus Christ, has perfectly kept the covenant's demands and so has achieved for us, his subjects, true life. As we follow our King, as faithful citizens of his kingdom, we will experience that life more and more.

The Persians had defeated the Babylonians, and God had moved the heart of the Persian king Cyrus to decree that the exiled Israelites could return to their homeland. A good number do exactly that and begin to rebuild the temple, the physical symbol of God's presence in their midst. That they undertake to do this is encouraging. It means that they have learned the value of their relationship with God and seek to embody it with this special building as soon as possible, even against significant opposition from their neighbors.

Theme of the Book

God brings the exiles back to Jerusalem and directs that his temple be rebuilt.

When the temple had been rebuilt and its services resumed (chaps. 3–6), Ezra arrives in Jerusalem with another group of returnees. But Ezra finds that though the people of God have reconstructed the temple, their relationship with God that the building represented is still in need of repair. They have opened themselves up to being drawn away from faithfulness to God by intermarrying with people who worship other gods. They had been warned against doing precisely this by Moses and Joshua (Exodus 34:16; Deuteronomy 7:3–4; Joshua 23:12–13), but they have once again rejected the word of God in favor of their own desires. The Persian king Cyrus had decreed that the exiled Israelites could return and build a temple for their God. The real temple where

God wants his name to dwell, however, does not consist of wood and stone, but of the committed hearts of his people.

> ### 🔖 Memory Passage: *Ezra 1:3*
>
> Any of his people among you may go up to Jerusalem in Judah and build the temple of the LORD, the God of Israel, the God who is in Jerusalem, and may their God be with them.

God's people had been brought back to the special place of fellowship with him. They had labored long and against fierce opposition to build the temple where he would visibly dwell among them. But the major obstacle to their progress was not the bureaucratic red tape strewn in their path by the jealous and suspicious local officials. No, their real obstacle was internal. The physical dwelling place of God in their midst was supposed to represent a deeper, personal, intimate dwelling place of God in the lives of each one of them. The external construction was accomplished, but there was some work left to do on the internal construction. Ezra served as building inspector for the internal construction work of the returned exiles. He pointed to significant structural issues that needed to be addressed, and thankfully the people agreed with him! They promised to work as diligently on their personal lives as they had in their communal effort at rebuilding the temple.

🔍 The Jesus Lens

In the course of time, God would dwell among his people in an even more personal and relatable way. He would send his Son, called "Immanuel" (meaning "God with us"), to initiate the construction of a new kind of temple. This new temple would bring together the visible place of God's presence among his people with a personal relationship with each one of his people. The key component of the construction is the one who correctly orients the entire building process and ensures the continued approval of its new resident. Each believer, aligned with Christ, interconnects with every other believer to become the living temple of God. The temple is no longer a place to visit God, but rather his very dwelling that we form as his people.

> You are … built on the foundation of the apostles and prophets, with Christ Jesus himself as the chief cornerstone. In him the whole building is joined together and rises to become a holy temple in the Lord. And in him you too are being built together to become a dwelling in which God lives by his Spirit. (Ephesians 2:19–22)

Ezra's concern was not primarily with the physical temple, but with the realization in the hearts of his people of the deeper reality the temple signified. He wanted the nations surrounding Israel to see the presence of their God not just in a shiny new temple, but also in the obedient, trusting lives of his people. Are we as concerned that unbelievers can see the presence of our God in our lives, his new temple?

Contemporary Implications

There is building to be done! Let's join God's construction crew! He provides the energy, the tools, and the blueprints. There is a job for everyone. By the power of God's Spirit, we continue to attach additions to his new temple. Occasionally we must also engage in some temple maintenance. Our perspectives might need to be hammered back into alignment or our visible Christlikeness might need a new coat of paint. And, as anyone who has done any building knows, it is vitally important that we take care that the temple always rests securely on its foundation. In our case, that foundation is Jesus Christ. As an exemplary temple-builder, the apostle Paul puts it this way:

> By the grace God has given me, I laid a foundation as a wise builder, and someone else is building on it. But each one should build with care. For no one can lay any foundation other than the one already laid, which is Jesus Christ. (1 Corinthians 3:10–11)

God has chosen to live within us. Let's make sure his house is in order! We need to dust off spiritual disciplines like Bible reading, prayer, fellowship, and evangelism so that we and others will be able to hear what God is saying. We need to wash the grime of worldly influence off the windows so that people can clearly see God in us. We need to open up and air out those parts of the house we have kept shut for too long so that God has access to every part of us. There is a lot involved with building and maintaining a divine dwelling, but God is delighted when we rely on his strength and get to it.

Hook Questions

- What are you building with your life? Are your efforts focused on God's kingdom or on your own? Are you aware that building of some sort is always going on? Wouldn't it be better to expend your efforts on something that lasts? What are the tools that God has given you to participate in the building process?
- What kind of life does this building demand? Have you committed yourself to something that is draining the life from you? Are you happy with how you've spent your years? Why not commit yourself to something that infuses you with life?

Ezra showed God's people that though they had been engaged with an external building process, they had neglected to build their internal relationship with God. They had been drawn away from their focus on God by those who were committed to other gods. This is something that easily happens to God's construction crew today as well. Let's be sure we're using quality building materials that are up to code. We have the resources of an almighty God given freely to us so that we can make our personal lives and our lives together a beautiful place for God to dwell.

13 | # NEHEMIAH
Distinctions

It had been fourteen years since Ezra's return to Jerusalem. Children had been born and grown to be teenagers. They had never known life in exile. For them, it was normal to live among ruins. It was normal to be looked down upon by the local population and their officials. Sure, they had heard their parents' stories about Jerusalem's glory in the past. But it was hard to imagine that these stones and burned timbers were once a shining city. Ezra had pleaded with their parents to keep their focus on the Lord and not allow themselves to be lured away from their devotion to him by the people around them who worshiped other gods. But it was hard to maintain such distinctions when the boundaries between the people of God and the people of other gods were so blurry. God sent Nehemiah to help them.

> 📖 **Theme of the Book**
>
> *God moves the returned exiles to rebuild the wall of Jerusalem.*

Nehemiah was the cupbearer to the Persian king Artaxerxes when news reached him about the situation of the Jews who had already returned to Jerusalem. Things were not good and morale was low. The wall of the city was a pile of rubble. Nehemiah's distress over the sorry state of his fellow Jews reduced him to tears. The king noticed his concern and, moved by God to do something for his servant, sent Nehemiah to Jerusalem with permission and provisions to rebuild it and its wall. Nehemiah arrived in Jerusalem and immediately began to take the steps necessary to rebuild the city wall.

> **♦ Memory Passage:** Nehemiah 2:17
>
> You see the trouble we are in: Jerusalem lies in ruins, and its gates have been burned with fire. Come, let us rebuild the wall of Jerusalem, and we will no longer be in disgrace.

Nehemiah's distress was not simply that a nice architectural feature of the city was missing. He was concerned that what it represented was also missing: the visible dividing wall between the people of God and those who didn't know him. God's people were beginning to blend into the local population so much that their distinctiveness was disappearing. How could God make his glory known among his people if exactly who his people were was becoming unclear? Nehemiah effectively communicated his concern to the exiles, and they got on board with the idea of rebuilding the wall of the city.

As you can imagine, the idea of erecting a wall of separation between themselves and the people around them with whom they had previously blended so easily did not go over well with the locals. There was significant opposition (chaps. 4 and 6) — as there always is when the people of God are distinct. Nevertheless, with sacrifice and great effort the wall was completed, and the visible distinctiveness of God's people began to have a parallel effect in their lives. They began to look after the poor in their midst (chap. 5), they confessed their sins (chap. 9), and they recommitted themselves to following the laws God had given them for their good (10:28–39). They were once again a distinct people — a channel of God's blessing to the nations that would one day come into focus in Jesus Christ.

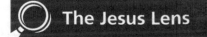

The Jesus Lens

Jesus, and those united with him by faith, are also distinct from those who don't know him. Our citizenship is in a new kingdom, the kingdom of heaven (Philippians 3:20). Our motivations and goals are different from those of our neighbors. We serve a different God than they do. Everyone recognized that Jesus and his followers were different than what they had come to expect from themselves and others. Even though they lived in the same country, ate the same food, and wore the same clothes, there was a recognizable distinctiveness. Of course, as Nehemiah experienced, difference often brings resentment and opposition. Jesus experienced both to a fantastic degree. Those who opposed the spiritual wall and city he was rebuilding finally decided they would rather crucify him than put up with that any longer. And Jesus knew that his disciples would experience that resentment and opposition as well. So he prayed to the Father on our behalf:

> I have given them your word and the world has hated them, for they are not of the world any more than I am of the world. My prayer is not that you take them out of the world but that you protect them from the evil one. (John 17:14–15)

Christ's true home (and that of his disciples) is not of this world. We live here for now, but our passports originate from a different place. They bear the stamp of the kingdom of heaven, where all the citizens look increasingly like the King.

Contemporary Implications

Notice that our Lord does not pray that his followers be isolated from the world of people who do not know him, but rather that their distinctiveness from such people will be preserved and protected. God wants to reveal truth about himself and the new humanity he is creating and calling people to in Christ. He can only do that if his people remain distinct from the rest of humanity in their relationship to him and each other.

> Therefore, since we have these promises, dear friends, let us purify ourselves from everything that contaminates body and spirit, perfecting holiness out of reverence for God. (2 Corinthians 7:1)

Let the world see what it means to be distinctively Christian. If, when others look at the community of God's people, they only see more of the same kind of life they already know, then what is the good news for them? Let's make sure that the alternative life and different kind of human community that God is making available through Jesus Christ are clearly visible to those outside his kingdom. This is what it means for us to be holy, set apart, or distinct.

Hook Questions

- What difference, if any, does your relationship with Christ make in your marriage, friendships, career, student life, or entertainment choices? Do you regard your distinctiveness as God's own child a source of joy or of disgrace?
- Is there a visible distinction between your life and that of an unbeliever? Would anyone looking at your life be able to see that you are a believer, or are you a stealth Christian — remaining largely undetected until you drop a gospel bomb? How do you maintain your distinctiveness as a Christian without putting off those who need to hear and see the good news?

It is not easy to resist the pressures to conform to the ways of thinking and acting that characterize those who live for this world. We are surrounded by those influences. We might not even recognize that the wall of distinction between us and unbelievers is in need of repair. And when we do take steps to repair it, we will often encounter opposition. Are we ready to answer those who ask with contempt, "Who do you think you are?" The answer, of course, is that we are subjects of a wonderful King, who grants his people a richer, more enduring and profoundly fulfilling life than anything available outside his kingdom. The walls that separate this kingdom from the outside world are unique. They let in anyone who wants to enter, but keep out anything that would fundamentally threaten those inside. Do those outside see anything inside this community of the king that would make them want to come inside? Do they even see a wall of distinction?

Providential Deliverance

Sometimes it seems as if God has left the building. Certainly it must have seemed so to Esther. She lived under the rule of a foreign world power. Her father and mother were dead, and she was raised by her crusty older cousin, Mordecai. Now she had even been taken from his care by royal decree and brought into the king's harem, where, obeying her cousin's instructions, she kept her Jewish ethnicity secret. Surely none of these events were on her list of life goals. But despite all of these twists and turns in her path, Esther's future looked bright. Of all the concubines in the harem, Esther pleased King Xerxes the most, and he made her his queen. God had not, in fact, left the building. Little did Esther know that God had providentially placed her in the queenship in order to bring about the deliverance of his people from Haman, who was bent on annihilating the Jews.

Theme of the Book

God providentially provides Esther and Mordecai to bring Israel deliverance from her enemies.

Mordecai regularly visited Esther, and during one of his visits he discovered a plot to assassinate the king. Esther revealed the plot to the king and gave Mordecai credit. Later, when Mordecai refused to kneel before Haman, the king's honored official, Haman was furious. He found out that Mordecai was a Jew and decided to take steps to eliminate not only Mordecai, but all of his people as well. Interestingly, one of Haman's complaints to the king about the Jews is the very emphasis of the book of Nehemiah: "There is a certain people ... who keep themselves separate" (3:8). Employing all of his slithery skills, Haman succeeded in persuading the king to issue a decree to annihilate the Jews. Mordecai informed Esther of the dire situation and that the life of every Jew was in jeopardy. He persuaded her to put her own life in jeopardy by going to the king unbidden in order to appeal for the lives of her people.

> **Memory Passage:** *Esther 4:14*
>
> Who knows but that you have come to your royal position for such a time as this?

That night, during a divinely induced bout of insomnia, the king had the official records read to him (which, evidently, were a potent sleeping aid), and he discovered written there Mordecai's previous whistle-blowing regarding the assassination attempt. The king decided to publicly honor Mordecai, further enraging Haman. Shortly therafter, at a banquet she had requested, Esther revealed to the king Haman's plan to exterminate the Jews. Now it was the king's turn to be furious, and Haman ended up impaled on the very pole he had prepared for Mordecai. Moreover, at Esther's request, the king decreed that the Jews had the right to protect themselves against any who might attack them. Thus, by God's providential working through Esther and Mordecai, the Jews were saved. There would one day be an even greater deliverance brought about by God, by an individual who would seem just as unlikely a candidate to do so—a lowly Jewish carpenter who lived under Roman occupation.

The Jesus Lens

For the Jews under Persian rule, the odds were stacked against them. Their only hope was that the one to whom all authorities must ultimately answer would somehow provide for their deliverance. And God did just that through Esther and Mordecai. God put Esther and Mordecai just where they needed to be, at just the time they needed to be there, to bring about his salvation. For human beings under the rule of sin, the odds are stacked against us. Our only hope is that God will somehow provide for our deliverance as well. And God did just that through his own Son. God became human, at just the right time, to bring about his salvation.

> When the set time had fully come, God sent his Son, born of a woman, born under the law, to redeem those under the law. (Galatians 4:4–5)

The Father provides Christ to deliver his people "when the set time had fully come." Jesus accomplishes this salvation in a way similar to what we find in the book of Esther. The threat of death is removed, we are given the means to defend ourselves (by the power of his Spirit), and the chief architect of our planned destruction has himself been sentenced to the same fate he desired for God's people. The Jews initiated a new feast day, called Purim, to commemorate their deliverance. It was a time of celebration and joy. Christians have such a day as well. We call it Sunday.

Contemporary Implications

God used Esther and Mordecai to bring about the deliverance of his people. But his people had to be notified! So Mordecai wrote in the name of the king and sent the news throughout the kingdom by mounted couriers on fast horses (8:10). God used Jesus Christ to bring about the deliverance of his people. But his people have to be notified today as well. We have the privilege and the responsibility to carry this news as fast and effectively as we can throughout the world. Okay, maybe not by mounted couriers on fast horses, but by word of mouth, by print and electronic media, by lives that communicate to everyone who sees us that we have good news to share.

> We are ... Christ's ambassadors, as though God were making his appeal through us. (2 Corinthians 5:20)

As Christ's ambassadors, we have been providentially provided to proclaim deliverance through him to those who are perishing. We have been made children of the King. And who knows but that we have come to royal position for such a time as this?

Hook Questions

- What does it mean to be Christ's ambassador? What does an ambassador do? Do you speak to others in the King's name and authority or in your own? How does your worshiping community work together to make the good news known?
- How could you be an agent of God's deliverance in the place where he has put you? What are the ways you could make the good news known to those who are perishing? How far are you willing to go to be used by God to bring about the deliverance of his people?

It was a dangerous thing for Esther to enter the king's presence without being summoned. She was risking her life. But the fate of God's people was at stake. God has other people whom he wants to deliver from the fear of judgment. He has put each one of us in a unique place, at just the right time, where we can be used to bring about that deliverance. Like Esther, we too might have to risk our own comfort or even safety as we carry out our divinely appointed task. But we can take comfort in knowing that as we do so, we are simply imitating our Lord, who has turned our sorrow into joy and our mourning into celebration (9:22).

15 | JOB

God and Suffering

If we are honest with ourselves, we will admit that sometimes we have questions or doubts about God's justice. Things happen that make us think, "How could God allow this to happen?" The book of Job addresses this concern about God's justice. It is a "theodicy"; that is, it is an argument for God's justice in the world, particularly in the light of the apparent counterargument of human pain and anguish, from which his children are in no way exempt. It is not enough to say, "In all things God works for the good of those who love him" (Romans 8:28), because sometimes it is hard to see any good at all in circumstances. It is also cruel to suggest, as so many well-intentioned but ultimately hurtful people do, that perhaps the hardship being endured by our brothers or sisters in the faith results from their sin. Of course, God is under no obligation to explain himself to us. But he graciously does just that in this book.

Theme of the Book

God is active in areas and realms beyond our understanding.

The book of Job begins with the title character enjoying an enviable life. Times are good indeed. But, Satan asks God, is Job happy with God because of the wonderful things God has given him, or is Job happy with God because of who God is? The only convincing proof of Job's love for God is to take away all of those things that have made his life so enjoyable. This God proceeds to do by sending disasters as rapidly and as painfully as machine-gun fire. Before we can escape the first chapter, Job has lost sons, daughters, servants, flocks, and herds. We have barely dragged ourselves into the second chapter before Job is afflicted with painful sores covering every part of his body. His own wife suggests that he take the easy way out (2:9).

Job's three friends show up to comfort him, but they end up only making things worse. They not so subtly suggest that Job must have done something wrong to merit his situation. Certainly God would not let such bad things happen to a good person. Consequently, Job must not be good. Job knows this is not right. He had enjoyed a close relationship with God, and yet God seems to have decided to use him for target practice. What's going on here? Job cries out for God to explain himself.

Memory Passage: *Job 42:3*

You asked, "Who is this that obscures my plans without knowledge?"
> Surely I spoke of things I did not understand,
> things too wonderful for me to know.

God finally does answer Job, but probably not in the way Job had hoped. God reveals himself in a storm and reminds Job that there is a huge difference between humans and God. For two chapters (38 and 39), God lists things in creation about which Job has some superficial knowledge, but then God goes on to explain how much more deeply he knows them. The point of this awe-inspiring list is that if we human beings cannot even fully comprehend the things we can see with our eyes, how can we possibly expect to understand things that take place in the divine realm—things we cannot see? For his divine purposes, and somehow incorporated into his redemptive plan, God may at times call on his children to suffer. And we, like Job, probably won't know why. Thankfully, the New Testament is full of explanations about why God called on his own Son to suffer.

The Jesus Lens

In Jesus, we see the problem of the suffering innocent in its sharpest focus. If anyone had the right to call foul over his situation, it was God's own Son. No one else was sinless like him. No one else had a closer relationship with the Father. And yet no one else suffered more. Jesus makes it perfectly clear that there is no necessary connection between suffering and goodness. A person can even be perfect and suffer.

> Christ also suffered once for sins, the righteous for the unrighteous, to bring you to God. (1 Peter 3:18)

Christ gives us the ultimate picture of the righteous sufferer as he accomplishes God's saving purposes. It was not easy for our Lord to endure what he did. He even asked that, if possible, God would exempt him from it (Luke 22:42). But he was willing to suffer because he trusted that this was the best way to get to the wonderful end the Father had in view—our salvation.

Contemporary Implications

When we submit to the lordship of Jesus Christ, we offer ourselves to him as living sacrifices (Romans 12:1). It should not surprise us, therefore, if God occasionally calls on us to make good on our offer by suffering, for his purposes—even if we, like Job, don't fully understand why. It could be for our own growth in faith, for the growth or encouragement of those who see us bear up under the load by the power of God's grace, or for a host of other reasons beyond our ability to grasp. What we can be sure of is that God is about his redemptive work, as he always is, and has chosen us to participate in that work by sharing, at least for a while, in some of the same kind of suffering his own Son experienced.

> Dear friends, do not be surprised at the fiery ordeal that has come on you to test you, as though something strange were happening to you. But rejoice inasmuch as you participate in the sufferings of Christ, so that you may be overjoyed when his glory is revealed. (1 Peter 4:12–13)

Job's horrible circumstances led him to question God's justice. Our circumstances, too, can occasionally lead us to doubt God's justice or goodness. Perhaps without our realizing it, we might be relapsing into the way of thinking that characterized our lives before we were Christians. That is, we might be placing *ourselves* at the center of our world.

Our understanding, *our* desires, and *our* comfort are once again asserting their control. God, not we ourselves, should be at the center of our Christian lives. It can be difficult to see God at work in our suffering. Like Job, we might not see how he could be at work in it at all! But suffering *is* used by God to accomplish his purposes just as effectively as the good times are.

To say otherwise is to say that suffering is meaningless—a cruel and unbiblical conclusion. To say that God is not somehow even using sin-originated suffering to accomplish his redemptive purposes is to assert that his sovereignty is suspended during suffering and that something or someone else is in control—another unacceptable conclusion. Yes, suffering is ultimately the result of the sin that human beings introduced into God's good creation. But, thank God, he has not abandoned us to sin's full effects. Even in the midst of those negative effects he is relentlessly pursuing our redemption and the redemption of the whole creation. This is a good thing indeed. Are we willing to be used by God to accomplish his redemptive work, even when that work includes suffering that we don't understand?

Hook Questions

- Where is God when it hurts? Are pain and suffering always bad? Was God wrong for allowing his own Son to suffer? What is the ultimate cause of suffering? Do you believe that God knows what he is doing?
- When things go the way you want, does that mean God is blessing you? Does the lack of any suffering mean that you are living a godly life?

There is a realm beyond the created in which God dwells. God is free to operate behind and beyond and above the created order to accomplish his purposes that, for the most part, remain known only to him. We must be willing to acknowledge our status as created beings on an entirely different level than the Creator, and to acknowledge the limitations our created status imposes on us. Primary among these limitations, although perhaps the most unacceptable to us, is the limitation on our understanding of how and why God acts as he does. God alone knows the end from the beginning, as well as the best way to get to the end from the beginning. God's redemptive plan involves nothing less than the liberation of creation and his people from sin and death. There can be no greater good than that! He has given us, his children, a taste of that redemption even now, along with an abiding relationship with him that no circumstance, however horrible it may be, can ever sever.

16 | PSALMS
Lament and Praise

The book of Psalms is all about relationship. It assumes that its readers are in a close relationship with God. In fact, the first psalm serves as a warning to those beginning the book that it is only those who delight in God's words who should continue to read any further. Of course, any good relationship requires communication, and the book of Psalms is a collection of those communications. A relationship has highs and lows, and so there are praise psalms and lament psalms. Because the Hebrew name of the book means "praises," one might not expect that the book contains more laments than praises. But the movement of individual lament psalms, and the movement of the book as a whole, is from lament to praise. When we get back to basics and direct our thoughts back to who God is and what he has done for us, we will always end up, eventually, in praise.

Theme of the Book

God the Great King provides the words of lament and praise that are appropriate responses to him.

The psalms also contain deep theological truths, but truths at their most vital and vibrant realization in a living relationship with God, the source of truth. It is interesting to note that through the psalms, God communicates to us not only on the cognitive level, but also on the emotional level. He created us as multifaceted beings, and he speaks to all facets of his human creations, including the emotional parts. It is reassuring to sneak peeks at the emotions of God's people of the past and find our own emotions reflected in them. We find frustration (43:2), depression (6:3), anger (101:3), feelings of distress and sorrow (13:1–2), as well as feelings of joy (33:3) and confidence (25:1). And we are reassured that within the context of our relationship with God the great King, these feelings are okay to have. No matter how and what we are feeling, we can tell God about it. In fact, he *wants* us to tell him about it. He already knows, but he invites us to spend some quality time with him.

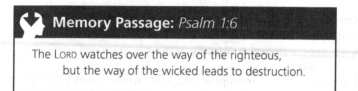

Memory Passage: *Psalm 1:6*

The LORD watches over the way of the righteous,
    but the way of the wicked leads to destruction.

All of us have hard times at some point in our lives, or even at many points for a few of us. For unbelievers there is absolutely nothing solid to lean on for strength. How often are we reminded how temporary and insubstantial the things we trust in really are? People fail us, memories and health decline, things get old and break, stock markets crash. But if we find our strength in the Lord, we will never be disappointed. He never fails, declines, ages, or loses value. And he has given much to have a relationship with us.

But he wants it to be an honest relationship, with nothing hidden or falsely represented — no creative online profiles. He wants to know when we are unhappy and when we are happy, when we are in distress and when we are excited, when we're in a loving mood and when we're downright angry. In short, he wants with us the kind of relationship he has with his Son.

The Jesus Lens

The intimate, personal relationship God desires for us is clearly displayed in the life of Jesus. Not only did Jesus enjoy the closeness with the Father that he wants us to know, he also demonstrated the relationship the Father wants with us. Jesus, in effect, embodies the psalms. The same aspects of God's relationship with his people that we see in the psalms, we also see even more consistently in Jesus. In Jesus we have the presence of God, the kingship of God, the blessings for obedience and tragic consequences for our disobedience, the forgiveness of God, and the compassion and love of God all lived out before us. God determined not just to relate to us with words, but with a human presence too. He has done everything possible to encourage our relationship with him, so that we might know the closest possible fellowship with him. The apostle Paul describes our relationship with God through Christ as an organic one:

> The Son is the image of the invisible God.... He is before all things, and in him all things hold together. And he is the head of the body, the church. (Colossians 1:15–18)

Jesus lives out the appropriate response to the Great King. He is in perfect relationship with the Father and desires his people to have that relationship as well. And he provides the means to have this relationship by reconciling us to the Father through the sacrifice of himself to pay for the sins that have alienated us.

Contemporary Implications

God wants us to be in a continual, close relationship with him. And he doesn't put any emotional qualifiers on this relationship. He doesn't specify that we may only pray to him when we are happy and content with the world. He doesn't require that we only sing praise songs — although it's rare to see a lament team in our churches. He doesn't ask that we hide our emotions under a blanket of doctrinal propositions. What he does ask is that we talk to him about everything. Within our secure relationship, we can pour out our hearts to God and rest assured that he will wrap our deepest concerns in his protective peace. He doesn't promise to deliver us from all of our problems right now. But he does promise to guard us from any relationship-disturbing threat they may pose. And ultimately, our relationship with God is the only thing that matters.

> Do not be anxious about anything, but in every situation, by prayer and petition, with thanksgiving, present your requests to God. And

the peace of God, which transcends all understanding, will guard your hearts and your minds in Christ Jesus. (Philippians 4:6–7)

We can talk to God about everything as we grow in the unbreakable relationship with the Father that Jesus has secured for us. And we have the confidence of knowing that the Creator of heaven and earth not only has the time to listen to us, but he has moved heaven and earth to be able to do so. He desperately wants to hear from us.

Hook Questions

- Is your faith strong enough for you to be honest with God? Are you trying to hide things from him? Do you share only the joyful and happy parts of your life with God, or also the darker parts of doubt, fear, and sadness?
- Is there room in your faith community for you to express these feelings? How would you rate the communication in your faith community's relationship with God?
- What is your motivation for prayer? Do you primarily want God to give you things or do things for you, like some great cosmic concierge? Or do you want to open up your life to God as you get to know him better? Have you spent some time lately thanking God for your relationship with him, which cost him so much to bring about?

It may take some practice to open ourselves up to God. We have probably assumed that only polished prayer-speak is acceptable to him. But take a closer look at the psalms. Some candid things are said there, in strong language. The writers of the psalms don't pull any punches when they talk about what is bothering them. They aren't even afraid to tell God when they're having trouble understanding what he is doing. And they speak just as candidly and powerfully when they have something good to say. That's what makes for a strong, honest relationship. And that's what God wants with us.

The book of Psalms focused on our relationship with God, the Creator. The book of Proverbs focuses on our relationship with the world, the created. God created the world with a structure. True, that structure has been damaged by sin, but God's grace keeps it from collapsing. So, if we learn the patterns and rhythms of natural phenomena and human behavior, we should be able to gain some advantage for living fruitful lives. The book of Proverbs provides those insights, and living according to them is a way to describe wisdom.

 Theme of the Book

God has placed an order in creation to which we should pay attention in order to live wisely.

The book of Proverbs is, therefore, a primer on street smarts. It helps God's people know how to avoid being taken advantage of by others and instead how to maximize their own human experience. But the proverbs are general principles that usually, but don't always, apply. Sin has damaged the created order, throwing sand into the gears, so that sometimes things don't happen as they should. Also, because we are created beings, our perception of the workings of the world designed by an infinite Creator is bound to be limited and even faulty. And, of course, God is always free to work behind the scenes and beyond the rules of nature to accomplish his purposes, as we have seen in the book of Job. So we must be careful as we read and apply these principles derived from observing the world. It takes a measure of wisdom to rightly understand wisdom.

The proverbs must be thought about, mulled over, and savored like chocolate tortes, one flavorful bite at a time. Of course, living according to the rhythms and patterns of the world presupposes those rhythms and patterns have been placed there by a wise God who made and designed the world for human beings. In other words, to gain maximum benefit from the wisdom of the book of Proverbs, one must acknowledge and submit to the God who makes the world work the way it does.

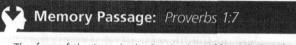

Memory Passage: *Proverbs 1:7*

The fear of the LORD is the beginning of knowledge, but fools despise wisdom and instruction.

The message of Proverbs is that when we live in harmony with the order found within creation and in the proper relationships with our fellow human beings, then we are wise. This is wisdom because it is living as God intended—alertly attending to the world, to our own responsibility to bear God's image, and to the interests of each other. When we live like this, we will experience a much greater enjoyment of life than if we ignore the order God has placed in creation. But sin has disrupted that order to some degree and has also affected our ability to always rightly perceive it. If only there were a human being we could see living in perfect wisdom, we would have a much clearer picture of how conforming to the created order would look in actual human experience. God sent his Son to be that picture.

The Jesus Lens

God became human in the person of his Son to pay the price for our sin and to restore our relationship with him. But Jesus could only accomplish this payment for our sin if he had no sin of his own; that is, he had to live a perfect life. The fact that he never sinned means that if we look at his life, we will be able to see how a human being should live as God intended. We can see what it means for a human being to be wise. Indeed, the apostle Paul tells us that all wisdom is found in Christ (Colossians 2:2–3). This wisdom doesn't look much like what the unbelieving world thinks it does. You'll be hard-pressed to find a dictionary that defines wisdom the way the Bible does:

> It is because of him that you are in Christ Jesus, who has become for us wisdom from God—that is, our righteousness, holiness and redemption. (1 Corinthians 1:30)

Wisdom from God involves living a righteous and holy life and expending ourselves in order to redeem others. Jesus shows us what this looks like. He is the wise one whose wisdom is credited to us before God, and he is also the one we try to imitate—not to earn credit with God, but to experience the fulfillment in life that comes from living as God intended, living wisely.

Contemporary Implications

The book of Proverbs repeatedly encourages us to seek wisdom. In chapter 8, wisdom is presented as a woman who invites into her house those who want to experience a fuller life. At the climactic end of the book, we are even invited to embrace wisdom just as a man would embrace a wife (31:10–31). The New Testament identifies Jesus as wisdom from God. What we are encouraged to do, therefore, in order to become truly wise, is to embrace Jesus. When we surrender our lives to him and let his Spirit begin to transform us, we will begin to experience the full lives God wills for us.

> Do not conform to the pattern of this world, but be transformed by the renewing of your mind. Then you will be able to test and approve what God's will is—his good, pleasing and perfect will. (Romans 12:2)

Because Jesus is the perfect human being—living exactly as God intended for us and bearing his image clearly, as well as giving his life for the sake of others—he communicates with his words, actions, and emotions what it means to be wise. Becoming wise, then, is nothing else and nothing less than becoming like Jesus. When we let our thinking and behavior be transformed by Christ's Spirit, therefore, we achieve the wisdom God desires for us because we become like his Son (Ephesians 1:17; Colossians 1:9).

Hook Questions

- How do we go about developing the wisdom that finds its fulfillment in Christ? Do your Christian habits indicate that this is important to you? Why would we want to become like Christ?
- Is it foolish to live according to biblical guidelines in today's world? How do you react to movies and television shows that portray Christians as mentally deficient? Do you find it humorous or tragic, and why?

When we run an engine without oil, it never turns out well. And we know that cell phones don't work well under water. We are aware that our man-made devices only operate as they were intended when certain guidelines are followed. Proverbs are guidelines to ensure our lives operate as they were intended. The design parameters of a rich human experience have been established by God, so we would do well to listen to what he has to say. Ultimately, the proverbs find their fullest explanation in Jesus, who shows us what it means to live as God intended. He gives us his Spirit to guide us into that life as well. Let's embrace him and become truly wise.

ECCLESIASTES

Life Purpose

It is difficult at times to understand the direction our lives are going, or the direction they should be going. It's as if we're driving in the fog on a curvy road. The book of Proverbs encourages us to follow the highway signs, but the book of Job reminds us that our little red wagon can be run off the road in a heartbeat. This real possibility leads to the profound question asked by the author of this book: If we try to live a life that is in harmony with the created order, seeking God's wisdom, and that life can nevertheless end up a disaster, then why should we even try? This is a fair question and one God answers for us by taking us along for the ride as "the Teacher" goes on a journey to the only possible conclusion.

Theme of the Book

God prompts the Teacher to question the purpose of life.

The name of this book comes from the Septuagint, the Greek translation of the Old Testament. It translates the Hebrew word for "Teacher" as *ekklesiastes*—that is, one who leads a congregation, or *ekklesia*. Whatever congregation was being led by the Teacher was in trouble, because he had concluded that life "under the sun" is without meaning. But, we have to ask, "meaning" to whom, and consisting of what? Usually, when we or others talk about meaning in life, we mean personal security and significance—something that makes us feel valued, worthwhile, and fulfilled. We want to know that it would have made a difference if we had not been born. Life, considered by itself, cannot provide this information. We are forced to look for meaning beyond the creation. Meaning is found in living our earthly lives as part of a bigger reality governed by the presence of God.

> **◆ Memory Passage:** *Ecclesiastes 12:13*
>
> Now all has been heard; here is the conclusion of the matter: Fear God and keep his commandments, for this is the duty of all mankind.

The Teacher of Ecclesiastes shows us that on our own we can't figure out the meaning of life. That meaning does not lie in our pleasures or conveniences, in our wisdom or in our foolishness, in our work or in our possessions. The Teacher discovers that life does indeed have meaning, but a meaning that is frequently beyond our ability to grasp when we limit our perspective to the created realm.

To find meaning and purpose in life, we are forced to turn our perspective from the realm "under the sun" to the realm that exists beyond the sun, beyond creation, where God dwells. We must turn to God in humility, acknowledging our creaturely limitations — and, with reverence, acknowledging that he has no such limitations — and submitting ourselves to his care and guidance. Ultimately, the meaning of life does not reside in things that we think will bring us satisfaction, but in things that bring God glory. Our goal in life is to make these the same thing. And there was one human being who has showed us just what that looks like.

The Jesus Lens

As we saw in the book of Job, our circumstances can change in a moment. If we look for contentment, significance, security, or meaning in those circumstances, we're going to have a hard time rebooting when our programs crash. It has taken the Teacher a while to arrive at the same conclusion as the book of Psalms: meaning in life is not found "under the sun" — in the human experiences and trappings that are subject to changes beyond our comprehension. Rather, meaning in life is found "above the sun" — in our *relationship* with our Creator.

It makes sense. Only by reconnecting with the source of life can we expect to know life in its fullest. That is what Jesus tells his disciples as they struggle to understand the suffering and death he would experience. As painful as those things are — things we ourselves might now even be tasting a bit of — they cannot affect our true life if that life is connected to the source of life, who never changes and who always satisfies the deepest cravings of our hearts.

> Jesus answered, "I am the way and the truth and the life."
> (John 14:6)

In Christ alone is found meaning, purpose, and direction in life. When we, like the Teacher, try to find meaning for our lives in anything else, we also will be forced to conclude, "Meaningless! Meaningless! ... Everything is meaningless!" (1:2; 12:8). Only by being reconciled to God through Jesus Christ ("the way") can we finally find what it is we've been looking for ("the life").

Contemporary Implications

The primary purposes of the New Testament are to show us that there is no life outside of Jesus Christ and to encourage us in every possible way to enter into a relationship with God through him so that we can experience that life in the fullest possible way. The Teacher was rummaging around "under the sun," looking under every stone for anything that would supply some explanation for what makes human life worthwhile. He found lots of things that made great promises, but ultimately failed to deliver. He was full of human wisdom and knowledge (1:16), but that wisdom and knowledge couldn't provide answers to the basic questions of life. That wisdom and knowledge are available only through Jesus Christ. That is why the apostle Paul worked so hard to make sure everyone had access to the answer to the meaning of life.

> My goal is that they may be encouraged in heart and united in love, so that they may have the full riches of complete understand-

ing, in order that they may know the mystery of God, namely, Christ, in whom are hidden all the treasures of wisdom and knowledge. (Colossians 2:2–3)

We may know in our Bible-trained heads how we're supposed to answer questions about life, but do we really believe those answers? We spend hours, days, even years of our lives chasing after things that we believe will make our lives significant, when we could have that significance any time we chose. There is an old joke about someone who is outside, looking in the grass for his lost ring. His friends show up and offer to help. They ask him where he lost it. He tells them he lost it in the house. When they ask him why he is looking for it outside, he tells them, "The light is better out here." How stupid to look for something where it can't be found! Let's stop looking for the meaning of life where it can't be found. Let's look for life's purpose in the eternal truths that God has revealed to us in Christ.

Hook Questions

- Why should we bother drawing in another breath? Have you become so focused on trying to gain meaning and direction for your life by your own effort that you have neglected the only avenue through which you can expect to find those things? How would you rate the meaningfulness of your life right now?
- Where do we go to find out about the true life revealed in Jesus Christ? Do you really believe, along with the Teacher, that trying to find fulfillment in things, status, or work is "meaningless"? Are you taking any concrete steps to enrich your life by getting to know Jesus better?

The statistics for teen suicide are alarming—and ultimately understandable. Some teenagers are coming to realize that their lives lack meaning, and it doesn't make any sense for them to continue on in a meaningless existence. Exactly right. It doesn't make sense to continue in that kind of existence; but there is another kind of existence bursting at the seams with meaning and purpose. It is found in a relationship with God through Jesus Christ. The Teacher tried just about everything to find meaning in life without any reference to God. Perhaps you have, too. But there isn't any. Only when we return to our Creator in reverence and acknowledge our need for him will the fog start lifting and our path into the future come into focus. We will have life—full, meaningful, energizing life.

19 | SONG OF SONGS

Love

The name in English might be a bit confusing. In Hebrew, whenever a noun is set apart from its plural form by the word "of," it signifies something that is the best in its category. For example, "Lord of lords" means the most exalted Lord; "Holy of Holies" means the holiest place; and "Song of Songs" means the best song. This book contains exquisite love poetry—expressions of deep love between a man and a woman. It describes that love as it was meant to be without the effects of sin: intimate, without shame, and characterized by genuine admiration and care for each other. God communicates with us on our level. If we are ever going to understand anything about his love for us, we must first understand human love at its fullest potential. And we can get a glimpse of it by looking at the best song ever written about it.

Theme of the Book

God depicts intimate human love as a gift and also as a key to understanding his own love for his people.

Although some of the descriptions about intimate love between a man and a woman that are found in this book can make a reader a little uncomfortable, we need to be reminded of the beauty and significance of this most magnificent expression of the close relationship between marriage partners. When a man and woman unite in marriage, God intends them to become one (Genesis 2:24). In this book we see that unity expressed in words of desire, contentment, and focus on each other. It is too bad that our understanding of this closest human relationship has been dirtied by Hollywood's cheap portrayal of it as irritating, confining, and unfulfilling. In the Song of Songs we see something different. We see the realization of the dream of every love-starved man and woman — a relationship that some of us are blessed to know, at least to some degree. Those who have tasted this kind of love wouldn't trade it for anything.

⚷ Memory Passage: *Song of Songs 8:7*

Many waters cannot quench love;
    rivers cannot sweep it away.
If one were to give
    all the wealth of one's house for love,
    it would be utterly scorned.

Such love is a beautiful gift from God to his human creations. It is also an aspect of the image of God he has placed in us. We can understand and even aspire to this relationship of love and commitment that is intended to describe the unity of the two marriage partners. And because we can understand that kind of love on the human level, we can begin to understand something of the divine love for us that it reflects, even if only dimly at times. Within the love relationship described in the Song of Songs, both partners give themselves wholly to each other. Elsewhere in the Bible, God describes his relationship with his people in terms of a husband and wife (Ephesians 5:22 – 33; Revelation 19:7; 21:2, 9; 22:17). And in the person of his Son, he too gives himself to us and for us.

○ The Jesus Lens

Unlike so many human relationships in which each person is most concerned with getting what they can from the other, the Song of Songs shows us that the deepest, most intimate relationships come from each person seeking to give what they can to the other. Jesus embodies this kind of love. Out of God's deep love for us, he gives what costs him the most—his own Son.

> God demonstrates his own love for us in this: While we were still sinners, Christ died for us. (Romans 5:8)

Christ demonstrates to us what God's love looks like. This divine love is an all-consuming focus on securing a relationship with those he loves. And that relationship is exclusive—it is a sacred bond that gives life completeness. This is what redemption is all about. God loves us and will stop at nothing to secure a relationship with us—even if it costs him his own Son. And there is nothing that can stand in his way—not even our own sinfulness. He continues to court us until we reciprocate his affection and say, "My beloved is mine and I am his" (2:16).

Contemporary Implications

When we begin to appreciate this self-giving, other-honoring love that characterizes the best human love and always characterizes God's love for us, we will grow secure and fulfilled in the relationship. Something else begins to happen as well. You may have noticed that a couple who has been married for decades begins to act, think, and even look like each other. They can finish each other's sentences. They know exactly what the other likes and dislikes. They have experienced so much of life together that it has worn them into a similar appearance. God wants our loving relationship with him to have the same effect in our lives. He wants us to become so close to him that we start resembling him.

> A new command I give you: Love one another. As I have loved you, so you must love one another. By this everyone will know that you are my disciples, if you love one another. (John 13:34–35)

We become like those we love. God loved us so much that he became a human being in order to secure our relationship with him forever. When we love God, we begin to reflect aspects of his character, and people begin to notice the resemblance. People need to see that there is a richer, deeper, all-consuming love like they've never known that is being offered to them by their Creator. That love is glimpsed in the intimate love of a husband and wife. As the church, the bride of Christ, grows old together with him, what his love looks like will also become more and more apparent in her appearance. And that's a wonderful thing.

Hook Questions

- Does our love for God or for each other look anything like God's sacrificial love for us? How would you describe to an unbeliever what love is?
- How would an unbeliever recognize the love of God in you? Does your experience or practice of love look any different from that of an unbeliever? How does your effort to love like God affect your Christian witness?

How can any of us hope to understand the infinite love of an infinite being? God has created us in such a way that the intimate, committed, secure, and giving relationship of a husband and wife can give us some idea. God delights in us and wants us in his presence all the time. As we become like his Son — the physical manifestation of his love — God's love will begin to describe our relationships more and more. God has woven reminders of his kind of love into our very DNA. Let's examine it, cultivate it, and share it with a world that has forgotten what it looks like.

20

ISAIAH

Divine Presence

Isaiah was married with children. He was highly educated and had easy access to royalty. No doubt his parents had planned for him a comfortable future in high society. But God had something else in mind. He called Isaiah to a long, thankless prophetic ministry during a tumultuous and frightening period in international affairs. Judgment was coming because God's people had rebelled against him. Isaiah and Judah had witnessed their northern neighbor, Israel, conquered and removed from their homeland in 722 BC by the fierce Assyrian war machine. That same destructive power threatened Jerusalem as well in 701 BC and was only turned back by divine intervention (chaps. 36 and 37).

If that weren't enough to put a scare into the most confident, Isaiah also saw with his prophetic eyes a gloomy picture of the not-so-distant future, when Babylon would rise in power and accomplish the destruction of Judah that Assyria had only threatened. In his vision there were also pictures of deliverance, but a deliverance that was inseparably linked to a mysterious servant figure. So Isaiah's prophecy envisioned two different outcomes: judgment because of rebels and deliverance because of servants. Each of these outcomes was entirely dependent on the response of God's people to his presence among them.

📖 Theme of the Book

The Holy One of Israel challenges his people to respond appropriately to his presence among them.

"The Holy One of Israel" is a title for God that occurs twenty-six times in Isaiah and only six times in the rest of the Bible. The repetition of this key phrase shows Isaiah's deep concern that his people respond to this holy, awesome God in their midst in reverent obedience, so that they may enjoy a rich and satisfying life and not experience the same fate as their brothers and sisters to the north. Isaiah had seen God's majestic, awe-inspiring presence firsthand when he received his prophetic call (chap. 6). In God's presence, Isaiah acknowledged his uncleanness and jumped at the chance to serve him. Isaiah's response to God's presence should have been a model for the people of Judah. But instead of responding to God's care with fruitful service, they were producing rotten fruit (5:1–7). They had chosen to be rebels rather than servants, and a day of judgment was inevitable. But amazingly, in the second half of Isaiah's prophecy he talks about a servant who *would* respond to God perfectly and therefore would be the means by which God would do wonderful things for his people.

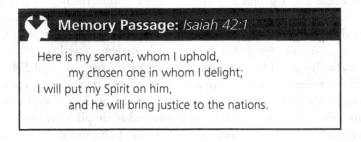

Memory Passage: *Isaiah 42:1*

Here is my servant, whom I uphold,
    my chosen one in whom I delight;
I will put my Spirit on him,
    and he will bring justice to the nations.

Anyone who is a servant of the Holy One of Israel responds to him appropriately (8:13) by doing his will. But through Isaiah, God talks about a special servant, a suffering servant (52:13–53:12). Of course, this makes no obvious sense. We can understand when a person who serves God is used by him to "bring justice to the nations," or is blessed with abundant life (65:13–14), or is delivered from harm (27:2–3; 54:17). We can't understand when such a person suffers. But in order for God to offer his people hope, something both profound and profoundly disturbing was going to happen: the obedient servant was going to experience judgment so that the disobedient rebels could be delivered from judgment. What?!

The Jesus Lens

As a visual component of his prophecy, Isaiah pointed toward a boy whose name reminded everyone that there were consequences for how they lived in the presence of a holy God. The boy's name was Immanuel, which is Hebrew for "God with us" (7:14). God had always been present with his people, guiding them, instructing them, and caring for them. But he would get even closer to his people. He would become one of them. The gospel writer Matthew quotes Isaiah's prophecy in reference to Jesus:

> The virgin will conceive and give birth to a son, and they will call him Immanuel (which means "God with us"). (Matthew 1:23)

God's presence with his people in the person of Jesus challenged them to respond appropriately so that they could have joy, peace, and rest. It didn't turn out well. Jesus reminded God's people that they were accountable to him for their actions — never a popular discussion topic. He also showed them by his own life how far they had deviated from the path God desired for them. It was easier to get rid of Jesus than to acknowledge a wasted life. So, the only true servant of God was tortured and crucified by those rebelling against God.

But it is through his suffering that God would bring deliverance and blessing to the rebels. Because God had become one of his people, he could secure his relationship with his people forever by his own perfect obedience. And he could exhaust his judgment on his rebellious people by allowing the only one who didn't deserve it to experience it for us. Amazing love! But wait, there's even more! So that his people might still come to know the rich life he desires for them when they walk in the path he has shown us in his Word, he sent the Spirit of this perfect servant to indwell each believer in order to transform us from rebels to servants.

Contemporary Implications

In 56:1–8 and 58:6–14 God tells us the sorts of things his servant does. Unsurprisingly, these are the very things that characterize Jesus' life and ministry. They include things like doing what is right, loving and honoring God, opposing injustice, and providing food and shelter to those in need. Basically, the servant of God responds to the presence of God by doing those things that mimic the love of God that we ourselves have experienced. And in doing so we will experience in our lives less and less the presence of our death-producing rebellious acts and more and more the presence of our life-giving God.

> How much more, then, will the blood of Christ, who through the eternal Spirit offered himself unblemished to God, cleanse our consciences from acts that lead to death, so that we may serve the living God! (Hebrews 9:14)

The Spirit of Christ is present within us and enables us to respond to our King with grateful service. God wants our lives no longer to produce the bad fruit that poisons everyone who eats it, but rather to produce nutritious, curative, attractive fruit that will fill the whole world (27:6). That is the only appropriate and natural response to his loving presence with us.

 Hook Questions

- Do our lives of service to God challenge people around us with his presence and invite them into his presence as well? Are we challenged by God's presence with us? How would you behave differently if God were physically present with you? How do we know what a life of service to God looks like for us in our particular circumstances?
- Is God's presence with you something that is obvious, or do you guard it more closely than your bank account number? Is God served and are people challenged by your Facebook page? What is one observable difference God's presence in your life has made?

Thankfully, our relationship with God is not dependent on our faithful service to him. We all fail miserably at that. The faithful service of Jesus Christ, our representative, secures God's presence with us forever. But the Spirit of that faithful servant dwelling in us massages and reprograms our understanding, our wills, and our emotions so that we can also serve God more and more faithfully and experience the joy in his presence that comes as a result. We are daily challenged by the presence of the Holy One within us to respond to his love for us with loving service, and we are daily enabled by his presence within us to enjoy the blessings of doing so.

21

JEREMIAH

New Covenant

Things had become much worse in the southern kingdom of Judah since the time of Isaiah. The people of Judah had reverted quickly from the sweeping reforms of King Josiah (640–609 BC) to the moral decay that characterized the reigns of his sons and grandsons. Jeremiah was called to spend his adult life being the voice of God, the ignored relationship partner, to these people who refused to listen. No wonder he resisted his call! God's people seemed bent on rejecting their covenant, their special relationship, with him. How could God allow them to remain in the land that symbolized their relationship with him when it was clear they didn't want that relationship?

Though it grieved him, God would bring the Babylonians in 586 BC to take his beloved people away into exile, where they could reflect on what they had done and what they had lost. But, amazingly, God was not through with them. Through Jeremiah, God announced that he would arrange for there to be another relationship with his people, unlike the previous one that had proved impossible for them to maintain. This relationship, this covenant, was going to be something entirely new.

Theme of the Book

God promises his people a new covenant beyond the necessary exile.

Jeremiah tried to get his countrymen to see that the things they were trusting in instead of God would ultimately fail them, but it was no use. For them, trusting in political and military allies, accommodating preachers, religious structures and routines, and even other gods all seemed so much more comfortable and expedient than reliance on the old-fashioned God of their ancestors. But Jeremiah kept trying. He explained to them that in any healthy relationship, each of the parties needs to listen attentively and respond to the other. God had always listened and responded to them, but they had stopped listening and responding to him. The relationship was in a desperate place. Nevertheless, God's people refused counsel, and so the relationship would be dissolved due to "irreconcilable differences." God removed his people from his presence. But before doing so, he made a promise that was as incredibly gracious as it was impossible to comprehend. After the period of exile, he would somehow enter into a new relationship with his people that could never be broken.

💭 Memory Passage: *Jeremiah 31:33*

"This is the covenant I will make with the people of Israel after that time," declares the LORD. "I will put my law in their minds and write it on their hearts. I will be their God, and they will be my people."

There are all sorts of practical and theological problems with God's promise of a new covenant. First, how is God going to do this? Judah's sin is so deep it is as though it is engraved with an iron tool, with a flint point, on their hearts (17:1). In this new relationship, God says that instead of sin, his law will be written on the hearts of his people. It sounds as if radical spiritual surgery is necessary. Second, how can God be just and forgive his people? What kind of judge turns a blind eye to sin? If sin is excused, then why should anyone obey the law? Finally, how can this new covenant be any more lasting than any that have preceded it? Won't human beings just mess up *any* relationship we enter into with God?

But the word "new" in "new covenant" does not mean what it does, for example, in the phrase "new car." It does not simply describe something that replaces an old, worn-out predecessor. No, the word "new" here means "of a different kind." It is something the world has never seen before. All of the practical and theological problems of this "new" relationship are resolved by Jesus Christ. The new something is made possible by a new someone.

The Jesus Lens

God became human in the person of Jesus Christ for two reasons, and both of them have to do with this new relationship. First, God requires an unfailing and representative human relationship partner if there is to be any possibility of an unfailing relationship with humans in the future. Second, this representative human being must experience divine judgment sufficient to pay for the failings of God's human relationship partners of the past, present, and future.

Jesus accomplishes both. His union with the Father is unbroken by any human failings (John 10:30; Hebrews 4:15). His perfect faithfulness within the divine-human relationship ensures that God's relationship with all those who make Jesus their representative is just as secure as the Son's relationship with the Father. This fantastic, eternal security comes at a dear price. There is still an enormous outstanding debt for unfaithfulness that has to be paid. God is holy and just. He cannot simply ignore the sins of his people, or for that matter the sins of anyone. There would have to be judgment. Jeremiah describes this judgment as a cup filled with the wine of God's wrath that everyone on the face of the earth would have to drink (25:15–29). This is the cup Jesus agreed to drink for us.

> In the same way, after the supper he took the cup, saying, "This cup is the new covenant in my blood, which is poured out for you." (Luke 22:20)

Holding a physical cup in his hand, Jesus alludes to the other, scarier cup that lay before him. In order for the new, unbreakable relationship his faithfulness had merited to become a reality for God's people, he would also have to pay the price for their sins. Jesus accomplishes the new covenant, the new relationship with God, at the cost of his blood. Only he could fully comprehend the magnitude of that judgment. That's why Jesus prays in the garden of Gethsemane that, if possible, that terrifying cup be passed from him (Luke 22:42). But it didn't pass from him, and he drank it down to the last drop so that every human being he represents is assured of a lasting relationship with God that is unbroken even by unfaithfulness on our part.

Contemporary Implications

We all know how sinful we are. It is hard for us to forgive ourselves, much less expect anyone else to. Surely God, who knows us better than we know ourselves, must be disgusted with us. But the book of Jeremiah tells us just the opposite. God knows our fallen human condition, but he wants a relationship with us just the same. So, in incomprehensible love and mercy, he sovereignly decided to do what we could not: be faithful for us and pay our outstanding debts. He would, in effect, become both relationship partners. Instead of a relationship between God and man, it would be a relationship between God and the God-man, Jesus Christ. All of us who put our faith in him as our divine-human representative can rest assured that nothing can ever again separate us from God's love.

> I am convinced that neither death nor life, neither angels nor demons, neither the present nor the future, nor any powers, neither height nor depth, nor anything else in all creation, will be able to separate us from the love of God that is in Christ Jesus our Lord. (Romans 8:38–39)

Our new covenant relationship with God is now as secure as the faithfulness of the Son. We are justified in doubting our relationship with God only if we can bring ourselves to doubt Jesus' faithfulness. When we trust Jesus Christ for our salvation, we acknowledge that we believe what God is saying about the new relationship he has gone to such lengths to secure with us. Having that kind of relational confidence will enable us to spend less time focused on ourselves and more time focused on enjoying and sharing the rich life that that relationship produces.

Hook Questions

- Is God's love for you conditional? Have you been living as though it is? Does your confidence in your relationship with God ultimately depend on your faithfulness or on Jesus'? Have you made Jesus your representative in faithfulness and in judgment?

- Are you more demanding than God is with yourself or others? Do you feel the need to pay for sins that have already been paid for? Is your behavior more motivated by guilt or by gratitude?

We have all seen people who are insecure in a relationship (maybe you're one of them). Instead of enjoying the relationship, it seems as if they always need to keep proving to themselves that they deserve to have it. Some Christians are like that too. They beat themselves up over every failing and doubt they have any right to their relationship with God. Sure, we want to nurture our relationship with God and not do those things that interfere with the fullness of life it provides, but the relationship itself is never in jeopardy. Not believing this is true is not believing God himself. When we take God at his word and accept his wonderful love expressed through his Son, we can grow in our relationship with him and more fully experience the abundant life he intends for us to enjoy.

22 | LAMENTATIONS
Comfort in Cataclysm

We don't really know who wrote Lamentations, but tradition ascribes it to Jeremiah. Certainly the situation it describes fits the circumstances of Jeremiah's day. God had brought the Babylonians to judge his people, and they had done a thorough job of it. All of the things God's people had been trusting in were gone. Jerusalem, the city of God, was gone. The temple, the place that symbolized God's presence among his people, was gone. The religious rituals were gone. Everything was gone. Was God gone too? The author of Lamentations has put his troubled thoughts to poetry, as rhythmic as sobbing. In the depths of his anguish, he clings to the one truth that gives him hope: even though we are unfaithful, God is not. His love tempers his wrath, and his compassion always accompanies his judgments.

Theme of the Book

God's loving compassion and faithfulness are present even during the cataclysmic destruction of Jerusalem.

The five chapters of these laments are arranged according to the Hebrew alphabet. The Hebrew alphabet has twenty-two letters and the number of verses of all five chapters is a multiple of twenty-two. This is an orderly arrangement, with each subsequent verse beginning with the subsequent letter of the alphabet. This orderly arrangement falls apart in the last chapter, where, even though there are still twenty-two verses, there is no arrangement of those verses according to the Hebrew alphabet. The order has fallen apart. That is exactly the concern of the author. His orderly world has fallen apart. This gut-punch to his faith produces the main question of the book (which is also the book's first word and its Hebrew name): "How?" How could this have happened? How can we survive? In the face of such circumstances, when our world is in chaos, what is there to cling to anymore? In chapter 3, the climax of the book, the author finds a lifeline in his sea of sorrow.

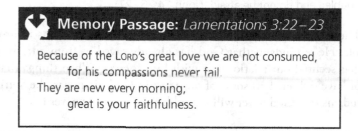

Memory Passage: *Lamentations 3:22–23*

Because of the LORD's great love we are not consumed,
    for his compassions never fail.
They are new every morning;
    great is your faithfulness.

God's people understood that they had merited the horrible judgment they had experienced. What was harder for them to understand was that God had not destroyed them completely. The only reason given to them was "the LORD's great love." Ultimately, this is all we can cling to in difficult times. If we are trusting in anything else to get us through, we, like the people of God who gazed in disbelief at the charred remains of their city, will be jolted into an awareness of our misplaced trust when those things disappear. In the coming storm of God's judgment against the sin of all humanity, it is only "the LORD's great love" once again that will keep us from being consumed. That love would become human and dwell among us.

The Jesus Lens

"Because of the LORD's great love" or, in the words of the New Testament, "[because] God so loved the world" (John 3:16), we are not abandoned to the horrible consequences of our sins. In his compassion God sent his Son to secure for us the new relationship that Jeremiah talked about. And the one who secured our relationship with him forever also preserves and nurtures that relationship when circumstances try to get us to doubt it. Jesus knew that just because our eternal future is secure, that does not mean that our contemporary present will be trouble-free. So Jesus has sent his Spirit to indwell each believer to give us peace and confidence even when our worlds turn upside down.

> The Advocate, the Holy Spirit, whom the Father will send in my name, will teach you all things and will remind you of everything I have said to you. Peace I leave with you; my peace I give you. I do not give to you as the world gives. Do not let your hearts be troubled and do not be afraid. (John 14:26–27)

The faithful presence of the Spirit of Christ comforts us in any trouble. He reminds us that God has already saved us from ourselves and has secured our relationship with him forever. When things that might have siphoned off some of our trust in God disappear, the Spirit reminds us that God never will—and his compassions never fail.

 ## Contemporary Implications

When we realize that we have been superglued to God in a bond so unbreakable that not even the worst pressures of life can ever separate us, we will be able to endure them. They won't be easy, but as the storms pass over we can take comfort in knowing that life can change, but God will not. Life can be cruel and unfair, but God cannot. Our world may fall to pieces, but God will still give us peace.

> Praise be to the God and Father of our Lord Jesus Christ, the Father of compassion and the God of all comfort, who comforts us in all our troubles, so that we can comfort those in any trouble with the comfort we ourselves receive from God. (2 Corinthians 1:3–4)

This kind of comfort, unable to be touched by changing circumstances, is something unbelievers do not have, but they are attracted to it. When we communicate to them through our own lives and words that there is someone who will never fail them as their own relationships, circumstances, and judgments have failed, we are communicating the same thing that God was communicating to his people so long ago.

We are reminding them, like the author of Lamentations was reminded, that our only true comfort is "the Lord's great love."

 ## Hook Questions

- Where do you find your security and comfort in life? Have the things you are trusting in ever failed you? Do you spend most of your time developing your relationship with God or developing your relationship with other things?
- Are you as compassionate with others as God has been with you? Are you ready to be merciful and compassionate to those who, in your estimation, don't deserve it? What if God were like you?

It is not easy sometimes to feel compassion for people who have messed up their own lives. Unless, of course, the people who have messed up their lives happen to be us! Then we want everyone to have compassion! In the book of Lamentations, God reminds us that we have made a huge mess of our lives, but we can take a step back from the edge of despair by remembering his unfailing love and compassion and redirecting our trust toward him. When we do this, not only will we find a comfort unavailable in those things that have proved to be so flimsy, but we will also be able to guide to that same comfort those who are desperately seeking it.

23

EZEKIEL

Life from God

Judah's end had not come all at once. Even before the fall of Jerusalem in 586 BC — an event lamented in the previous book — Babylon had already devastated the nation. Judah had come under Babylon's control in 605 BC. Several years later, in 597 BC, after Judah's King Jehoiakim had rebelled against Babylonian rule, King Nebuchadnezzar paid the capital city an unpleasant visit. He took away the treasures of the royal palace and temple, put a new king on the throne (Zedekiah), and took away into exile 10,000 people, including the king (2 Kings 24:1, 8 – 17). One of those people taken was a young man named Ezekiel, whom God called to be a prophet from his place of exile in Babylon. With graphic imagery, picturesque language, symbolic acts, and powerful words, Ezekiel's prophecies showed God's people that the slow death they were experiencing was a natural consequence of their gradual but relentless turning away from the one who gives life.

Theme of the Book

God's presence is the key to life.

In his visions, Ezekiel saw something alarming: God's presence was leaving the temple (8:3 – 4; 9:3; 10:4, 18 – 19; 11:22 – 23). The consequences of that fact were disastrous to contemplate. When God withdraws his presence, life departs as well. Ezekiel experienced firsthand the displacement and discouragement, the chaos and death that results from the lack of God's presence. He pleaded with his people to run for their lives back to the source of life. But they were surrounded by so many things that, like late-night infomercials, promised solutions to all of life's difficulties so that they were blinded to the true source of that life. They had turned to other gods to provide life for them (chap. 8) — idols they had set up in God's own temple! Without God in their midst, death, destruction, and exile quickly followed.

Even after the fall of Jerusalem, Ezekiel continued to prophesy. Through him God reminded his chastened people that life is found in him alone. Though they had rejected him and experienced his judgment, they could still have life in him. Apart from him they were nothing more than dry bones; when they return to him, God can yet make their dry bones come to life.

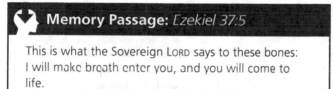

Memory Passage: *Ezekiel 37:5*

This is what the Sovereign Lord says to these bones: I will make breath enter you, and you will come to life.

Even as God's people were experiencing the consequences of their rejection of him, their gracious and merciful God was encouraging them with prophecies of restoration to life. And that life in God's presence was so abundant that it extended beyond simple return from exile to a new day. In symbolic language Ezekiel describes a future place where God will dwell that will exude life. This place will teem with fish and animals, and fruit trees of all kinds will grow and produce abundant fruit. From this new place of God's presence, described in terms of a new temple, life-giving and life-healing water would flow (47:1 – 12). About six hundred years later, long after Ezekiel was dead and buried, God's presence among his people was manifested in a different way, in a human being. And this human being, Jesus Christ, God's presence with us, informs a Samaritan woman he met that he is the life-giving, life-healing water Ezekiel had described (John 4:1 – 14).

The Jesus Lens

Jesus became God's presence with us in a unique way. Just as God's presence with his people in the Old Testament involved the entrance of his glory into the temple, so Jesus reminded us that he is that glory when he entered the temple. Then he went even further and referred to himself as the temple — God's visible presence with his people (John 2:13 – 21). The challenge for the people of Jesus' day was the same as for the people of Judah in Ezekiel's day: Would they welcome and treasure God's presence among them and experience the life that flows from it like a river, or would they resist and reject his presence among them and become like a valley of dry bones? The apostle John makes it clear that in Jesus' embodiment of God's presence was life more than sufficient for all who received him.

> In him [Christ] was life, and that life was the light of all mankind.
> (John 1:4)

Life is found in Jesus Christ, and he has demonstrated in words and actions that he has plenty to share. He raised people from the dead; he healed the sick and mended those with broken bodies; he multiplied food (and is himself the bread of life); and he calmed life-threatening natural forces. Even when it appeared that death had overcome him, he burst open its doors and appeared in radiant light and life — an unambiguous display of the abundant life that will one day overtake absolutely everything. All who acknowledge him as the source of life participate in the life he gives (6:47) — a life that is as eternal and rich as the God who gives it.

Contemporary Implications

Ezekiel spoke of a restored temple in which the glory of God would enter once again (chap. 43). This is the temple from which the living water would flow (47:1 – 12). God is indeed building a new temple, one that is being erected one believer at a time. God's presence fills this new living temple in the person of his Holy Spirit (Ephesians 2:19 – 22). Let's not forget how precious is this life-giving presence within us, as God's people of the Old Testament did. Instead, let us do everything we can to keep it in the front of our minds so that our life in Christ grows and deepens, and flows out to those around us.

> Set your minds on things above, not on earthly things. For you died, and your life is now hidden with Christ in God. When Christ, who is your life, appears, then you also will appear with him in glory. (Colossians 3:2–4)

Let us keep our eyes focused on Christ, who is our life. The view out the rear window is nothing but death and decay. There is no future in looking at those things—we all know what happens when we take our eyes off the road for too long.

Hook Questions

- Does your focus enrich your life or deplete it? Where are you looking for life? Do you look for life from the author of life, or from something that is a cheap imitation? Whose warranty do you think is better? How could you enhance God's presence in your life?
- Does your life point others toward the source of life? When people look at your life, can they recognize God's presence with you? Does your abundant life spill over into other people's lives?

A lot of us have spiritual attention deficit disorder. We get so distracted by the things that surround our lives that we forget where our life comes from in the first place. When we honor God in our midst, we will really know life, and his glory will fill the temple of his people. When those who are still in spiritual exile see the death-erasing, chain-busting life that his presence produces in us, they will conclude, "The Lord is there" (48:35). Then they too will be drawn to his life-giving, life-healing presence.

24

DANIEL

Cosmic Authority

Daniel was taken into captivity by the Babylonians earlier than Ezekiel. Nebuchadnezzar, the king of Babylon, had invaded Judah in 605 BC, the first year of King Jehoiakim's reign (2 Kings 24:1). Jehoiakim submitted to him and paid him off with tribute and hostages—including one scared young boy named Daniel. So Daniel grew up in a foreign land, where he was groomed for the king's service. No doubt he had some internal struggles about that! Not only had he been taken from his homeland by the king who had destroyed it; now he was being forced to serve that very king, as well as the others who would follow.

Daniel must have been tempted to conclude that God had lost control of the situation, that human kings and military generals were directing the course of world events. The question of who is ultimately in control comes to a head in this book, when a human king demanded that Daniel do something his heavenly King had forbidden. Nebuchadnezzar, Daniel himself, and all of God's people needed to be reminded that even though circumstances may argue the contrary, God is still, always has been, and always will be in control of his creation—even of its most egotistical creatures.

Theme of the Book

God asserts his authority over human kingdoms.

Three of Daniel's friends among the exiles who had been brought into the king's service were the first to be used by God to demonstrate his superiority over human rulers. When those young men chose to obey God rather than the king by defying the royal command to worship the large golden statue he had set up, they were tied up and thrown into an incinerator like so much trash. But the one who made the sun was not impressed by the one who made the incinerator, and God rescued Daniel's friends unharmed (chap. 3). After another, subsequent humbling in which God made Nebuchadnezzar spend some time living like a wild animal, the king got the point. However great he thought he was, the God of Daniel was far greater. King Nebuchadnezzar burst forth in praise to this God, using words that paralleled Daniel's own.

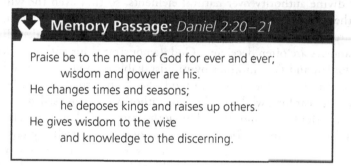

Memory Passage: *Daniel 2:20–21*

Praise be to the name of God for ever and ever;
　　wisdom and power are his.
He changes times and seasons;
　　he deposes kings and raises up others.
He gives wisdom to the wise
　　and knowledge to the discerning.

Later in Daniel's life, the Babylonian kings had indeed been deposed, and God had raised up a new bully on the block—the Persians. Daniel then served Darius, who also needed to be taught that there was one who was greater than he or any other king. God used human conniving to initiate the lesson. Daniel's jealous fellow officials were able to persuade Darius to make a decree that anyone who worshiped or prayed to any god or human being besides him would be thrown into a lions' den (chap. 6). As is always the case, their scheming only served God's purposes.

Daniel, of course, refused to stop worshiping or praying to God and was ultimately thrown into the lions' den. But God delivered him as he had his three friends earlier, and Darius too got the point. He issued a decree that everyone on earth should "fear and reverence the God of Daniel" (6:26–27). Daniel then received a series of visions that enabled him to see into the future. In those visions full of symbolic imagery, God "deposes kings and raises up others" in the course of accomplishing his redemptive purposes, and there is no one who can oppose him. The Most

High asserts his authority over one human kingdom after another, until his everlasting kingdom and authority are established. That same authority accompanied the one who would come to usher in that kingdom.

 ## The Jesus Lens

Jesus brought his divine authority into focus by his teaching (Matthew 7:29), by his forgiving sins (Matthew 9:6), and by his driving out evil spirits and healing every disease and illness (Matthew 10:1). He exercised divine authority over natural elements, so that even the winds and the waves obeyed him (Matthew 8:27). In the book of Daniel, it appeared for a while as if God's authority had been superseded. But appearances are often deceiving. God demonstrated his authority over Babylonian and Persian kings by unmistakable demonstrations of his power. And it was the same with God's Son. The crucifixion of Jesus made it appear for a while that human authority had superseded divine authority. But God demonstrated his authority over jealous Jewish leaders and petty Roman officials, and even over death itself, by raising Jesus from the dead (Romans 1:4). The resurrected Lord appeared to his eleven disciples and communicated by his words what had already been communicated by his actions.

> Then Jesus came to them and said, "All authority in heaven and on earth has been given to me." (Matthew 28:18)

Jesus has divine authority over all things in heaven and on earth. This authority was given to him by the Father (John 5:27) — an authority that he continues to exercise (Ephesians 1:20 – 21). Like Nebuchadnezzar and Darius, sometimes people get a little full of themselves and need to be reminded that there is one with far more authority than they have to whom they must give account. One day everyone will acknowledge that authority (Philippians 2:9 – 11).

 ## Contemporary Implications

Our risen Lord follows his assertion of authority in Matthew 28:18 with a command that he links to it as a logical consequence: "*Therefore* go

... make disciples ... baptizing ... and teaching" (Matthew 28:19–20). We have a mandate from God himself to advance his kingdom. And the kingdom service of Jesus' disciples is not based on the authority, the influence, and the ability of his faithful subjects, which is quite limited, but on his own power and authority, which is limitless.

> If anyone speaks, they should do so as one who speaks the very words of God. If anyone serves, they should do so with the strength God provides, so that in all things God may be praised through Jesus Christ. To him be the glory and the power for ever and ever. Amen. (1 Peter 4:11)

As was the case with Daniel and his friends, our commitment to serve God may very well put us in scary situations where we are forced to decide whose authority holds greater sway in our lives—the immediate human authority who may take our life or the divine authority who gives us life. When faced with such threatening situations, we, like Daniel and his friends, will be fortified by remembering that to God alone belong "the glory and the power for ever and ever."

Hook Questions

- Are you embarrassed to speak the truth? Does your faith in God seem misplaced in the face of the apparently greater forces and influences that the world offers and values? Has God's authority been surpassed for you by modern technology, science, or charismatic leadership? Whose authority has more effect on you in your daily life, God's or someone else's?
- Do you trust your source? Do you believe God is who he has said he is? Do you believe that God has done what he has said he has done?

We all know the rules of our culture: we are not supposed to believe in one truth to the exclusion of others, and we are not supposed to judge. But God shows us in the book of Daniel that it doesn't matter what human authorities say or how forcefully they say it. God is the one with ultimate authority, and his words are the ones that count. When we judge which path to take, it is not necessarily the most expedient, the most comfortable, or the least scary path that is best, but rather the one that conforms to God's authority. When we judge what words to say to others, it is not necessarily those that express our own preferences or inclinations, those that express the prevailing human sentiment, or those that will win us the most favor that are best, but rather those that express God's authority—because our divine King always directs his power and authority toward the good of his subjects.

25

HOSEA

Divine Faithfulness

Hosea was the last prophet to prophesy to the northern kingdom of Israel before it fell to the Assyrian Empire in 722 BC. During his long and discouraging ministry, which began around 750 BC, he saw Israel go through six kings in about thirty years, with most of them coming to power by assassinating the previous king. Clearly, Israel was on its last legs. They had turned away from God and had cut themselves off from his life-giving presence. Their society was decaying from within and was vulnerable from without. God used Hosea to give them a visual picture of what they were doing. He called the prophet to enter into a marital relationship that had more unfaithfulness than a daytime soap opera so that Israel could see what their unfaithfulness to God looked like.

Theme of the Book

A faithful God contends with his unfaithful people.

God directed Hosea to marry a promiscuous woman (1:2) — not exactly the romantic dream. But God wanted Israel to see Hosea's anguish over the unfaithfulness of his wife, Gomer, so that they would understand more clearly the grief their unfaithfulness was causing him and the negative consequences that unfaithfulness would produce. The people of Israel devalued their relationship with God, and it was bringing them ruin. As a further reminder of this logical connection between unfaithfulness and its negative consequences, Hosea was directed to give his three unfortunate children names that indicated the coming relational break: Jezreel (meaning "God scatters"), Lo-Ruhamah (meaning "not loved"), and Lo-Ammi (meaning "not my people"). The fruit of unfaithfulness for Israel would be the loss of her distinctiveness. She would be scattered, stripped of the protective love of her divine spouse, and sent away from his life-giving presence.

> ### Memory Passage: *Hosea 1:2*
>
> Go, marry a promiscuous woman and have children with her, for like an adulterous wife this land is guilty of unfaithfulness to the LORD.

God, with relentless mercy and grace, does not end his message to Israel there — although he would be justified in doing so. No, incredibly, amid prophecies of devastating judgment God also promises hope. In fact, Hosea's name reminds God's people where their hope lies, because it means "he [God] delivers." Just as Hosea was directed to love his unfaithful wife once again and buy her back from the slavery that her loose life had brought about (chap. 3), so God would love his unfaithful people again and deliver them from the judgment their faithlessness had brought about (13:14; 14:4). In spite of the utter faithlessness on the part of one relationship partner, the faithfulness of the other partner would hold fast and be a ray of hope in an otherwise dark future. That ray of hope becomes a supernova in Jesus, the light of all people (John 1:4).

The Jesus Lens

Jesus' faithfulness to the Father undoes the judgment for unfaithfulness represented by each of Hosea's children. Instead of "God scatters" (Jezreel), through Jesus God promised to gather his people from "every nation, tribe, people and language" (Revelation 7:9); instead of "not loved" (Lo-Ruhamah), through Jesus God demonstrates just how much he loves us; and instead of "not my people" (Lo-Ammi), through Jesus we are now the "people of God" (1 Peter 2:10). Jesus came to people who had turned their backs on their divine relationship partner, just as Israel had done during Hosea's day.

Yet, even during that unfaithfulness, just as Hosea did for Gomer, God continued to love his people. He even sent his own Son to buy us back from the slavery our unfaithfulness had brought about. But Jesus did something that Hosea was unable to do. Jesus took on the roles of both relationship partners. He is God, so the sacrificial, self-giving love he expresses for us is a demonstration of God's own love. He is human, so the sacrificial, self-giving love he expresses for God is a demonstration of the love of all who claim him as their representative.

> Let us rejoice and be glad
>   and give him glory!
> For the wedding of the Lamb has come,
>   and his bride has made herself ready.
> Fine linen, bright and clean,
>   was given her to wear. (Revelation 19:7–8)

Jesus' faithfulness makes the church a faithful bride. His faithfulness to God as our representative in our divine marriage is described as "fine linen, bright and clean." In other words, because of Jesus' perfect relational loyalty, those united with him by faith always appear spotless to their divine spouse. In God's eyes, through Jesus we're not Gomers anymore!

Contemporary Implications

Unless a person enjoys misery, anyone in a marriage relationship seeks to enhance the relationship. In the book of Hosea and in the New Testament, the relationship between God and his people is described as a marriage relationship. God himself has secured this relationship forever against anything that could break it, but he wants us to experience the wonderful life that comes when this relationship grows deeper. So, he sent the Spirit of the perfect relationship-keeper, Jesus Christ, to lead us into a deeper experience of the relationship.

> May God himself, the God of peace, sanctify you through and through. May your whole spirit, soul and body be kept blameless at the coming of our Lord Jesus Christ. The one who calls you is faithful, and he will do it. (1 Thessalonians 5:23–24)

Every Christian struggles to some degree with living as a faithful relationship partner with God should live. But we may take comfort in knowing that the faithfulness of Jesus is counted as our own. We can also take comfort in knowing that we don't have to rely on our own abilities to achieve a deeper relationship with God. And that's a good thing. For some of us, our relationship skills are about six fries short of a Happy Meal. No, *God* is at work within us to help us realize the life he desires for us. He is the one who is faithful, "and *he* will do it."

Hook Questions

- Are any of us faithful? Even when we feel closest to God, are our hearts entirely devoted to him? How would you evaluate your own consistency in your relationship with God? Would your spouse let you get away with the lack of attention and care that you give God?
- Is our Lord ever unfaithful? Do you live as though you doubt his faithfulness? What are you looking at for your security in your relationship with God, your own faithfulness or Jesus'?
- Are we trying to become more like our faithful Lord, with the strength he himself provides by his Spirit? What should motivate us to deepen our relationship with God?

When we read about Hosea's sad life, we can be both frustrated and disgusted. Why doesn't Hosea just dump Gomer and move on? Why doesn't he just let her spend the rest of her life in the mess she created? It would serve her right. But when we judge her like this, we are judging ourselves. Isn't it amazing that God didn't just dump his faithless people (a.k.a. "us") and move on, leaving us to spend the rest of our miserable lives in the mess we had created?! Hosea's relentless love for Gomer is a picture of God's relentless love for us, shown even more clearly in his own Son. For his own reasons, God has decided to commit himself to us. Of course, relationships require reciprocity. So God courts us, cajoles us, and transforms us by his Spirit so that we dare to wade deeper and deeper into the waters of abundant life, until we're fully committed to him as well.

26

JOEL

Day of the Lord

Give me what I deserve! We all might want to think twice about demanding that, because what we think we deserve might diverge significantly from God's judgment on the matter. The prophet Joel ministered during the time when a severe drought and locust plague were crippling the land. God's people had evidently assumed that divine blessing was their right, no matter how corruptly they lived. But God reminded them by means of these natural disasters that abundant life was realized only in relationship with him. When that relationship was ignored or allowed to fade, then the protective barriers against death and destruction were lowered and the enemies of life could charge in. In Joel, this phenomenon is called "the day of the LORD." It is a day when the consequences of turning away from God and the need for his salvation are realized.

Theme of the Book

The day of the Lord is coming and brings judgment before restoration.

God's people were looking forward to the day of the Lord as a day when God would judge all those *other* people who had rejected him and gone their own way. It was hard to come to terms with the fact that God's judgment could include them as well. They needed to return to him and recommit themselves to their relationship with him in order for there to be any rescue from the dangers that stalked them down the dark alleys they had taken. So Joel called for fasting, prayer, and mourning (2:12). For God's people the good things of life would not come about because they were somehow better than other people, but because they were plugged into the unfailing, life-generating power source. Joel reminded them that when by their faithlessness they unplugged themselves, it wouldn't take long before things in their lives got awfully dark.

♥ Memory Passage: *Joel 1:15*

Alas for that day!
    For the day of the LORD is near;
      it will come like destruction from the Almighty.

Joel saw in the immediate disasters of drought and locust plague vivid reminders of the coming day of the Lord when God's judgment would be amplified to a global scale. Everyone on earth would come to a place called "Jehoshaphat," which means "the LORD judges" (3:2, 12). The ultimate day of the Lord is coming when comprehensive and final divine judgments will overwhelm mankind like a colossal tsunami and make the devastating drought and locust plague of Joel's day seem like minor inconveniences. Then, too, the only island of life in a sea of death and destruction will be found in relationship with God.

The Jesus Lens

The apostle Peter quoted from Joel's prophecy on the day of Pentecost after Jesus' resurrection and ascension (Acts 2:17–21), indicating that Jesus' death on the cross was our day of the Lord, when God's judgment for our disobedience was experienced on our behalf by our sinless representative. Joel told God's people of his day that the disasters they were experiencing were the natural result of abandoning God, and their effect was intended to remind them that their life was found in God alone.

On the coming final day of the Lord, when all nations will gather before the Lord for judgment, the one and only criterion that will hold any sway before the Judge of all the earth will be relationship with him. Those who have such a relationship through faith in Jesus Christ will enjoy the life that flows from that relationship. Those who don't have such a relationship will experience the dire consequences. Jesus experienced those dire consequences so that all who come to the Father through faith in him can be assured of life. He is the one who will do the judging on the day of the Lord, and he knows the sheep that belong to him.

> When the Son of Man comes in his glory, and all the angels with him, he will sit on his glorious throne. All the nations will be gathered before him, and he will separate the people one from another as a shepherd separates the sheep from the goats. (Matthew 25:31–32)

Jesus will return to judge the living and the dead. The day of the Lord is coming. Joel sees "multitudes, multitudes in the valley of decision" (3:14). Those who decide to turn to God for life through faith in his Son will have nothing to fear on that day. They will be safe and secure inside the stronghold of his love (3:16). Why would anyone choose plan B?

 ## Contemporary Implications

Believers today live between "days of the Lord." Jesus has already experienced our day of judgment and has enabled us even now to enjoy a foretaste of the restoration of all things that will take place when he returns again on the final day. To experience that foretaste, however, we have to make sure our chairs are scooted up to the table of God's grace. Only in our relationship with the source of life can we expect to realize true life for ourselves. We can only really live when we live together with him.

> God did not appoint us to suffer wrath but to receive salvation through our Lord Jesus Christ. He died for us so that, whether we are awake or asleep, we may live together with him. (1 Thessalonians 5:9–10)

We may look forward to the day of Christ's return with confidence that he has paid the price for our sin. But more than that, we may look to our Lord for life. As long as we are trusting in him, we will never be disappointed and we will never have to fear. Instead of the day of the Lord being a "dreadful" time for us (2:11), it will be a time of rejoicing, of fruitfulness, and of security (2:19–27).

Hook Questions

- Why should a righteous judge *not* find us guilty? Do you feel connected to the source of life? Do you recognize any negative consequences in your life that have come from a weak connection? How could you make your relationship with God more vibrant?
- Do you regard painful experiences in your own life as divine judgment? What is the difference between discipline and judgment? How have difficulties in your own life enhanced your relationship with God? How could you use those experiences to encourage others in their faith?

There are many who are hoping that their lives will have been "good" enough to merit a pass on the day of judgment. Others are waiting for the day to come when they can finally experience life. Some are just trying not to think about the coming day of judgment. How easy it is to resolve all of these concerns about that day through faith in Jesus Christ! Jesus offers us his own righteousness to replace our blameworthiness, unshakable joy to replace our circumstantially determined happiness, and justifiable confidence in him to replace our justifiable doubt in ourselves. The day of the Lord is near in the valley of decision (3:14). Let's decide for life in Christ.

Amos didn't mince words. He was a hard-working, blue-collar guy from the countryside. God sent him to the northern kingdom of Israel around 750 BC to deliver an unambiguous message. God's people were enjoying good times. The economy was booming, the nation seemed secure, and life was easy. But as anyone with children discovers at Christmas, sometimes they can be more fascinated with the box than with the gift that is inside. God's people had become more fascinated with the trappings of their relationship with God than with God himself. Their relationship with him had become routine and mechanical. They had forgotten what he had done for them that sprang from his love and compassion. As a result, they had also forgotten their obligation to treat their countrymen with love and compassion. Instead, they were enriching themselves on the backs of the powerless. Instead of helping the needy among them, they were adding to their troubles. They needed to be reminded of what that felt like.

 **Theme of the Book**

God judges his people for their social injustice.

The rich life that God desires for his people is not only to be experienced individually, but also communally. The whole world should be able to see what God is like by looking at the community that bears his name. But in Amos's day, the other nations were not getting the right picture. In fact, it seemed as if they were tuned to another channel altogether. In Israel there was corruption, indulgence, immorality, and oppression of the poor. These things communicated exactly the wrong message about God, and the lion was roaring with anger (1:2). God was not interested in their religious routines that had nothing to do with religious substance (5:21–23). It was time for reminders of how powerless they really were apart from his gracious care. In one generation, the northern nation would be conquered and their injustice and unrighteousness would be swept away, along with that of all their neighbors.

> ### 🕊 Memory Passage: *Amos 5:24*
>
> Let justice roll on like a river,
>   righteousness like a never-failing stream!

But unlike the smug and complacent to whom Amos prophesied, God is unfailingly gracious. Though Israel would have to experience judgment, God would still deal mercifully with them. Amos ends his prophecy with a promise of restoration (9:11–15). He sees a distant day when the people of God will be gathered again under a Davidic king. Only this new people will include other nations, and their relationship with God will never again be broken. This time of restoration will culminate in a restored creation so fruitful that the harvesters won't be able to keep up. Hundreds of years later this prophecy will begin to be realized by a distant descendant of David who broadens the definition of "God's people" to include all nations. It is through this one that God will one day restore all things (Acts 3:21).

◯ The Jesus Lens

Jesus came to establish this new community of God's people. Unlike the people in Amos's day, this new community would be characterized by justice and righteousness, and so demonstrate attributes of God's own character. In his Sermon on the Mount, Jesus described in practical detail what this kind of life looks like (Matthew 5:1–7:29). But he went far beyond mere description. Jesus lived out the truths he taught. He demonstrated what it meant to live in a way that reflects God's character. He healed the sick, fed the hungry, forgave sins, spoke out against hypocrisy and injustice, and guided people into an understanding of the truth. He took the role of a servant and ultimately gave his life to save his people.

> Jesus went through all the towns and villages, teaching in their synagogues, proclaiming the good news of the kingdom and healing every disease and sickness. When he saw the crowds, he had compassion on them, because they were harassed and helpless, like sheep without a shepherd. (Matthew 9:35–36)

Jesus communicates by his words, his actions, and his emotions God's compassion, mercy, and justice. And he also does this on our behalf. We don't have to worry that we don't measure up. Of course we don't! But the representative of our community does. And he sent us his Spirit to guide us into that kind of human existence as well.

Contemporary Implications

When we read the prophecy of Amos, if we're honest with ourselves we will have to admit that God's people there often look an awful lot like us. Religion had become disconnected from life and had been sealed off in an airtight ziplock bag so that its aroma wouldn't mingle with the other activities on the daily menu. But there is no life apart from God. When we root our lives, with all their intersocial complexity, in him, it is no surprise that our behaviors will begin to say something true about him. And when we grasp the magnitude of what he has done for us, those behaviors will be consciously motivated by a profound gratitude.

> The King [Jesus] will reply, "Truly I tell you, whatever you did for one of the least of these brothers and sisters of mine, you did for me." (Matthew 25:40)

As those called to Christlikeness, we should communicate truth about God's compassion, mercy, and justice through the way we live. As redeemed human beings transformed by the Holy Spirit, when we begin to reflect more and more of God's true character in the way we interact with others, we will increasingly realize what it is to be fully human. Because we will simply be doing what we were created to do — bear God's image.

Hook Questions

- How do others see God's compassion, mercy, and justice by your behavior? How would someone describe God if they only had you, his representative, to go by?
- Have you given false testimony about God's character by the way you have lived? How might you modify your behavior to better communicate truth about your God?
- Do you regard social justice as something you must do, or how you must be? Are you relying on the power of the Holy Spirit to transform you from the inside out? Do your interactions with others flow out of a grateful heart, or are you looking to your good deeds to earn points with God?

When we see others in need, it is easy to feel superior. We may think, "If only they were as capable as I am, they would not have allowed themselves to get into that horrible situation." But we aren't superior, and the situation of those in need might not have anything to do with their ability. God, however, really is superior to us, and yet he loved us and rescued us from the horrible situation that we had, in fact, allowed ourselves to get into. When by the transforming work of the Spirit of God, we become more like him, we will begin to treat others more as he has treated us—with compassion, mercy, and justice. When we do this, we will experience human life more fully, and our relationship with God will grow deeper. Then our lives will be like beacons of light to those around us still living in darkness.

We know almost nothing about Obadiah apart from this prophecy. In this shortest book of the Old Testament, Obadiah prophesies against the nation of Edom, a southeastern neighbor of the kingdom of Judah. The Edomites were descendants of Esau, Jacob's twin brother. Despite this family connection, the Edomites had taken advantage of the Babylonians' attacks against Judah to kick her when she was down. Wrong move! God had promised Abraham that those who cursed him (and his descendants) he would curse (Genesis 12.3). So when the Edomites messed with God's people, they were messing with God himself. And none of the things they were trusting in — their mountain stronghold, their allies, their supposed wisdom, and their military strength — would be able to save them when God directed his attention toward them for vengeance.

Theme of the Book

God will avenge Edom's mistreatment of Israel.

Historically, Edom had been dominated by Israel and Judah. When the kingdom of Israel had been defeated by the Assyrians and the kingdom of Judah had been weakened by the Babylonians, Edom took advantage of the situation to take a little vengeance on Judah. They offered no help when Judah was attacked by Babylon. In fact, they were delighted that it happened. Not content with gloating from the sidelines, they even contributed to Judah's problems by taking their belongings, adding to the bloodshed, and handing over to the enemy those who had managed to escape (vv. 11–14). Edom herself felt immune from such problems. Her people dwelt in mountain strongholds, and she had strong alliances and a reputation for wisdom (vv. 3–8). But she had not calculated on Israel's God. There is no place inaccessible to him, no strength or wisdom greater than his, and no one more zealous to avenge his people than he.

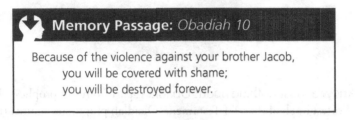

Memory Passage: *Obadiah 10*

Because of the violence against your brother Jacob,
    you will be covered with shame;
    you will be destroyed forever.

By wronging God's people, Edom had wronged God himself and would pay a dear price. Edom would be totally destroyed (v. 18), and Edom's judgment points toward the judgment of "all nations" (vv. 15–16). God will judge the pride, the arrogance, the inhumanity of all those who set themselves against him. But if everyone who was guilty of Edom's crimes would be destroyed, who would escape God's wrath? Apart from God's compassion and mercy, no one would. That compassion and mercy become flesh in Jesus Christ.

The Jesus Lens

In Jesus Christ the prophecy of Obadiah comes to pinpoint focus. In Obadiah, God's people are being oppressed by their own relatives. Jesus "came to that which was his own, but his own did not receive him" (John 1:11). Instead, his own relatives mocked him, regarded him with contempt, mistreated him, and handed him over to be executed — exactly what the Edomites did to the people of Judah. Jesus did not take matters into his own hands when he was mistreated, but rather waited patiently for God to avenge the injustice.

> When they hurled their insults at him [Christ], he did not retaliate; when he suffered, he made no threats. Instead, he entrusted himself to him who judges justly. (1 Peter 2:23)

As he promised in the prophecy of Obadiah, God avenged himself on those who dared do such a thing to this representative of his people. Even more, in one act of vengeance, God unleashed his full judgment on everyone who had or ever would set themselves against him. But the one who would bear the judgment was the only one who didn't deserve to. Jesus bore the vengeance of God against Edom's sin — and against our sin. By satisfying God's vengeance, Jesus provides the way of deliverance for prideful, arrogant, and inhumane people — like us.

God shows that his vengeance has been satisfied by raising Jesus from the dead. When we put our faith in Jesus, his experience of divine vengeance becomes ours too, and we die with him on the cross. Then, together with him we are raised to new life — no longer as enemies of God, but as belonging to his own people, for whom God will one day right all injustice.

Contemporary Implications

Who could have imagined that the scary prospect of God's vengeance on his enemies would be accompanied by such an amazing expression of his love? By our faith in Christ, God destroys his enemies and re-creates us as his people. If we couldn't possibly have predicted how God was going to judge his enemies in the past, how could we think we have the ability to imagine how he will do so in the future — and then do it *for* him? If God could effectively execute his vengeance on those who opposed him, he is surely able to deal with those who oppose us.

> Do not repay anyone evil for evil. Be careful to do what is right in the eyes of everyone. If it is possible, as far as it depends on you, live at peace with everyone. Do not take revenge, my dear friends, but leave room for God's wrath, for it is written: "It is mine to avenge; I will repay," says the Lord. (Romans 12:17–19)

The Edomites believed it was their right to exercise vengeance. They felt they had been wronged by Judah and had the opportunity to give some payback. But they were taking for themselves prerogatives that belonged to God alone. He alone knows all the details and the best way to bring resolution to injustice. When we are tempted to take matters into our own hands, we are guilty of the sin of Edom. We have surrendered our lives to God. We can trust that he will use them well.

Hook Questions

- Whom do you trust more to judge fairly, yourself or God? How would you fare if you judged yourself the way you judge others? How would you fare if God let happen to you what you want to happen to others?
- What is the problem with taking matters into your own hands? What happened when you were in control of your life instead of God? How should you put perceived injustices into God's hands?

Everyone will experience God's vengeance. There are only two ways this can happen. Either we can accept Christ's experience of God's vengeance on our behalf, or, if we refuse that, we will have to experience God's vengeance directly. In the end, no human kingdom (corporate or individual) that opposes the Lord will survive his vengeance. There will only be one kingdom and "the kingdom will be the LORD's" (v. 21). Let's pray that those who oppose the Lord's kingdom will cease to exist by becoming new creations in Christ (2 Corinthians 5:17).

JONAH

Extended Compassion

Assyria was a kingdom for whom Israel, and many other nations, would have liked bad things to happen. They were a ruthless, terrorist nation that frightened other nations into submission by the horrible things they did to any nation who opposed them. It was good to read in the prophecy of Obadiah that God would judge Edom for her mistreatment of his people. We would certainly expect to read something similar here regarding Assyria. We like it when good things happen to good people and when things turn out badly for bad people. It doesn't sit with us so well when the reverse happens. So, we can understand why this book about a prophet named Jonah describes his reluctance to go to Nineveh, the capital of Assyria, and preach there. What if they respond and God has compassion on them?

Theme of the Book

The Sovereign Lord's compassion extends beyond Israel.

The book of Jonah divides conveniently into two parts with two chapters each. In the first part, Jonah runs away from his divine calling to preach to Nineveh by hopping a boat to Tarshish. But the sailors on the boat toss Jonah overboard when it becomes clear that God is preventing their voyage from succeeding. God then gives Jonah some time to reconsider his choices from within the belly of a great fish provided for just this purpose (a piscatorial time-out). Responding more promptly to divine command than Jonah, the fish subsequently ejects Jonah on dry land, chastened but unharmed. In the second part of the book, Jonah does go to Nineveh, and there he proclaims God's coming judgment on that city. But the people of Nineveh repent, and God shows them compassion, just as Jonah feared. This outcome is very, very wrong in Jonah's estimation and prompts his complaint to God.

> ## Memory Passage: *Jonah 4:2*
>
> That is what I tried to forestall by fleeing to Tarshish. I knew that you are a gracious and compassionate God, slow to anger and abounding in love, a God who relents from sending calamity.

In the last chapter of the book, God drives his point home to both Jonah and his people as a whole, whose attitude Jonah represents. Both Jonah and Israel are being stingy with God's salvation. They are happy to experience it themselves, but are unwilling that others should too. Like Jonah, Israel had been given the task of being "a light for the Gentiles" (Isaiah 42:6; 49:6), but they had resisted their prophetic calling. God rebukes Israel by rebuking Jonah and reminds them that they are as unworthy of divine compassion as the people of Nineveh. God dispenses his compassion indiscriminately, without consideration of the worth of its objects, because no one is worthy. In fact, God would send his own Son to be the vehicle of this indiscriminate compassion to every nation, tribe, language, and people (Revelation 14:6).

The Jesus Lens

John the Baptist described Jesus as "the Lamb of God, who takes away the sin of the world" (John 1:29) — not just the sin of Israel. And Jesus went out of his way to bring his message of salvation also to those outside the community of Israel. He spoke to Samaritan and Canaanite women (Matthew 15:21 – 28; John 4:5 – 26), military officers (Matthew 8:5 – 13), and government officials (Matthew 27:11 – 14; John 4:46 – 53).

He himself declared that "whoever" believes in him has eternal life (John 3:16).

> I have other sheep that are not of this sheep pen. I must bring them also. They too will listen to my voice, and there shall be one flock and one shepherd. (John 10:16)

Jesus is the good shepherd, who gathers his sheep near and far. The sheep may be those who belong to ethnic Israel as well as those who do not. They may be those who seem morally good to us as well as those who are morally repugnant to us. Those who comprise the "whoever" who believe in him could even include those we might describe as horrible people, like the Assyrians of Jonah's day. But we, like Jonah and Israel, cannot appreciate the depth of God's compassion for us that he has demonstrated in Jesus Christ until we realize that we ourselves are horrible people and that God has chosen to show us his compassion anyway (Romans 5:6–8).

 ## Contemporary Implications

We have been given the Great Commission to take God's compassion to those to whom, for a variety of reasons, we might feel uncomfortable going. But God's indiscriminate compassion should increasingly characterize our communication of the good news in word and action as we become transformed to the likeness of Christ. God's Spirit is at work in us so that we become ready and willing to share his compassion out of a sense of gratitude for experiencing it ourselves.

> Therefore, as God's chosen people, holy and dearly loved, clothe yourselves with compassion, kindness, humility, gentleness and patience. Bear with each other and forgive one another if any of you has a grievance against someone. Forgive as the Lord forgave you. (Colossians 3:12–13)

Let us clothe ourselves with the compassion of Christ as we spread his good news to those near and far. When we are upset that God shows forgiveness and mercy toward sinners, we forget that that is exactly what he has done for us. We become like the Pharisee in Jesus' parable, who was thankful that he was not like those he considered more sinful than himself (Luke 18:9–14). But it was not the Pharisee but the one who recognized his own sinfulness and looked to God for compassion who "went home justified before God." The ship of the whole human race has sunk, and we are all splashing around helplessly in a sea of sin and death. We have been hauled aboard a lifeboat by unseen hands. Let's get busy helping to haul aboard as many others as we can.

Hook Questions

- What does your life say about God's compassion? Do you put limits on the exercise of compassion?
- What *should* God's compassion look like in your circumstances? Like Jonah, do you, at times, run away from your responsibility to communicate divine compassion?
- Do you push yourself to extend to those who are different from you (perhaps even hostile to you) the good news of the compassion of God in Jesus Christ? To whom do you have the most difficulty showing compassion? Why might this be so?

As we share the gospel with others, it is easy to let ourselves behave like doormen at exclusive clubs, only willing to let in those trendy people who are dressed well and look like models. But if God's compassion were only made available to model human beings, *none* of us would be allowed inside his kingdom. God has thrown open the doors of his salvation to all who have faith in Jesus Christ. He doesn't check our references, reputations, or rap sheets. That is not to say that entrance into his presence is cheap. No one can afford the cover charge. But the impossibly steep charge is waved for all who know the owner's Son. Our efforts at sharing with others God's expansive offer of salvation will improve and be energized to the degree we realize our own unworthiness to have experienced it.

30 | MICAH
Justice and Mercy

The prophet Micah, like Isaiah and Hosea, ministered during the chaotic time in the history of God's people when the northern kingdom of Israel would fall and the fate of the southern kingdom of Judah hung in the balance (around 740–700 BC). Micah saw that God's judgment was coming to both kingdoms, but he also saw the vague outlines of a coming time of restoration in a distant day. Through his prophet Micah, God justifies the harsh sentence he has passed on his people. He testifies against them, presenting irrefutable evidence "beyond a reasonable doubt" that his judgment was just. God's people had not acted justly with each other and had not shown mercy to those in their midst over whom they had power and influence. So God would show them what justice and mercy looked like.

📖 Theme of the Book

God will punish his rebellious people, but promises future salvation.

Micah's prophecy alternates between the rationale and description of the coming judgment (chaps. 1–3 and 6:1–7:7) and the merciful promise of a coming restoration (chaps. 4–5 and 7:8–20). In the case for the prosecution, God calls a discouragingly long list of witnesses. Among these shady characters are property barons who enrich themselves at the expense of their countrymen (2:1–2), opportunists whose moral compass is stuck on greed (2:8–9), government officials who use their power to enrich themselves on the backs of those they govern

(3:1–4), self-appointed prophets and corrupt priests who are ready to preach health and wealth as long as the offering plate is full (3:5–7, 11), and dishonest businessmen who use every trick to extort more profit (6:10–12). God's own people, who were supposed to represent his character, had turned away from justice. Now they would experience justice; they would be handed over to ruin (6:16). But God is not done speaking through Micah (whose name means "Who is like the LORD?"). In incomprehensible mercy, God commutes their sentence.

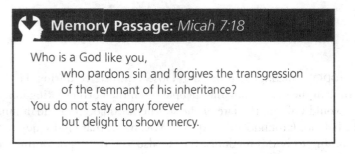

Memory Passage: *Micah 7:18*

Who is a God like you,
> who pardons sin and forgives the transgression
> of the remnant of his inheritance?
You do not stay angry forever
> but delight to show mercy.

God promises a time when he will bring about a restoration that will include far more than Israel and Judah. "Many nations" will come to the Lord to learn his ways (4:2). This new, expanded people of God will be led by a just and merciful shepherd (5:2–5). Under his guidance and care, this new community will live securely and eternally (4:4–5). Micah's prophecy of judgment was fulfilled in part when God's people were conquered and removed from the land by Assyrian and Babylonian forces. Micah's prophecy of merciful restoration was fulfilled in part years later when a Persian king allowed them to return to their land. But God's judgment against human injustice and his mercy in the face of human mercilessness would be realized more fully when the just and merciful shepherd arrived. The fuzzy pictures of Micah's prophecy come to multi-megapixel resolution in Jesus Christ.

The Jesus Lens

Jesus came to bear fully the judgment for human injustice and mercilessness that had been experienced by Israel and Judah only in part. He is the one from Bethlehem whom Micah foretold, who would "be our peace" (5:2, 5). But unlike every human kingdom, the realm of this different kind of ruler would be based on and characterized by justice and mercy. The first one of those, of course, is the most difficult. For there to be no possibility of outstanding warrants, fines, or penalties against any citizen of his kingdom, he would have to provide a way for the penalty to be paid for all past, present, and future crimes. Only someone who had committed no crimes of their own would be able to accomplish this. So, in an amazing display of mercy, and to satisfy the demands of justice, righteous Jesus took the judgment for our unrighteousness upon himself.

> For Christ also suffered once for sins, the righteous for the unrighteous, to bring you to God. (1 Peter 3:18)

Jesus bears our judgment so that we can experience God's mercy. Now that our time has been served, our record has been expunged, and our citizenship rights restored by our righteous and merciful representative, we no longer need to fear judgment. Justice has been served in the uniform of mercy. After laying the foundation of justice, our merciful shepherd returned to the Father until a future time when the restoration his actions have initiated will be fully realized. Until then, he has sent us his Spirit to indwell us and guide us so that the divine justice and mercy we have experienced will begin to leak out all over our human experience.

Contemporary Implications

As the people of God today, we have the same responsibility to manifest God's justice and mercy as did Judah and Israel in Micah's day. Of course, if we rely on our own strength to do this, we will be just as ineffective as they were. But God has resolved this problem by means of his own Son. Jesus' death was God's judgment on him for our failure to fulfill the creation mandate to bear God's image, to represent his justice and mercy. But his death and resurrection were followed closely by the coming of his Spirit, whom he sent to guide us into the truth and to give us the ability we lack to carry it out.

> And he [Christ] died for all, that those who live should no longer live for themselves but for him who died for them and was raised again. (2 Corinthians 5:15)

Christ died for us so that by his Spirit we may live for him, practicing justice and mercy. As we rely on his Spirit to do this, we will be becoming more like our Lord himself and more like what he intended his human creations to look like—a new humanity experiencing life in its fullest possibility as we assimilate more and more the divine characteristics of justice and mercy. These characteristics are described in detail in the pages of the Bible, where God's dealings with his human creations throughout time unfailingly manifest them. And we have an uninterruptible, continuous Wi-Fi connection to the God of justice and mercy to whom we can pray for strength and guidance by his Spirit as we try to imitate his justice and mercy in our daily circumstances.

Hook Questions

- Are you carrying around a load of guilt? Are you afraid of God's justice? Do you feel unworthy of God's mercy? Are you unwilling to let Jesus be your representative in matters of divine justice and mercy? Why?
- What is the motivation for your life, fear or gratitude? Where do you look to see what real justice and mercy look like? How do you let the Spirit guide you in the exercise of justice and mercy?

It may be difficult for us to accept God's mercy in Jesus Christ because we realize how much we deserve his judgment. But it is just that realization that should cause our faith to grab with white knuckles even tighter on to the realities that God has brought about through his Son. By the sacrifice of his Son, God's judgment on us is emptied out, but his mercy is still overflowing. And by the Spirit of his Son, we are learning to be people of justice and mercy, who look more and more like the God of justice and mercy who has done all of this for us. When unbelievers see this kind of justice and mercy exercised by this new, God-shaped humanity, they will recognize something they haven't experienced but desperately want and will be drawn like moths to a porch light. This is the beginning of the time of the restoration of all things that Micah saw dimly in the distance—a time when "many nations will come and say, 'Come let us go up to the mountain of the LORD, to the temple of the God of Jacob. He will teach us his ways, so that we may walk in his paths' " (4:2).

It seems odd that the prophecy that is all about God's unleashing his wrath on his enemies comes from a prophet whose name means "comfort." But God's people can be comforted by Nahum's prophecy because it was directed against Nineveh, a capital city of Assyria, one of the most brutal and heartless empires the world has ever known. The people of Nineveh had seemed to repent under the ministry of Jonah, but it hadn't taken them long to return to their old ways. When Nahum prophesied, the northern kingdom of Israel had already fallen to the Assyrians (722 BC). One nation after another had been mowed down by the blades of its seemingly unstoppable military machine. Its control had even extended to the ancient kingdom of Egypt, whose capital city of Thebes was destroyed by the Assyrians in 663 BC. Little Judah seemed alone and vulnerable. But God was with Judah, and he regards the enemies of his people as his enemies. Assyria was messing with the people of God and had therefore been messing with the Sovereign Lord of all creation. Not a wise move! Nahum informed the people of Nineveh that God had had enough; they would now experience the horror of his divine wrath.

📖 Theme of the Book

The Lord is sovereign over all and will judge Nineveh.

Nahum begins his prophecy with a description of the God whom the Ninevites had provoked. Although he is good, slow to anger, and a refuge for all who trust in him (1:3, 7), he will not leave the guilty unpunished (1:3). And when he comes to punish the guilty, it is a world-convulsing, mountain-shattering, sea-emptying tornado of judgment that nothing can withstand (1:3–6). Assyria regarded herself as a lion, the king of the beasts for whom the rest of the world was just prey to be devoured (2:11–12). But when the true King of heaven and earth comes against them, the lion will become the prey. Assyria's doom is sealed when the one whose "wrath is poured out like fire" says to them, "I am against you" (1:6; 2:13; 3:5).

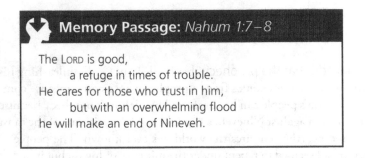

Memory Passage: *Nahum 1:7–8*

The LORD is good,
 a refuge in times of trouble.
He cares for those who trust in him,
 but with an overwhelming flood
he will make an end of Nineveh.

To secure comfort and "peace" for God's people, God will completely destroy the wicked who threaten them (1:15). In the midst of these euphemistically termed "times of trouble," there is only one refuge, one fortress, one secure place where there will be safety and protection: the Lord. Those who reject this one place of safety, trusting in their own man-made fortresses, will leave themselves exposed to an overwhelming flood of divine wrath. "It is a dreadful thing to fall into the hands of the living God" (Hebrews 10:31). But God provides a way for everyone to enter into the protective walls of his fortress. Jesus is that way.

The Jesus Lens

Jesus came to experience that firestorm of divine wrath for us, to become in his own person a fortress against divine judgment in the future. All who trust in him are brought inside his protective walls. But for those outside, there will be no escape. For those inside, there is light and life. But for those outside, there will be "darkness, where there will be weeping and gnashing of teeth" (Matthew 22:13). Jesus is the one who will bear our judgment on himself when we come to him in faith. But those who refuse his incredibly gracious offer and who continue to insist on being the enemy of his people and, therefore, the enemy of him, will know him not as their redeemer but as their judge.

Like the people of God in Nahum's day, we can look forward to comfort and relief from those who trouble us, because God "will pay back trouble to those who trouble you and give relief to you who are troubled.... This will happen when the Lord Jesus is revealed from heaven in blazing fire with his powerful angels" (2 Thessalonians 1:6–7). Jesus is the one who will judge between those who are his people and those who are against his people. And the Judge is coming.

> He [God] commanded us to preach to the people and to testify that he [Jesus] is the one whom God has appointed as judge of the living and the dead. (Acts 10:42)

God has raised up Jesus to be the righteous Judge of the living and the dead. Jesus is coming in judgment, but in mercy he himself has experienced that judgment already for those who have faith in him. The doors of his protective fortress are wide open until the day comes when they are shut and judgment comes. Outside are terror, destruction, and death; inside are life, safety, peace, and joy. Who would insist on staying outside?

 Contemporary Implications

We don't usually hear sermons from the book of Nahum. And it is rare to see a cross-stitched verse from this book hanging on the wall of a believer's home. God's wrath makes us uncomfortable—as well it should! When we trust in Jesus, we die with him on the cross and are made new creatures, who have his resurrection life. We have been brought out of the darkness outside and into his wonderful light (1 Peter 2:9).

> You turned to God from idols to serve the living and true God, and to wait for his Son from heaven, whom he raised from the dead—Jesus, who rescues us from the coming wrath. (1 Thessalonians 1:9–10)

The righteous Judge bore our judgment himself so that we are free to serve him without fear. This grateful, fearless service includes letting others know, with all the ability and urgency we can, the good news of the alternative to bearing God's judgment themselves. God wants our enemies to become our siblings in the faith, just as we who were at one time enemies of God have become siblings of his Son by faith. Now that's a remarkable conversion.

Hook Questions

- Why should God *not* judge us for our offenses against him? Has God dismissed our sins through our faith in Christ, or has he judged our sins through our faith in Christ? How are Nineveh's sins like ours before we were Christians? What are the opposites of Nineveh's sins that we can see in the life of our Lord and, hopefully, increasingly in our own lives?
- Who ultimately calls the shots in our lives? Is our professed submission to God observable in our treatment of others? Do we rely on God's strength or our own? How might the way we are living as Christians indicate how we regard the return of the one who will judge the living and the dead?

The book of Nahum is an uncomfortable book to read. Readings from Nahum are not even included in formal schedules of Scripture passages to be read regularly in churches. We don't like to hear about judgment. But without a deep appreciation of judgment, salvation is meaningless. Who needs salvation if there is nothing to be saved *from*? By reading about the judgment that will surely come against the enemies of God and his people, we understand more fully what Jesus has saved us from by bearing the judgment for us. We also are uncomfortably, but necessarily, reminded of what we were before God made us new creations by faith in Christ, and what we should be becoming increasingly unlike as we are conformed to the likeness of our Lord by the transforming power of his Spirit. God's judgment is just; God's judgment is total; God's judgment is certain. God miraculously converted us from his enemies to his friends. Let's do what we can, by his power, to eliminate a few more of his enemies in the same way.

32 HABAKKUK
Comfort in God

It is surely no coincidence that after a book describing God's judgment comes a book that points us toward comfort in God—even though that comfort might not be found where we might be looking for it. The prophet Habakkuk ministered after Nahum's prophecy had been fulfilled. God had, in fact, judged Assyria by raising up the Babylonian empire to defeat the Assyrians. With the threat of external attack removed from immediate concern, Habakkuk turns his attention more inward, to the interrelations of God's people. And he doesn't like what he sees. In this book, Habakkuk voices the concerns of all God's people who are troubled by the continued presence of sin in their midst. Habakkuk also learns, as we all have to, that God offers a comfort that is not found in the places where the world looks for it.

 Theme of the Book

God is my only comfort in life and in death in a world of seemingly unchecked evil.

When we read the book of Habakkuk, we are overhearing a conversation between a person concerned for justice (hopefully resembling us) and God, who isn't behaving as expected in this regard. Habakkuk complains that there is violence, conflict, and injustice among God's people and that God doesn't seem to be doing anything about it. God's answer to Habakkuk troubles him even more than the situation he is complaining about. God tells Habakkuk that he is planning to raise up the Babylonians to judge his people for their behavior.

Habakkuk is shocked! How can God bring judgment against his people by means of a nation whose morality is even worse than that of his people? God reassures Habakkuk that the Babylonians will receive their own judgment at the appropriate time. After reflecting on how God has acted through past history for the good of his people, Habakkuk comes around to the insight that God wants him to have: comfort is not found in our own understanding, in the behavior of God's people, or in having things turn out the way we would like. Our comfort and confidence are found instead in the one who can never fail, change, or disappoint.

Memory Passage: *Habakkuk 3:19*

The Sovereign LORD is my strength;
   he makes my feet like the feet of a deer,
   he enables me to tread on the heights.

Habakkuk had probably experienced the great national reforms under good king Josiah. But after Josiah's death in 609 BC, the nation quickly reverted to their old ways. Habakkuk wants God to do something about this. And God is going to, but not in the way Habakkuk expects. That is a double disappointment for Habakkuk. But God rebukes him for forgetting some basic truths: he has never failed his people in the past and there is nothing that can thwart his plans. Habakkuk spends the entire last chapter of his prophecy reorienting his thinking according to those truths. The world around him might appear to be coming apart at the seams, but the all-powerful God is still in control. And God's strength and faithfulness are Habakkuk's comfort. Centuries later, the Sovereign Lord became flesh and once again encouraged those who were stressed, strained, and frustrated by the injustices and cruelty of others to find their comfort, their security, their rest in him.

The Jesus Lens

The people of God in Jesus' day were wrestling with some of the same issues Habakkuk was. How could God allow the hypocritical religious leaders to load down his people with burdens they couldn't possibly carry (Luke 11:46)? How could God allow a pagan nation like Rome to have power over his people? Like Habakkuk, God's people were tired, weary, and confused. They needed to know that God was still in control and that he still cared for them. God's Son reminded them that God's power had not waned by a single microjoule. Jesus' miracles demonstrated that he had divine power far beyond anything that human beings could effect, and that power was being directed toward our benefit. Jesus reminded them and us that even when circumstances are beyond our ability to understand, our comfort comes in our relationship with this all-powerful God. Jesus invites us to find that reassuring comfort in him.

> "Come to me, all you who are weary and burdened, and I will give you rest." (Matthew 11:28)

Jesus offers true comfort and rest to those who come to him. He is the good shepherd who leads us beside still waters—even though those waters might flow in the presence of our enemies (Psalm 23:2, 5). If we listen closely, even during the cacophony of discordant and jarring static that threatens to drown it out, we will be able to hear our shepherd's voice calling us into his protective peace.

Contemporary Implications

Like Habakkuk, when we get confused or discouraged, we may need to reorient our thoughts. We must remember that God is in control and that he has never failed his people in the past. Jesus has secured our relationship with God so strongly that nothing can snatch us out of his hand (John 10:29), no matter how troubling or tragic the situation may be. Habakkuk was encouraged to have patient hope, patient trust, and patient confidence in God. One thing Habakkuk did right was to bring his concern to the only one who could do something about it. We are urged to do the same thing.

> Cast all your anxiety on him because he cares for you. (1 Peter 5:7)

In any trouble, we may find comfort in God and in his care for us. Our circumstances may change in a heartbeat, but God's care for us never will. Our future is secure. God's authority over death and all the disgusting and discouraging effects of sin has been proven by Jesus' resurrection from the dead. We now have a "living hope" of an inheritance that God will certainly bring about (1 Peter 1:3–5). Now that's something we can take comfort in!

Hook Questions

- When things go wrong, where do you turn for comfort? What are the amazing things God has done for his people, and for you, in the past? Does God change?
- Do you really believe that God knows what he is doing? Do you believe that you know best? Are you able to believe in God's power and wisdom when things don't go as you want?

Like Habakkuk, it is easy for us to lose focus. Sometimes things happen that we can't understand. Sometimes the things we lean on give way. God occasionally pushes us, like Habakkuk, out of our comfort zones so that we remember where our true comfort lies. How God works is beyond our understanding, but his power and faithfulness are not. When we redirect our focus on our always reliable, always faithful, and all-powerful God, then we will able to say along with Habakkuk, "Though [fill in the disturbing thing], though [fill in the disturbing thing], though [fill in the disturbing thing], yet I will rejoice in the LORD, I will be joyful in God my Savior" (3:17–18). The disturbing things won't go away, but they will be filed in the appropriate place in our minds — under "things God can handle."

33

ZEPHANIAH

Coming Judgment

Zephaniah traces his ancestry back to King Hezekiah. So he is a blue blood who would have been able to gain a hearing among the elite of his day. "His day" was probably sometime during the reign of good king Josiah (640–609 BC), when the feared empire of Assyria was in decline and the Babylonians were still gaining power. The national judgment foreseen by Habakkuk had not yet materialized. Perhaps the officials of Judah thought the worst was over. It was easy to lapse into reassuring routine and think, "The LORD will do nothing, either good or bad" (1:12). Perhaps this prophet who belonged to the royal line would give his country-club buddies welcome news of coming blessings in spite of their refusal to promote the pathway toward the abundant life that the Lord had graciously communicated to them. Oh, but they couldn't have been more wrong!

📖 Theme of the Book

God announces to Judah the approaching day of the Lord.

If the court officials expected a message about coming blessings, it didn't take long for their minds to be blown. In the first sentence of his prophecy, Zephaniah let them know what God had planned for them: "I will sweep away everything from the face of the earth" (1:2). And noble birth or position would be no protection (1:8). They had ignored God for too long. In the day that was coming they would be unable to ignore him any longer. He would cause them to experience the darkness, gloom, clouds, and blackness that were the inevitable consequence of their rejection of his light (1:15). The kingdom of Judah, God's unfaithful relationship partner, would be thrown on the brush pile together with all the other nations, to be consumed by the fire of God's wrath (3:8). The only ones who would be able to survive the backdraft of God's firestorm of judgment would be those who "trust in the name of the LORD" (3:12).

Memory Passage: *Zephaniah 2:3*

Seek righteousness, seek humility;
   perhaps you will be sheltered
   on the day of the LORD's anger.

God had shown his people where life was to be found. His people could know rich, full, dynamic human life if only they would value and enjoy their relationship with their wonderful God. But they put their trust in other things instead of in God (3:2). They ignored correction and felt no shame for doing so (3:2, 5). Even their religious officials had turned away from God to the temptations of the popular culture (3:4). It was time for them to realize that if they turned away from God, they were no different from the rest of the nations. They would be judged by God along with everyone else. There was one storm shelter where refuge could be found — one place where the fire of divine judgment would not reach them. And that place was the firebreak of trust in God. The judgment that would come in 586 BC pointed toward a final divine judgment that is just as certainly coming. And when the one who would preside over that final judgment became flesh, his message echoed Zephaniah's.

The Jesus Lens

Preparing for the coming of the Judge of heaven and earth, John the Baptist called for repentance in order to escape "the coming wrath" (Matthew 3:7). John made the choice clear: put your faith in Jesus

Christ, the "Son of Man," and escape judgment and enjoy life, or reject his payment for your sin and insist on paying for it yourself. In John's words: "Whoever believes in the Son has eternal life, but whoever rejects the Son will not see life, for God's wrath remains on them" (John 3:36). Justice demands that sin be punished. But the Son himself credits his own unmerited punishment to the account of everyone who has faith in him. Those who reject him are refusing their immunity from prosecution on the coming day of judgment.

> For he [God] has set a day when he will judge the world with justice by the man he has appointed. He has given proof of this to everyone by raising him from the dead. (Acts 17:31)

The Son of Man is coming to judge. Those who have faith in him will be sheltered on the day of judgment. Jesus encourages us to choose life and escape the judgment and death that lurk outside the borders of our relationship with him: "Whoever hears my word and believes him who sent me has eternal life and will not be judged but has crossed over from death to life" (John 5:24). Immigration from the land of darkness to the kingdom of light requires only faith in Christ. The steep price for your new life in this new kingdom has already been paid by Christ himself.

Contemporary Implications

Abundant life, security, safety, and protection are found in a relationship with God through faith in Jesus Christ. Outside this safe zone are all of the corroding, weakening, and wasting effects of sin. Our good God is coming to purge sin and its destructive effects from his creation once and for all. Those who are still in sin's grip will be carried away along with it in the coming judgment. Zephaniah's appeal still has traction today: escape while you can! Even those of us who have found safety in God occasionally are tempted to take field trips to our old way of life. When we wander outside of the safe zone, we expose ourselves to those corrosive effects of sin, and our lives suffer. We need to help each other nurture the life God has for us in Christ so that when the fires of judgment come, we don't get singed.

And now, dear children, continue in him, so that when he appears we may be confident and unashamed before him at his coming. (1 John 2:28).

Let's encourage one another to enter into and remain in the safe zone of life-generating relationship with the "Judge of all" (Hebrews 12:23–24). He is coming soon to judge every human being. Those who are represented by Jesus Christ will always have their cases dismissed.

Hook Questions

- Do you look forward to the Lord's return, or do you fear it? What might be causing fear? Do you want God to remove sin from the world, or would you like to play with it a little longer? What makes sinful behavior attractive to you?
- In what will you take confidence on the coming day of judgment? How is your relationship with Christ? Is it growing deeper or are you growing apart? What is causing this?

No doubt it was surprising for Zephaniah's hearers to learn that God's judgment would include some of them too. Wait a second! Sure, God would judge the *other* nations, but us? Ancestry, inheritance, religious or political practices, position, or titles would not protect them or us from divine judgment. There is only one thing that can—a relationship with God himself. But that's just considering the negative. In a relationship with God we find true life in all of its richness—human life as the one who created it intended it to be. That is the life that can be enjoyed by anyone who leaves the land of judgment for the kingdom of God by faith in Jesus Christ.

34

HAGGAI

Priority of God

God had been doing exciting things. In 539 BC he had moved the heart of Cyrus, the king of Persia, to allow the exiled Israelites to return to the Promised Land. Tens of thousands jumped at the chance to make the journey back. Immediately the returned community began to address the damage done to their homeland. On the top of the list was the temple. The place that was the visible sign of God's presence with them had to be rebuilt! In two short years they had already completed the foundation and set their sights on finishing the job.

Their neighbors, however, were less enthusiastic and did all they could to prevent these newcomers from maintaining their distinctiveness and identity as the people of the only true God. This unrelenting opposition and the distractions of other pursuits finally wore down the resolve of God's people, and their work on the temple ground to a halt. The temple, like the people's commitment to give God priority, stood incomplete for over a decade. Ironically, God finally sent a prophet whose name means "festive" to a community who was anything but. Haggai urged God's people to reorient their priorities toward the one who gave them true security and significance.

Theme of the Book

God directs his people to give priority to him and his house, and so to be blessed.

The returned exiles had allowed themselves to be hypnotized by the discomfort of conflict, the lure of self-interest, and the busyness of everyday life to the point that they were giving all their efforts to things that led nowhere and ignoring the things that actually led to blessing. God reminded his people, through Haggai, that their identity and their contentment in life were inextricably tied to doing the work of their God. Right then, that work involved building the place that communicated to the whole world that God's presence was in their midst. They needed to be building the house of God.

> **Memory Passage:** *Haggai 1:8*
>
> "Go up into the mountains and bring down timber and build my house, so that I may take pleasure in it and be honored," says the LORD.

It is not as though Haggai were some idealistic youth unfamiliar with the painful experiences others had gone through. He was probably an older man, who had perhaps even seen Solomon's temple before it had been destroyed by the Babylonians in 586 BC. He knew firsthand the physical, spiritual, and moral problems of the exiles. But with his keen prophetic vision Haggai saw amazing things that God's people could not. He saw the wonderful things God had in store for this temple. It would be filled with glory and would stand secure as a place of peace even when the whole world was shaking (2:7–9). At the center of these remarkable promises is a man with the ungainly name Zerubbabel. He was the administrative governor of Judah and, more importantly, a son of David and the ancestor of the Messiah (Matthew 1:12).

The Jesus Lens

God said he would make Zerubbabel like his "signet ring" (2:23). A signet ring had a raised design on its outer surface that could make impressions in soft surfaces such as wax. That impression guaranteed the authority, power, and trustworthiness of its owner. Here God is saying that Zerubbabel, this descendant of David, is a powerful guarantee of the promises God made with regard to this new temple. In fact, these promises are realized when a later offspring of David — Jesus

Christ, God in the flesh—would himself enter the temple, bringing the Father's glory and peace (Luke 19:41–46). Unlike the exiles of Haggai's day, Jesus' central focus was on accomplishing the Father's will.

> "My food," said Jesus, "is to do the will of him who sent me and to finish his work." (John 4:34)

Completing the building of God's house and establishing it as a place of peace and blessing is another way of describing Jesus' redemptive work, because the Father's house is nothing other than the community of believers whom Christ came to save (John 14:1–4). It is through faith in Jesus Christ that we experience blessing and unshakable peace in the household of God.

 ## Contemporary Implications

The apostle Peter tells us that God is still building his house. He says that each person who comes to God through faith in Christ is like a living stone that God is using to build a spiritual house: "As you come to him, the living Stone ... you also, like living stones, are being built up into a spiritual house" (1 Peter 2:4–5). God used somebody in our lives to bring us to Christ. He now wants us to be that somebody in someone else's life. How can we reprioritize our lives so that our gifts and abilities are utilized more fully in God's divine construction work? We can be confident that we will be blessed if we seek to serve God as our first priority. Jesus tells us that we don't need to give priority to our own self-interests. Our Creator knows very well what we need and where our efforts in life will produce the maximum satisfaction:

> Seek first his kingdom and his righteousness, and all these things will be given to you as well. (Matthew 6:33)

"All these things" include "what you will eat or drink" and "what you will wear" (6:25). More important than even these fundamental concerns is a life that gives priority to God. Practically, this means looking for those materials and tools that God has placed in our lives that we can put to use in his magnificent building program in Christ. Let's get busy building the house of God, and we can trust our Foreman for everything else.

Hook Questions

- If you had only one day left to live, what would you do? What does your answer tell you about where your priorities lie? Do you believe that real fulfillment in life comes from doing what God wants you to do or what you want to do? (Answer truthfully here.) What does the Bible say God wants you to do?
- How would someone else see that God is the first priority in your life? If someone followed you around during the course of your day, would your actions make it clear to that person that you placed priority on honoring God? Or would that person see no real difference between what your actions showed that you valued and what unbelievers' actions did?
- What specific changes could you make in your life so that you could be more actively engaged in building the Lord's house?

It is difficult these days to keep ourselves from adopting the same values as those who do not know the Lord. It is tempting to believe that fulfillment in life can come from the things we own, the wealth we can store up, or our professional titles or positions. But our own Creator reminds us through Haggai that our meaning, purpose, and fulfillment in life lie in keeping our focus on him and not on ourselves. When we come to the point in reorienting our lives where we are able to find our joy and contentment in being used by God to build up his spiritual house, then we too will hear him saying to us, "From this day on I will bless you" (2:19).

35 | ZECHARIAH
Temple Building

Zechariah's ministry overlaps Haggai's, but it continues long after his. They both address the same issue — temple building — but Zechariah takes the topic to a whole other level. With highly figurative (apocalyptic) writing that points toward events in the distant (eschatological) future, Zechariah continues to encourage the returned exiles to build the temple. Whereas Haggai encouraged them by making the connection between their progress in building and their progress in making God the priority in their lives, Zechariah encourages them by making the connection between the temple and everything in the present and future that its presence represents and symbolizes.

 Theme of the Book

God uses apocalyptic, eschatological imagery to encourage his people to complete the rebuilding of the temple.

At the beginning of his prophecy, Zechariah has eight mysterious visions (1:8–6:8) in which we encounter horses of different colors, horns, measuring lines, a stone with seven eyes, a lampstand and olive trees, a flying scroll, a basket with a woman inside, chariots, and bronze mountains. To say that these visions are difficult to understand is like saying that shark bites hurt — a little bit of an understatement. Nevertheless, the ideas expressed in these visions are further developed in the rest of Zechariah's prophecy, and all describe the worldwide significance of the construction project that seemed so pointless and pedestrian to

God's people. God's visible presence in the midst of his people, communicated by the presence of the temple, declares that he has drawn a line of distinction between those who are his people and those who are not — those who will experience his mercy and blessing and those who will experience his judgment. God's temple must be rebuilt because its very presence is divine communication of vital truth.

> ### 🕊 Memory Passage: *Zechariah 1:16*
>
> This is what the LORD says: "I will return to Jerusalem with mercy, and there my house will be rebuilt. And the measuring line will be stretched out over Jerusalem," declares the LORD Almighty.

The temple signified a distinction between those who had a relationship with God and those who did not — a distinction between blessing/life and judgment/death (1:14; 12:1 – 5). Its rituals signified God's cleansing of those who would enjoy his life-giving presence (5:5 – 9; 13:1 – 6). Its liturgies described its inhabitant, the King of the entire earth, to whom all nations would one day submit (2:11; 8:20 – 22; 14:9, 16). And its high priest, who performed the sacrifices that cleansed God's people, pointed toward that High Priest who would come and sacrifice himself to secure an eternal, unbreakable relationship between God and his people (3:8 – 9; 6:9 – 13).

This coming High Priest will himself be God and so will combine the offices of priest and king in himself. By purifying judgment he will make the inhabitants of the earth and those who are in relationship with him the same group of people. The place of the relationship with God made possible by this perfect priest-king will then be the entire earth. The temple means all these things even though it is hard for God's people to see that. These prophecies begin to unfold through the birth of the prophesied Branch (6:12), who will bring about this worldwide temple building, though the implications of his birth are also hard for many to see, unaided by the Jesus lens.

🔍 The Jesus Lens

So many of the details of Zechariah's prophecy are clearly fulfilled by Jesus (see, for example, Matthew 21:5; 26:31; John 19:34, 37). But the connection between the coming of Jesus and Zechariah's encouragement to rebuild the temple is less obvious. The temple Zechariah encouraged his people to build was itself prophetic. It pointed toward realities that ultimately found their full realization in the coming of Christ, because the temple was the place that confirmed God's relationship with his people. Jesus makes that relationship more personal and more accessible by becoming one of us and offering himself to us and for us.

The Word became flesh and made his dwelling among us. (John 1:14)

Jesus "made his dwelling" among us. That is, he himself became the place where God was dwelling in our midst, the place where people might meet God, the one through whom people can have a relationship with God. Jesus is, therefore, the ultimate temple. His dominion, or the boundaries of this holy dwelling place of God, will one day encompass the entire earth (9:10; 14:9). Only those who have been purified by the self-sacrifice of the messianic high priest will have access to God in this world temple. For the rest there will only be the death that always lies outside the safe zone of his life-giving presence.

Contemporary Implications

God's people in Zechariah's day had to be reminded of the gigantic implications of the project before them so that they would not lose heart as they faced the hard work it involved. God's people in our day might also need to be reminded of the gigantic implications of that Old Testament temple-building project so that we too won't lose heart as we face the hard work before us.

Don't you know that you yourselves are God's temple and that God's Spirit dwells in your midst? (1 Corinthians 3:16)

Our union with Christ makes us expressions of the presence of God and therefore living pieces of his temple — the place where God dwells. Working to bring others into the church is another way of saying that we are adding pieces to God's temple (1 Peter 2:4 – 5). We join in the building of God's new temple as we seek to expand the church by the Spirit's power. For every believer, then, there is an urgent need to be "building the temple," or to be proclaiming the good news of salvation in Jesus Christ to those who are still outside the protective walls of the place of relationship with God. Zechariah's encouragement to his people is an encouragement to us as well: "Let your hands be strong so that the temple may be built" (8:9).

 ## Hook Questions

- In the building of God's new temple, are you more a craftsman builder or a construction-site gofer? Do you even recognize that you are on God's construction crew, building a glorious temple whose building site is the whole earth?
- What kind of building materials should we use for this new temple? Where do we get them?

Sometimes we forget the profound implications of what our relationship with God means. God's glory is in our midst. We, as sinners cleansed by the self-sacrifice of our high priest, Jesus Christ, have access to his holy presence. We are assured of a full, vibrant life safeguarded and energized by the antioxidants of his mercy, grace, care, and compassion. By the power of his Spirit, we have the privilege of participating in the expansion of his temple until his glory fills the whole earth. Let's allow Zechariah's jarring visions to jar us back into an energized enthusiasm for divine construction!

36

MALACHI
Honor God

Like Haggai and Zechariah, Malachi ministered to the returned exiles in Judah, but about a hundred years later. During his days, the temple had finally been rebuilt and, thanks to the efforts of Nehemiah, the walls of Jerusalem had been rebuilt as well. The formal rituals of worship had been restored. All things appeared to be ready for the restoration of God's people to their former situation. Surely now God would come in power and glory to reestablish his people as preeminent among the nations.

And yet nothing happened. And nothing continued to happen. The expected, glorious manifestation of God in their midst (that all the other nations would not fail to notice) was not taking place. They continued to scrape by as a small province on the margins of the world powers and dependent on their good graces. It began to look as if things were never going to get any better. The people began to suspect that God had really given up on them. They began to believe that God no longer loved them (1:2)—he wasn't going to exalt them and he wasn't going to judge their enemies as he had promised. And if God wasn't going to remember them, well then, what point was there in honoring him? Routine, insincerity, and compromise began to infect their worship. Their growing belief in God's unfaithfulness to them led to unfaithfulness toward him and toward one another. They needed to be reminded of some important truths, and God charges his prophet Malachi to do just that.

Theme of the Book

When he comes to judge, God will spare those who honor him.

Malachi reminded God's people that God indeed loved them and still had amazing things in store. If they continued to trust and honor him, and if they demonstrated those heart attitudes by their behavior, they would surely participate in the glorious future he had planned. Malachi urged God's people not to turn away from him but rather to dig in the heels of their faith and patiently serve him, even in their less than desirable circumstances, as they awaited the day when he would return to deliver his treasured possessions (3:17). He had certainly not forgotten them.

> **Memory Passage:** *Malachi 3:7*
>
> "Ever since the time of your ancestors you have turned away from my decrees and have not kept them. Return to me, and I will return to you," says the Lord Almighty.

"Returning to God" means living the kind of lives that reflect truth about God. It means giving him honor, because he is honorable (1:6–2:9). It means maintaining unity, because God is a unity (2:10–16). It means pursuing social justice, because he is a just God (2:17–3:5). It means giving tithes and offerings, because he is a giving God (3:6–12). It means serving him in humble trust, because he is trustworthy (3:13–15). The Lord takes notice of those who trust and honor him by living like this (3:16–18). Those people will certainly be vindicated when God comes to fulfill all his promises — a coming that will be preceded by the coming of the prophet Elijah (4:5).

The Jesus Lens

About four hundred years later, Jesus makes clear that the Elijah foretold by Malachi had indeed come in the person of John the Baptist (Matthew 17:11–13). The fulfillment of God's promises had begun through Jesus (2 Corinthians 1:20), but not in the way most expected. In the unexpected suffering of Jesus, God demonstrated his love for his people (Romans 5:8). But again, this divine communication calls us to honor God as we trust and wait for its implications to be fully realized. Even the one who communicated most clearly God's love and power to his people also demonstrated what it meant to honor God in the midst of trying circumstances. If ever there was someone whose experiences should have caused him to doubt the love, justice, and goodness of God, it is Jesus. Yet, in spite of what the immediate circumstances presented him, Jesus was able to keep his attention focused on the Father and to carry out his will faithfully.

> He was faithful to the one who appointed him, just as Moses was faithful in all God's house. Jesus has been found worthy of greater honor than Moses.... Moses was faithful as a servant in all God's house.... But Christ is faithful as the Son over God's house. (Hebrews 3:2–6)

Because Jesus is both divine and human, he shows us truths about the Father—that he does love us, that he is faithful and trustworthy, that he is giving. And he shows us truths about God's people—that we should love God, trust him, and honor him with our lives. A day is coming when God will fulfill all the promises he has made to his people. He has told us this, but has also shown us his love and given us indisputable evidence of his firm intentions through the sacrifice of his own Son. Beyond these amazing things, God sends the Spirit of Christ to give us strength and courage to honor him during our own trying circumstances as we await his coming.

Contemporary Implications

It is easy to lose focus on eternal, spiritual truths when everything around us pushes us to give all our attention to our immediate, urgent, and often seemingly more interesting circumstances. But when we honor God by focusing our lives on him by serving him to the best of our ability (2 Timothy 2:15), by maintaining love and unity among ourselves (John 17:11), and by standing firm in confidence and hope in him (Hebrews 3:6), we will find that our circumstances will certainly be no less interesting. Our lives will be rich with contentment now and pumped full of promise for an even richer future (Malachi 4:2).

> Whoever serves me must follow me; and where I am, my servant will also be. My Father will honor the one who serves me. (John 12:26)

Our Lord urges us to follow him. This will not be an easy path, but it will be a rewarding one. God has sent his Spirit to indwell believers to give us the strength to live in faith and obedience. When, in the power of the Spirit, we begin to live like our Lord, we will more and more honor God because we will be doing what he created us to do — bear his image. Living in relationship with God like this is how human beings honor God and experience full life.

Hook Questions

- Does your life bring honor to God? Have you allowed the demands of your immediate circumstances to crowd out the joys and responsibilities of a God-centered life? What is the ultimate end of a life focused on something other than God? What is the ultimate end of a life focused on God?
- What one thing could you do right now in your present circumstances to honor God? What is keeping you from doing it? Where can you find the strength to do it?

This last book of the Old Testament urges us to honor God and serve him faithfully even though our present circumstances may suggest that God has forgotten us, or at least is not concerned with us. Nothing could be further from the truth! In fact, in the next book of our Bibles, God will demonstrate just how much love he has for us by sending his own Son to die for us so that we can have the full life he always intended for his human creations to have — a life of unbroken fellowship with our Creator. God honors us with undeserved salvation, vibrant life, and sure promises so that we can honor him by delighting in that salvation, enjoying that life of grateful participation in his redemptive work, and trusting in those wonderful promises.

37

MATTHEW

Torah Fulfillment

This book, named for a tax collector turned apostle, is a fitting beginning to the New Testament because it is all about new life in Christ—a life, surprisingly, that was already described by the Old Testament law. Matthew wrote for predominantly Jewish readers to show them how that law they so cherished ultimately finds its fulfillment in Jesus. But Jesus interpreted the law in a way these readers did not expect. They had made the law a prison, interpreting it as an unachievable means to an uncertain end instead of a gracious provision by the Creator to guide his creatures into the fullest possible human experience in fellowship with him and with one another. By his words and his life, Jesus would make this positive goal of the law plain to them and possible for them. He would pay for all their violations of the law's relational purpose and at the same time accomplish its relational purpose by giving himself as a sacrifice.

📖 Theme of the Book

Jesus is the new Moses who reinterprets Torah.

Like Moses, Jesus came to deliver his people from their bondage to the law into a place of rich life. That place is found in relationship with him. And when the law is *correctly* understood, it points to the same thing. Some Jews, at least, had missed the point. They had focused so narrowly on the law that they hadn't seen the expansive life to which it pointed. They were like someone who stands too close to an impressionistic painting. Near the painting all the dabs and strokes of paint seem to be a random jumble of unrelated color. But as you back away, the larger coherence and purpose of all those details come into focus.

Jesus leads his hearers to this new vantage point by explaining to them the deeper significance of the law: "You have heard that it was said.... But I tell you ..." (5:21–22, 27–28, 33–34, 38–39, 43–44). The law was always intended to guide human beings into a deeper relationship with their Creator and, consequently, with one another. Sin had kept that from happening. Jesus came to deliver us from sin's penalty and power so that what was once unattainable has now become possible because of his divine power, authority, and continuing presence with his people by means of his indwelling Spirit.

> **Memory Passage:** *Matthew 28:18–20*
>
> All authority in heaven and on earth has been given to me. Therefore go and make disciples of all nations, baptizing them in the name of the Father and of the Son and of the Holy Spirit, and teaching them to obey everything I have commanded you. And surely I am with you always, to the very end of the age.

In the first verse of his gospel and frequently throughout it, Matthew describes Jesus as the Messiah, or the Christ. As the memory passage makes clear, this title signifies that Jesus was the divinely authorized and appointed agent of God's redemptive work. That redemptive work involves the restoration, enhancement, and perpetuation of the life-giving and life-sustaining relationship with God. A healthy relationship with God is inseparably related to a healthy relationship with those made in God's image. Of course, as Jesus himself says, these two emphases summarize the entire law (22:36–39).

These wonderful goals of the law are in no way eliminated by Jesus' redemptive work but rather finally made possible! We should note that in the last verse of his gospel, Matthew records Jesus as commanding his disciples "to obey everything I have commanded you." It is in a life lived within the parameters of divine instruction that we find our deepest contentment. And the last words of this gospel remind us where our ability to do this comes from: "I am with you always, to the very end of the age."

The Jesus Lens

In presenting his particular perspective of the good news, Matthew focuses on Jesus' dual role as Messiah (divinely appointed, Moses-like deliverer) and teacher (Moses-like lawgiver). These two ideas are combined in 23:10: "You have one Instructor, the Messiah." By quoting the Old Testament more than any other New Testament author, by repeatedly indicating that what was written in the Old Testament finds its realization in the life and ministry of Jesus, and by structuring his gospel around five key discourses (to parallel the five books of Moses), Matthew makes his unique perspective clear: Jesus fulfills the Old Testament. He fulfills its demands, and he fulfills its intention. He has not come to replace the Old Testament revelation with something different, but to cause the intent and purpose of the Old Testament to finally be realized.

> Do not think that I have come to abolish the Law or the Prophets; I have not come to abolish them but to fulfill them. (Matthew 5:17)

Jesus fulfills the Torah, or law, of Moses. But he fulfills its original intent, which was far different from what the teachers of the law understood it to be. The Torah, as Jesus describes it, was not intended to be a fence to keep out life, but rather a fence to keep out death. It was not intended to be an enemy of life, but rather a description of life. Jesus reinterprets the law of Moses by stripping off the layers of paint that had been applied to it by the religious leaders and revealing its original beauty and character underneath. When restored to its luster, the law emerges as a description of the deepest possible human experience of life with our Creator and with those who bear his image. Because Jesus reveals that kind of life perfectly, and because he is the one who makes that kind of life possible for us, he is the fulfillment and focus of the entire Old Testament. This is good news worth exploring and experiencing!

Contemporary Implications

In a world of broken relationships, broken promises, and broken dreams, who wouldn't want to experience something whole and healthy? Thankfully, we don't have to rely on our own sketchy efforts to do so. When we make Jesus our representative by putting our faith in him, his payment for our relational unfaithfulness with God is credited to us. And our relationship with God is secured by Christ's relational faithfulness with God. That relationship remains just as secure and unbroken, just as whole and healthy, as his obedience is perfect.

> Christ is the culmination of the law so that there may be righteousness for everyone who believes. (Romans 10:4)

Our desire to enhance and cultivate our secure relationship with God that our Lord has achieved for us by his adherence to the life-giving prescriptions of the law will motivate us to want to become more like him. And a life lived in the way our Lord has demonstrated and described is a life lived in conformity to the intent of the law that he fulfills—namely, that our relationship with God deepens and is accompanied by a growing relationship with those who bear his image. The indwelling Spirit of the one who has already accomplished this gives us the ability to realize this intent.

 ## Hook Questions

- Are you a good person? What is good? Do you describe "good" in terms of actions or of being? Can someone *do* enough good things to compensate for not *being* good?
- How good is good enough? What is the standard? Is it possible for you to meet your or God's standards? What is the goal of the standards? How is that goal accomplished in Christ?
- Is there any use for the law of God in a Christian's life today? Why might Jesus command his disciples "to obey everything I have commanded you"?

We often have a negative view of law. We view it as restrictive and somehow limiting to life. But Jesus reinterprets the law to show that it points toward the same vibrant life he brings. The law shows us how to enjoy the healthy life God desires for us and to avoid the fatal diseases that result from sin. Jesus' death has provided the antivenin to sin's bite, but there is more to life than avoiding death. Through the power of the Spirit of Christ we can follow God's direction toward the extraordinary, extreme life that exists in relationship with him.

38

MARK

Suffering Servant

Mark was a companion of the apostle Peter who recorded Peter's reflections and remarks concerning the life and ministry of Jesus. Things hadn't ended well for Peter. Tradition holds that he was crucified in Rome. And for the Christians in Rome to whom Mark was writing, things weren't going well either. They were suffering severe persecution. There seemed to be a lot of bad news and not much gospel, or good news. Mark reminds the believers of his day and ours that just as Jesus suffered, so those who follow him should not be surprised to encounter suffering. But the life that Jesus' suffering accomplishes for us is one that no circumstance, however painful, can ever extinguish.

Theme of the Book

Jesus is the suffering Son of Man.

Christians in Rome were living in one of the most progressive, upscale, cosmopolitan cities in the world. It was easy for them to be drawn into the value system of their neighbors, for whom such things as vacations at the shore, public amenities, and fine dining defined a rich life. But all of these things could change with the wind, and the wind had changed for Roman Christians. The emperor Nero had found them to be a convenient scapegoat for the public discontent caused by his own incompetent leadership. He burned Christians alive and otherwise abused them in order to draw attention away from himself. It was a confusing, dispiriting time for believers. But Mark encourages them to remember that their true life is found in fellowship with God through the sacrifice of his Son, and that becoming like God's Son means being ready and willing to serve others just as he did, even when it might cost everything.

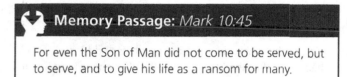

Memory Passage: *Mark 10:45*

For even the Son of Man did not come to be served, but to serve, and to give his life as a ransom for many.

Jesus taught that by giving our lives we find life (8:35). For Christians whose lives were in peril, this was a profound truth. No one could take from them what they were already willing to give. Nero's error was in thinking that by taking away from Christians the things that unbelievers valued most—even life itself—he could stop a movement that had no necessary connection to such things. Jesus had achieved for these believers eternal life and fellowship with God that no tyrant's vicious schemes, no culture's horrible oppression, and no Christian's anguished suffering could touch—good news indeed for believers whose faith in Jesus was leading them to experience those very things. In fact, it is through the suffering of the King of kings that he ultimately gains victory over the things that cause that suffering. Jesus' suffering, ironically, is "the beginning of the good news" (1:1) of deliverance for us.

The Jesus Lens

Mark describes Jesus by means of two titles—the Son of God and the Son of Man. The first title emphasizes Jesus' divine authority. He is the divinely authoritative and designated Messiah (1:1), who demonstrates his divine power by driving out evil spirits (1:1–28, for example), healing the sick (1:29–34, for example), calming a storm (4:35–41), raising the dead to life (5:21–43), feeding thousands of people with scraps of food (6:30–44; 8:1–9), walking on water (6:45–52), and rising from the dead (16:1–8).

The second title, Son of Man, emphasizes Jesus' willingness to experience humanity for our sake. He does so not just by becoming a human being, but by becoming a *servant* to other human beings. And he does not just become a servant, but a *suffering* servant (8:31; 9:31; 10:33 – 34), who gave his life to enable us to have an enduring relationship with God (14:21 – 24). It may seem odd that the King of kings would become a suffering servant of all. But as the apostle Paul later explains to King Agrippa, this gracious, redemptive, restorative act of God was just what the Old Testament had always pointed to:

> I am saying nothing beyond what the prophets and Moses said would happen — that the Messiah would suffer and, as the first to rise from the dead, would bring the message of light to his own people and to the Gentiles. (Acts 26:22 – 23)

The Son of God became flesh in Jesus Christ, the Son of Man, to suffer for our sakes. The apostle Peter had a hard time getting his head around this idea. In fact, when Jesus taught that he would not immediately assume his rightful place of authority but instead "suffer many things," Peter couldn't take it. He had to set Jesus straight. But Jesus had to set *Peter* straight. He explained to Peter that not only was it necessary for God's redemptive plan that Jesus would suffer on our behalf, but anyone who wanted to be his disciple would have to as well (8:31 – 34).

Contemporary Implications

If our Lord suffered in the course of his redemptive work, then it is at least conceivable that those who are called upon to participate in that work should experience the same thing. Jesus makes it clear that those who follow him must, like him, be "the servant of all" — even if that service comes at the cost of our lives (8:35; 10:44). Later, when the reality of suffering in the service of God and others began to hit the young church, the apostle Paul reminded them that it comes with the territory.

> For it has been granted to you on behalf of Christ not only to believe in him, but also to suffer for him. (Philippians 1:29)

We should anticipate and be willing to suffer as a consequence of our faith in Jesus Christ and our service to him. Only when our faith or communication of the good news begins to cost us something do we see how strong or genuine it is. Unfortunately, faith in Jesus and talk of the need for and path to salvation are less and less tolerated in many cultures. As resistance mounts and opposition increases, our willingness to sacrifice and suffer for the truth will display our family resemblance to Jesus, who is working through us by his Spirit to continue his redemptive work.

Hook Questions

- Do hard times cause you to question your faith? Is it right for God to allow his children to experience trouble? Was it right for God to allow his own Son to experience trouble? Can suffering ever be good?
- How does suffering fit into your understanding of salvation and service? Does suffering result in salvation? Does salvation result in suffering?

In our convenience-oriented, leisure-valued, comfort-seeking culture, the idea that suffering could ever be filed under "good" is hard to accept. But Jesus shows us that even one with his divine authority had to suffer to bring about a tremendous good—our salvation! No one likes suffering. Certainly no healthy person seeks it out. Even Jesus prayed that if possible the cup of his suffering would be taken away (14:35–36). But when our salvation or the salvation of others lies on the other side of suffering, we, following the path of our Lord and drawing on his strength, should not hesitate to wade into it. On the other side, Jesus assures us, there is life, honor, and a divine welcome (8:35; 9:35, 37; 10:29–31, 43–44).

Luke is the only Gentile author of a New Testament book. He states that the purpose of his writing is to set out an orderly account (for a person named Theophilus) of the things that had been taught by "those who from the first were eyewitnesses and servants of the word" (1:2). Because Luke is a doctor (Colossians 4:14), his unique perspective on Jesus' life and ministry involves a diagnosis of the problem of sin, the prescription for sin's treatment (including the tremendous physical cost that treatment requires), and the prognosis for those who have been saved from sin's malignancy. Luke presents Jesus as the great physician who brings the only saving remedy for those lost to the plague of sin.

Theme of the Book

The Son of Man came to seek and to save what was lost.

Luke sits us down in the office of his gospel and breaks the bad news to us. Sin has infected us, and it is a terminal disease. Unfortunately, it is often misdiagnosed, or missed entirely, by its victims and by the professionals who should be qualified to spot it. The Pharisees and teachers of the law, the credentialed experts in sin and its treatment, were failing even to recognize that they too were contaminated by it. And if sin was pandemic among the Jews, who had divine revelation to guide them, how much more helpless against its contagion were Gentiles! The only cure for this rampant disease is a human being who is immune to it.

This would have to be a perfect human being, a divine human being. Luke describes in detail the coming of this Savior (1:26–38; 2:1–21).

> **Memory Passage:** *Luke 19:10*
>
> For the Son of Man came to seek and to save the lost.

In Jesus, "God has come to help his people" (7:16). The first thing necessary for him to begin the process of administering curative treatment is for the afflicted to recognize they are sick and in need of healing (5:31–32). So Jesus taught tirelessly of the need for honest spiritual self-examination (for example, 5:36–39; 6:20–26, 41–50; 7:40–47; 8:4–15). Yet, for this divine-human physician to effect a cure for those otherwise lost to the debilitating and ultimately lethal power of sin, he would have to suffer and die (9:22, 44; 17:25; 18:31–33). Sin has invaded the whole human race. Effectively combating this systemic infection will require nothing less than the life of the sinless representative of the whole human race. The prescription is certainly drastic, but so is the disease.

The Jesus Lens

Jesus seeks out sin from every place it hides within us and from every quarter of society. He associates with tax collectors and sinners (5:30; 15:2), with Jews and non-Jews (2:32), with religious leaders (14:14–23), and with those shunned by religious leaders (8:43–48). To demonstrate his power and authority over sin's *ultimate* effect, he delivers people from sin's *immediate* effects. Jesus drives out evil spirits (4:33–35), heals "various kinds of sickness" (4:40; 5:15), and raises the dead (7:11–14; 8:40–42, 49–55). In fact, Jesus explicitly ties these two facets of healing together when he heals a paralyzed man (5:17–25).

The motivation for this seeking and saving is simply, but incomprehensibly, God's love for us. In a series of parables involving the recovery of lost items or people (15:1–7, 8–10, 11–32), Jesus reveals that God rejoices when a person is extracted from sin's deadly grip and restored to life with him. Like cancer-targeting drugs, Jesus targets his life against the cancer of sin. He seeks us out for salvation and he seeks out sin for eradication — though it must cost him his very body and blood.

> This is my body given for you.... This cup is the new covenant in my blood, which is poured out for you. (Luke 22:19–20)

Jesus came to give his life to bring life to sinners. The great physician refrained from saving himself (4:23; 23:35) so that his own life would infuse all of us who were as good as dead. Those of us who have experienced this miraculous cure are called upon similarly to expend our lives in bringing the life-giving gospel to others still suffering.

Contemporary Implications

Luke the physician has diagnosed the problem and prescribed the divine cure. But, like any good doctor, he leaves us with a prognosis. Those who have been sought out and healed by means of the sacrifice of God's own Son will begin to transform into the likeness of that Son, because his Spirit indwells us and is resequencing our spiritual genetic code. We will follow in the path Jesus has cleared, even to the point of death (9:23–24), as we go and proclaim repentance and the forgiveness of sins to all nations (24:46–47). Luke was a traveling companion of the apostle Paul and so had seen firsthand how much the application of the cure for sin could cost spiritual caregivers. But Paul's motivation through his many ordeals looks an awful lot like the divine joy Jesus describes:

> Therefore I endure everything for the sake of the elect, that they too may obtain the salvation that is in Christ Jesus, with eternal glory. (2 Timothy 2:10)

With the strength God provides, we must be ready to endure hardship to bring the gospel to the lost. God has spared us from certain death so that we, like the seventy-two disciples Jesus sent out, can use the new life we enjoy to let everyone know that God's healing has come, and like the seventy-two, rejoice with God when the lost are restored (10:1–20).

Hook Questions

- How much would you pay for your salvation? Do you regard Jesus' sacrifice for you as helpful, or necessary, for life?
- Has your faith cost you anything? How would you respond if it did?
- How much would you be willing to pay for someone else's salvation? Jesus was willing to give his life to save us; would we be willing to do that for someone else?

We sometimes find ourselves in the situation of the Pharisees — aware of sin, but not realizing its extreme toxicity. Unaware of the seriousness of our problem, we undervalue the magnitude of the treatment that is necessary. Our neighbors, our friends, our families, and perhaps even we ourselves are suffering from a life-draining, future-extinguishing illness whose symptoms include blinding its victims to its very presence (4:18). Luke makes both the illness and its remedy clear. Jesus has come to seek out and save those who are lost. Let's imitate our Lord by distributing the good news of new life in Christ to those who are still languishing under the wasting effects of sin — even when it might cost us as much as it did our Lord to do so.

John, the brother of James and the son of Zebedee, wrote his gospel from a different perspective than Matthew, Mark, and Luke. His gospel is much more relational. John was perhaps one of the first two disciples who followed Jesus (1:35–37) and the only one present at his crucifixion (19:25–27). John would benefit from years of Jesus' personal teaching, and among the twelve apostles, he had a relationship with Jesus that was closer than most. He even describes himself as "the disciple whom Jesus loved" (13:23; 19:26; 20:2; 21:7, 20). So John was in a unique position to know what life in relationship with Jesus was all about, and he wants everyone else to know that live-giving, life-nurturing union with God as well.

Theme of the Book

Jesus, the Word, is God.

In his account of the life and ministry of Jesus, John is careful to report those things that you need to know "that you may believe that Jesus is the Messiah, the Son of God, and that by believing you may have life in his name" (20:31). There is a necessary order in this twofold purpose. Before we can believe that Jesus can secure for us eternal life, we have to believe that he is the only one who could do such a thing. That is, we have to believe that he is God. So John begins by describing and giving evidences of Jesus' divinity (1:1–12:50). Once he has established this profound truth beyond question, John goes on to explain how Jesus' death, resurrection, and promised Spirit achieve that life in fellowship with him (13:1–20:31). But the essential truth on which any possibility of light in the darkness of sin depends is that Jesus is the one who created light in the first place. For the salvation John describes in his gospel to be true, Jesus must be God.

Memory Passage: John 1:1

In the beginning was the Word, and the Word was with God, and the Word was God.

"In the beginning" God created light and life by his word. He spoke, and they came into being. John uses some of the same words used in Genesis to describe God's creation of light and life to describe the coming of Jesus Christ to provide light in the darkness (1:4–9; 11:10; 12:35, 46) and life in the midst of death (3:16; 11:25). Because Jesus "is himself God and is in the closest relationship with the Father," he is the one who is uniquely qualified to make the Father known (1:18). Our union with the Father is only possible, then, through our union with his Son. In the words of Jesus, "If you really know me, you will know my Father as well" (14:7).

The Jesus Lens

John spends much of the first half of his gospel describing the miracles of Jesus, which are further proofs of his divinity, or "signs through which he revealed his glory" (2:11). Jesus changed water into wine (2:1–11), healed the son of a royal official (4:46–54), healed an invalid at the pool called Bethesda (5:1–15), fed five thousand people with five small loaves and two small fish (6:5–12), walked on water (6:16–21), healed a man blind from birth (9:1–12), and raised dead Lazarus from his grave (11:1–44). In the second half of his gospel, John describes the dreadful steps Jesus would take to enable us to know that union with the Father ourselves—a union that would be sealed and perpetually strengthened by the Spirit (16:13).

I and the Father are one. (John 10:30)

Jesus and the Father are one. Jesus is God, but Jesus is also human. Because he is a sinless human being, he has no penalty to pay for his own sins and is therefore able to pay for ours. Jesus, the God-man, came to offer himself in payment for our sin so that we could have the union with God that he enjoys and that was not possible for us to achieve in any other way. Jesus entered into a union with us so that we could enter into a union with God. After he paid the tremendous debt of our sin, he sent his Spirit to indwell those who believe in him to guide us into the deepest experience of life in union with God. It is a union that generates, safeguards, and perpetuates life.

Contemporary Implications

John wrote his gospel so that we may believe in Jesus and that by believing, we may have life in his name (20:31). Our union with God — the desired union for which Jesus suffered and died — requires us to respond in faith. Jesus is the bread of life (6:32 – 58) that we must eat; he is the living water (4:10 – 13) that we must drink. Jesus himself prayed that those of us who hear the good news may respond in faith so that we will experience union with the Father, who is the source of all life.

> I pray also for those who will believe in me through their message, that all of them may be one, Father, just as you are in me and I am in you. May they also be in us so that the world may believe that you have sent me. (John 17:20 – 21)

We have union with the Father through Jesus Christ, and that union is with a powerful life-generating force that will necessarily flow from us to others. In the words of Jesus: "Whoever believes in me, as Scripture has said, rivers of living water will flow from within them" (7:38). In another image, Jesus describes the life that courses from him through us to others as the life-giving nourishment that flows from the vine to the branches. Such branches bear much fruit (15:1 – 8).

Hook Questions

- How close do you feel to God? What enhances your relationship with God? What interferes with it?
- How closely do people associate you with God? What is the one attribute or activity in your life that makes your union with God most visible to others?
- How does your union with God affect your behavior? Is your union with God reflected in your union with other believers? Is your union with God producing any fruit?

We are in a love triangle. But this one is a good one. This one defines life, power, meaning, purpose, and truth. This one is as secure and eternal as the divine Trinity. Jesus is in union with the Father; Jesus is in union with believers through the Spirit; believers are in union with the Father through Jesus. This is the union that John the apostle enjoyed and wrote his gospel to urge us to enjoy too. This is the union that Jesus was willing to be crucified for us to enjoy. It is a union with the Father that is sealed for us forever by the indwelling Spirit of our Lord. This Spirit tugs us ever deeper into the experience of full human life that our Creator wants for us (10:10). The Spirit also nudges us ever more strongly to share this good news with others so that they can know this union with their Creator as well.

41

ACTS
Witness

In this sequel to his gospel, Luke writes again to Theophilus (and those of us reading over his shoulder) how God has been working out, and continues to work out, his intention to bring life to those who are spiritually dead. The period Luke covers in this second volume spans the time from Jesus' ascension into heaven after his resurrection all the way to the imprisonment of the apostle Paul in Rome—about thirty years. This time in the early history of the church was as volatile as nitroglycerin. Believers were mistreated, arrested, imprisoned, chained, flogged, interrogated, beaten, and even stoned to death. Yet what seemed humanly impossible in the face of all those painful complications was able to take place because it did not ultimately depend on human strength or ability. The fledgling church grew, and is still growing, because God is at work through his Spirit. Luke faithfully recounts these "acts" of God that take place through his faithful people in the power of his Spirit.

Theme of the Book

God expands and empowers his church through his Spirit.

The Holy Spirit came at Pentecost (Acts 2), and Peter immediately explained the significance of this event to those who witnessed it. The Holy Spirit is the evidence and guarantor of the life that comes by faith in Jesus Christ. The Spirit testifies to life in Christ, and those in whom the Spirit dwells testify to life in Christ. And the testimony of the believers in Jerusalem resulted in the daily expansion of the church there. But

God never intended the church to be restricted to Jerusalem. And he never intended it to be restricted to Jews either. It would take a "great persecution" of the believers in Jerusalem (8:1) and a vision by a Roman centurion and the apostle Peter (chap. 10) for the gospel to break out of its geographic and ethnic shell and spread to the ends of the earth.

> **Memory Passage:** *Acts 1:8*
>
> You will receive power when the Holy Spirit comes on you; and you will be my witnesses in Jerusalem, and in all Judea and Samaria, and to the ends of the earth.

Jesus' statement right before his ascension effectively provides the outline for the book of Acts. The initial work of the empowering Holy Spirit who came at Pentecost was focused in Jerusalem (chap. 1–7) and was spearheaded by the apostle Peter. After "a great persecution broke out against the church in Jerusalem," the believers fanned out "throughout Judea and Samaria" (8:1), spreading the good news of life in Christ. The witness of the gospel spread even more broadly after Peter, responding to a vision, proclaimed the good news to Gentiles and observed the Holy Spirit poured out on them as well. Acknowledging that the gospel had burst the seams of its ethnic confines, the believers in Jerusalem praised God that "even to Gentiles God has granted repentance that leads to life" (11:18).

It is through the tireless ministry of Paul, the chief persecutor of the church who had become its chief promoter, that the gospel began its relentless spread to the ends of the earth. In three wide-ranging missionary journeys (chaps. 13–21), Paul planted churches, defended the faith, and encouraged believers. Though at the end of the book Paul is under house arrest in Rome, the gospel witness is certainly not similarly arrested. In fact, the last two words of the book describe the unstoppable progress of the Spirit-empowered witness: "without hindrance."

The Jesus Lens

In the first verse of Acts, Luke refers to his earlier writing in which he wrote about what "Jesus *began* to do and to teach." By implication, then, the present work is an account of what Jesus *continued* to do and to teach. Jesus continues to act through his Spirit, who indwells every believer. Jesus declared that his food was to do the will of the Father and to finish his work (John 4:34). The will of the Father is that the gospel be proclaimed throughout the whole world (Matthew 24:14; 28:19–20; Mark 13:10; Luke 24:46). Through Spirit-empowered, gospel-proclaiming Christians, Jesus is finishing his work.

> "Come, follow me," Jesus said, "and I will send you out to fish for people." (Mark 1:17)

The Spirit of the risen Christ empowers witness about him. Jesus was a living witness of the Father. When the Spirit of Jesus indwells us, we too become living witnesses of the Father. And what is the message of the Father that he communicates through us by the power of the Spirit of Christ? Simply this: "Believe in the Lord Jesus, and you will be saved" (16:31). Those who follow Jesus will tell people of the life that is found in him. In fact, our participation in the redemptive work of our Lord is evidence of the Spirit's presence in our lives.

🏙 Contemporary Implications

The implication for us today is inescapable. "You will receive power when the Holy Spirit comes on you; and you will be my witnesses" (Acts 1:8). We have power by the indwelling Spirit to be witnesses of the gospel. It's a package deal. The fact of the Spirit's presence necessarily leads to our participation in spreading the gospel. God is well aware that our testimony about salvation achieved by and accessed through faith in his Son will be just as resisted as Jesus was. But God has given us his Spirit so that we may powerfully, lovingly, and diligently continue to speak.

> For the Spirit God gave us does not make us timid, but gives us power, love and self-discipline. So do not be ashamed of the testimony about our Lord. (2 Timothy 1:7–8)

We must let the Spirit of the risen Christ empower our witness to the gospel. That witness will certainly require divine power to confront the opposition that is always present to the truth. In his gospel account, Luke described the opposition to Jesus. In this, his continuing account of the acts of God through his Spirit, Luke describes the opposition to those in whom the Spirit of Jesus dwells. But the subtext of both accounts is that God ultimately achieves victory—through his Son, and through those who in the power of the Spirit witness to his Son.

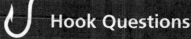

Hook Questions

- When was the last time you told someone the good news of salvation in Christ? What prevents you from doing so more often? How did you hear the gospel?
- Is the effectiveness of your witness of Christ ultimately up to you? How do you acknowledge and draw on the strength of the indwelling Spirit for your witness to life in Christ?
- In your present circumstances, what is one way you could make the gospel clear to others?

The book of Acts contains the last recorded words of Jesus, and those words are a command to his people to transmit the truth about him to the whole world. He himself provides the power to do that by sending his Spirit to indwell every believer. The rest of the New Testament is an encouragement to believers to maintain that witness to the truth in the face of all sorts of internal and external threats to the church. Let's take our rightful and expected place among those ancient and ongoing witnesses as we draw on the strength of the Spirit and witness to life in Christ.

42

ROMANS

Death to Life

In Acts, Luke focused on the responsibility of believers to witness to the salvation available in Jesus Christ by faith in him. In his letter to the young church in Rome, the apostle Paul outlines the content of that witness. Earlier in his life, Paul had done his best to squelch the church (Acts 8:3; 9:1 – 2). But after his radical conversion, he did everything he could to nurture and encourage believers. So even though he had not had the opportunity to visit the believers in Rome personally, he had heard good things about them (Romans 1:8) and wanted to make sure their understanding of the faith was well grounded. In this letter to them, therefore, Paul touches on every necessary doctrine — but doctrine clothed in the genuine love and care of one who desires his readers to know and experience as fully as possible the new life they have been given in Christ.

Theme of the Book

Through Christ, God brings his chosen ones from death to life.

There can be no appreciation for salvation unless there is an appreciation of the need for salvation. No one will grab for the life ring unless they are aware they are drowning. So Paul begins with an unflinchingly honest assessment of the human situation: "They have together become worthless; there is no one who does good, not even one" (3:12). Having effectively pulled out the cheap rug of self-esteem from underneath everyone, Paul then replaces it with a surer foundation for life: the righteousness of God given through faith in Jesus Christ to all who believe (3:21 – 22). Paul goes on to describe what this new life looks like. It involves daily offering ourselves to God as those who have been brought from death to life (6:13). It involves being led by the Spirit of God (8:1 – 17) to experience more and more the divine gift of abundant life that expresses itself in serving God and others (12:1 – 15:13).

> **Memory Passage:** *Romans 6:23*
>
> For the wages of sin is death, but the gift of God is eternal life in Christ Jesus our Lord.

Paul explains that the eternal life we have been given is not a life that is focused on earthly things that pass away. Those have about as much in common as ice cream and sardines. Our life in Christ is in tune with eternal realities, in tune with God and led by the Spirit. Paul offers the believers in Rome the example of his own life. His words and actions are directed by the Spirit in service to God and others: "I glory in Christ Jesus in my service to God. I will not venture to speak of anything except what Christ has accomplished through me in leading the Gentiles to obey God by what I have said and done—by the power of signs and wonders, through the power of the Spirit of God" (15:17 – 19). When believers live such a life—nurturing their relationship with God, serving others even when that service comes at great personal cost, and directing their behavior to give expression to the truths they promote— they are clothing themselves with the Lord Jesus Christ (13:14), who did all these things to perfection and gives us his Spirit so that we can do them too.

The Jesus Lens

Paul describes our old lives as enslaved to sin. Like zombies, we hardly realized we were already dead as we lurched around from one disaster to another. Our real, our Christian, lives begin and end with Jesus. He is the one in whom our new lives have their origin, and he is the one toward whom our new lives have their goal. Paul holds up the life of Jesus as an explanation and pattern for believers today. Jesus died to the effects of sin — its penalty and all of its noxious by-products. He rose from the dead to a new life that perpetually glorifies God. He went through this whole tortuous ordeal all for our sakes, because of his great love for us.

> The death he [Christ] died, he died to sin once for all; but the life he lives, he lives to God. (Romans 6:10)

It is the Spirit of this Christ who indwells each believer and makes all of these things true for us as well (8:9 – 11). In the words of Paul, when we put our faith in Christ, our old zombielike selves are crucified with Christ on the cross (6:6). Then, just as Jesus rose from the dead, we are snatched from the realm of death to live a new life (6:4) — a life, unsurprisingly, that looks increasingly like that of Jesus.

 ## Contemporary Implications

The penalty for sin has been paid. When Jesus was crucified on the cross, our old selves were crucified with him. We now live new, different lives energized by the Spirit of the resurrected Christ. What is a spiritual reality for us will take some effort in becoming a practical reality. Like a snake that continues to wriggle and bite even after it's dead, sin continues to try to inject its poison into our new lives. Every day we must remind ourselves that the snake really is dead.

> In the same way, count yourselves dead to sin but alive to God in Christ Jesus. (Romans 6:11)

Just as we have died to sin through the death of Christ, through the resurrection of Christ we live for God's glory: "If we live, we live for the Lord" (14:8). The apostle Paul gives the believers in Rome and us a demonstration of what "living for the Lord" looks like. It means proclaiming the good news of life in Christ through words and behaviors, love and service for others, hard work, prayer (15:17 – 19), and even suffering (8:17 – 18). In short, it means becoming like Christ.

Hook Questions

- What harmful habits are you having a hard time kicking? Why might that be?
- What is standing in your way to a more fulfilling life? How would you describe a more fulfilling life?

Our daily struggle to grasp hold of this new life we have been given can be hard. It is difficult to keep the proper orientation to God and others when so much of the world around us — and, let's be honest, so much of what we still allow to rent space inside us — is still aligned with our old, meaningless, and dead-end lives (7:14 – 25). Moreover, going against the grain of the world can, and often does, result in hardship for believers (8:17 – 18). But Paul reminds us that we have within us nothing less than the Spirit of the Almighty God, who leads us in the right path and weans us away from death, fear, and emptiness to the peace, confidence, abundant life, and ultimate complete victory that is ours by faith in Christ (8:31 – 39).

It had been a few years since Paul had led many Corinthians to the Lord during his second missionary journey, and the young church was experiencing growing pains. The believers were living in one of the most prominent cities in Greece. They were surrounded by temples to pagan gods whose followers engaged in sexual practices as part of their worship, and that moral confusion was influencing the church. Corinth was also a bustling commercial center, and the moral failings that often characterize those striving for personal economic advancement were also seeping into the church. Paul writes to his spiritual children to help them recognize and deal with these dangers and to guide them back toward healthy growth in and experience of the life God had given them in Christ and equipped them for by his Spirit.

Theme of the Book

God gives guidance to the spiritually gifted but immature Corinthian church.

Never one to wade slowly into a pool of problems, Paul jumps straight into the deep end. In the first several chapters of his letter, he exposes the ugliness of the Corinthians' divisiveness (1:11 – 12), their unacceptable toleration of sexual immorality (5:1 – 2), and their unbrotherly readiness to bring their disagreements before unbelievers for legal resolution (6:1). Paul's response to these problems emphasizes the same things as his later instructions regarding marriage (7:1 – 40), cating food that had been sacrificed to idols (8:1 – 13), and propriety in worship (chaps. 11 – 14). He explains that problems arise in the church when we, like unbelievers, seek to elevate ourselves instead of God and our brothers and sisters in Christ. The principle that should govern all of our behaviors and interactions is a Christlike love, and Paul spends a whole chapter describing it (chap. 13). When believers allow the motivations of unbelievers to squeeze out this kind of practical, self-giving love, their distinctiveness as children of God disappears.

> **Memory Passage:** *1 Corinthians 3:3*
>
> You are still worldly. For since there is jealousy and quarreling among you, are you not worldly? Are you not acting like mere humans?

The believers in Corinth were immature. Like babies whose whole worlds revolve around themselves and who kick and scream whenever their desires are not met, the Corinthians were self-focused. The result was divisiveness instead of unity in Christ (3:21 – 23). Some were giving their bodies over to sexual gratification instead of giving them over to the Lord for his use (6:20). Believers were focusing on themselves instead of seeking the good of others (10:24). They had even turned the use of their spiritual gifts into an opportunity to bring attention to themselves instead of building up the body of Christ (14:12). The worm at the center of all of the problems in the church at Corinth was a self-focus instead of an other-focus. Paul turns their attention away from themselves and toward Christ. He reminds them about the resurrection of Christ to urge them even now to begin to take on the characteristics of that new resurrection life, so that they might begin to look more and more like him (15:42 – 49).

The Jesus Lens

Jesus said, "I love the Father and do exactly what my Father has commanded me" (John 14:31). Jesus demonstrated the kind of love that is completely focused on the Father and on those he came to save. When we use our abilities and spiritual gifts for the service of God and the body of Christ, we will be becoming like Christ himself, because he gave everything for us. He gave up his divine glory to become human. He gave up human comforts to serve his people. He gave up his life to give life to his people. And he gave his people his Spirit so that we could continue this selfless giving and so become like him in the process. Christians become mature by growing up into the likeness of the giving Christ.

> So Christ himself gave ... to equip his people for works of service, so that the body of Christ may be built up until we all reach unity in the faith and in the knowledge of the Son of God and become mature, attaining to the whole measure of the fullness of Christ. (Ephesians 4:11 – 13)

Jesus shows us that Christian maturity is other-focused, not self-focused. When we are united with Christ by faith and his Spirit indwells us, we begin a growth process that ultimately transforms us into the likeness of Christ. Self-centeredness inhibits this growth. Using all the resources God gives us to participate in his redemptive work stimulates it.

🏢 Contemporary Implications

When the object of all of our efforts is ourselves, there are bound to be clashes because everyone is unique. There are as many personal interests as there are persons. But when we focus our efforts on Christ and his body, the church, all the tangles and snarls of our disunity are combed out into a coherent and unified goal: doing all for the glory of God so that many may be saved (10:31 – 33). The indwelling Spirit of Christ gives us the ability to realize this goal.

> Since you are eager for gifts of the Spirit, try to excel in those that build up the church. (1 Corinthians 14:12)

Trying to use our God-given gifts and abilities to build up ourselves is like trying to use a lawnmower to peel a grape. We're going to make a hash of things and there will probably be scars, because we're trying to use something to do what it was never intended to do. Instead, let us grow in spiritual maturity by using our divinely bestowed gifts for their intended purpose: to build up the body of Christ. Making the needs of others our concern shows that we are members of the family of Christ, because this is what he did for us.

Hook Questions

- Are you a mature Christian? Do you focus more on satisfying yourself or on satisfying the needs of others? Which is more important, the presence of spiritual gifts or the use toward which those gifts are put?
- How do you measure maturity? How does God measure it? Would there even be new life in Christ if Jesus focused his life on the same things you do?

Paul practiced what he preached. He imitated his Lord by giving himself for the benefit of the body of Christ, and he urges his spiritual children to follow in his footsteps. When we're busy tending to the needs of others, there will be less insistence on our own rights and less friction as a result. Paul ends his letter by providing the believers in Corinth an opportunity to begin to practice what he has so strenuously urged. He encourages them to give to the needs of their brothers and sisters in Jerusalem (16:1–3). As an expression of our appreciation for and grateful response to Christ's giving of everything to us, we give to others, whether it is with money, with time and effort, with the use of our spiritual gifts, or with putting their interests ahead of ours. The last line of his letter puts into words what Paul's life has demonstrated: "My love to all of you in Christ Jesus" (16:24). This is the succinctly stated goal of every mature Christian.

2 CORINTHIANS

Self-Giving

Less than a year had gone by since Paul wrote 1 Corinthians. In the meantime Paul had briefly visited the church and had written a stern letter of warning to them (2:4; 7:8). Now he writes to them again after hearing that they had taken his words to heart. But there were wounds, and there were still some in the church causing problems. They were masquerading as teachers, or even as apostles, and were trying to lead the believers away from the truth (11:12–15). Once again Paul reminds his spiritual children by words and example what life in Christ is all about. It is about expending ourselves in the service of others, just as our Lord did. The strength to do this is not found in any of us but is provided by God himself.

Theme of the Book

God directs Paul to explain and vindicate his apostolic authority while encouraging the generosity of the Corinthian church.

Paul accomplishes his two main goals of explaining his apostleship and encouraging generosity by holding up giving as the concept that unites them. He encourages the believers at Corinth to be generous in giving their forgiveness and comfort to those troublemakers among them who had subsequently repented (2:5–8). He encourages them to be generous in giving materially to their brothers and sisters in need (8:1–15). And most important, Paul urges them to give *themselves* gencrously in service to God for the spread of the gospel (5:15; 6:1). Paul also holds up his own self-giving as the authentication of his apostolic authority and as a model that they could imitate. Unlike the false teachers who had infiltrated their ranks and commended themselves (10:12), Paul lets his self-giving on the Corinthians' behalf testify to his true Christian character and authority. His ministry had been without any cost to them (11:7 – 8), but it had already cost him plenty physically, materially, and emotionally (11:23 – 29).

> **Memory Passage:** *2 Corinthians 2:17*
>
> Unlike so many, we do not peddle the word of God for profit. On the contrary, in Christ we speak before God with sincerity, as those sent from God.

Instead of profiting from his ministry to them, Paul insists that he would gladly give everything he had for the believers in Corinth because of his sincere love for them (12:15). The source of this love is not some spurious altruistic wild hair, but rather a reflection of his own transformation into the likeness of Christ. His giving is a reflection of a divine attribute that he encourages believers to imitate (1 Corinthians 11:1). God gave his own Son because of his sincere love for us (John 3:16). This "surpassing grace" and "indescribable gift" God has given us in Jesus Christ is the motivation and the resource for the giving that should characterize the life of any believer who receives it (2 Corinthians 9:14 – 15).

The Jesus Lens

We are being transformed into the likeness of Christ by the work of the Spirit of Christ, who indwells us (3:18). When we look closely at this one into whose image we are being transformed, we see giving everywhere. He voluntarily laid down his life for us (John 10:14 – 18). In fact, the very reason he came was to give his life for our sakes (Romans 5:8). And what a tremendous giving it was! Christ gave up his divine prerogatives and gave himself over to his rebellious human creations. He gave himself to serve us with his life, to endure us in his suffering, to pay for our sins by his death, to guarantee our life by his resurrection, and to equip us to become like him in this life by sending his Spirit. There is nothing more he could have given. As the old song goes, he "emptied himself of all but love."

> For you know the grace of our Lord Jesus Christ, that though he was rich, yet for your sake he became poor, so that you through his poverty might become rich. (2 Corinthians 8:9)

Jesus gave himself completely for the welfare of his people. Those who claim to be united with him by faith must certainly increasingly give evidence of the same tendency toward self-giving for the benefit of others. And, perhaps unexpectedly, we find that the maximum return on our giving does not come from hoarding our capital, but in investing it in the lives of others.

Contemporary Implications

As parents, sometimes we give our children money to put into the offering plate so that they can experience the joy of giving, even though they have nothing of their own to give. Paul explains to the believers in Corinth that we have been given treasure by our heavenly Father so that we too can know the joy of giving ourselves, even though whatever we give has been supplied by God (9:10–11). Through the gift of his Son, God has given us "boundless riches" (Ephesians 3:8) so that we can give back to him by using these riches to serve others.

> Each of you should give what you have decided in your heart to give, not reluctantly or under compulsion, for God loves a cheerful giver. And God is able to bless you abundantly, so that in all things at all times, having all that you need, you will abound in every good work. (2 Corinthians 9:7–8)

God will provide for our needs as we give ourselves to others in our service to God and his kingdom. Of course, this kind of giving is not easy. We have to battle against attempted cultural reprogramming that tries to make us believe just the opposite — that looking out for ourselves should be our first priority. But God reminds the Corinthian believers and us, through the apostle Paul, that we're pretty unreliable, pretty weak, and a pretty poor resource for this kind of investment capital. Our unfailing strength and resource for giving comes from God himself (1:21; 3:5 – 6; 4:7), and his reserves are incalculable.

Hook Questions

- Is it really better to give than to receive? Which would you rather do? What if giving involves giving up comfort, safety, or even your life? Why would anyone give like that?
- Is it possible for you to give any more than you have already received? What have you already received from God?

We've probably all had the experience. At Christmas, someone surprises us with a gift and we have nothing to give them in return. Awkward! Somewhere deep inside us we realize that expressions of affection like this should be reciprocal. And it won't do to scrounge up any old thing to give in return. The gift should be roughly equivalent. Our situation with God is similar. His Son, Jesus Christ, gave his life for us so that we could have life. It is only appropriate that we should give our lives back to him as a reciprocal expression of gratitude. Of course, we can hardly match the gift of eternal life in fellowship with God that we have been given. But we can try. And God even gives us the strength, the resources, and the opportunities to do so. When we give of ourselves like this, we become more like our Lord and so realize the close relationship with God that he desires for us. And every time we give, he gives even more.

Insanity is sometimes described as doing the same thing over and over again and expecting different results. The apostle Paul had joyfully discovered that salvation comes by faith in Jesus Christ to those who believe and not by vainly striving to do the impossible — obey the law of Moses in all its detail. Paul had spent much of his life trying to do exactly that until his wonderful conversion on the road to Damascus (Acts 9; Galatians 1:14). Scrupulously obeying the law had not been possible for anyone in the past (Galatians 3:10), and it would not be possible for anyone in the present or future either. Imagine his dismay when he heard that churches he had visited, and perhaps even helped to found, were again being tempted to gain some sort of justification by trying to obey the law (4:11). Paul calls on the Galatian believers to "Stop the insanity!"

Theme of the Book

God calls for rejecting the legalistic demands of the Judaizers and embracing the gospel of grace.

Paul is outraged! Certain people ("Judaizers") were trying to get the believers in the Roman province of Galatia to accept the notion that Mosaic law was still binding on them and that they therefore had to observe certain Jewish customs, especially circumcision, as a necessary component to their salvation. These people were trying to drive a wedge between Paul and the Galatian churches in order to get them to abandon the gospel of grace by faith that Paul preached and instead to adopt a gospel of human effort (4:17). Paul will have none of this! He calls such a notion "no gospel at all" (1:7). If obedience to the law was a workable way of earning salvation, there would have been no need for Christ to come and die for us (2:21). Paul insists that the righteousness that is credited to us is (and can only be) earned by Jesus Christ and is obtained "by faith" and not by observing the law.

Memory Passage: *Galatians 2:16*

A person is not justified by the works of the law, but by faith in Jesus Christ.

Justification is not the result of some cobbled together hodgepodge of Christ plus adherence to the law. Those two things go together like balloons and porcupines! If adherence to the law could contribute in any way to justification, then why is Christ necessary? And if Christ is sufficient for justification, then why is adherence to the law necessary? It is all or nothing with Jesus Christ. The congregations in Galatia had allowed their focus to be redirected away from Christ and back on to themselves and their own miserable efforts. Paul holds up the Jesus lens to refocus their understanding.

The Jesus Lens

Any correct understanding of the gospel begins and ends with Jesus Christ. By faith his payment for our violations of the law and his perfect obedience to it are both credited to us. Like debt-slaves held in slavery by our inability to pay our incalculable debt, we are redeemed into freedom by the incalculable payment of God's own Son. The freedom purchased at this enormous price comes to us by faith, and we receive it through the Spirit of that same Son, who reminds us of who we are and leads us into an experience of true life in fellowship with him.

Christ redeemed us from the curse of the law by becoming a curse for us.... He redeemed us in order that the blessing given to

Abraham might come to the Gentiles through Christ Jesus, so that by faith we might receive the promise of the Spirit. (Galatians 3:13–14)

Christ redeemed us from the curse of the law so that by faith we could participate in the blessing given to Abraham. The key words here are "by faith" — not "by our own efforts"; not "by faith and our own efforts." Paul will not let the Galatian believers forget that they owe their redemption and their new lives to God's own mercy and not their own ingenuity or industriousness. He won't let us forget it either.

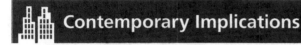

Contemporary Implications

Paul does not argue that there is no place for hard work in the Christian life. Just look at how hard he worked! No, he is insisting that it be filed in the right place in our understanding. Our hard work is never going to be adequate to earn our salvation. So filing hard work *before* receiving salvation as though our work somehow can earn it is a big mistake. Our debt is too great and our efforts too feeble for that possibility. Only our Lord could do it. Through Christ we have been freed from that impossible task.

It is for freedom that Christ has set us free. Stand firm, then, and do not let yourselves be burdened again by a yoke of slavery. (Galatians 5:1)

So, we shouldn't file hard work *before* salvation, but *after* it. Our efforts are no longer hopeless attempts at doing the impossible, but rather "faith expressing itself through love" (5:6), which is somehow used by God to advance his kingdom and bring himself glory. We express our joy and gratitude to God for a salvation that was beyond our ability by using our gifts and talents to "serve one another humbly in love" (5:13). Let us live and serve in the joy of our freedom in Christ and not as slaves to the law.

Hook Questions

- Do you think of yourself more as a human being or a human doing? What is the motivation for all of your busyness? Why do you do what you do?

• If faithfulness to God in the new covenant is not measured by obedience to the law, how is it measured?

It is not clear why the Judaizers were so intent on thinking of justification in connection with adherence to certain provisions of the law, or why believers were willing to listen to them. Perhaps a kind of muscle memory led them to follow the old patterns of behavior without conscious thought (3:3). Perhaps it was like a child's reluctance to remove the training wheels when the goal of the training wheels has already been achieved. Perhaps it was a fear of what others who were doing those things might say if they didn't (6:12). Perhaps they really believed that adherence to the law was necessary for salvation.

In any case, to the degree we look to our own efforts to merit salvation is the degree to which we are undervaluing Christ's efforts on our behalf. It is also the degree to which we're denying ourselves the freedom that is only found in Christ and choosing instead to place ourselves under a weight of obligation that will flatten us like a bug. Let's heed Paul's warning and choose the good news of the gospel of grace through faith in Jesus Christ!

Sin brings brokenness. It causes broken relationships, broken dreams, broken promises, and broken lives (2:1–3). Paul writes to the community of believers at the important and prosperous city of Ephesus, a congregation he had helped to establish and lived among for over two years on his third missionary journey (Acts 19), to remind them of the only remedy for that brokenness—the shalom that is found in Jesus Christ. *Shalom* is a Hebrew word that is usually translated as "peace," but its meaning is far richer. It includes the ideas of wholeness, health, normalcy, and fullness (3:18–19). In other words, shalom is the opposite of sin. Shalom describes life as it should be: vibrant, unquenchable, full, and unrestrained. How ironic that Paul should write about such a thing while imprisoned in Rome (3:1; 4:1)! Yet that is part of the power of his point. In spite of his circumstances, sin cannot cause brokenness for him, because Paul knows and enjoys the shalom that comes from Jesus Christ.

Theme of the Book

God establishes the church as the firstfruits of his shalom.

Through Jesus Christ, the brokenness of sin is undone. It is God's will "to bring unity to all things in heaven and on earth under Christ" (1:10). By faith in him, believers experience a restoration of the broken relationship between themselves and God. We are made members of his family and our sins are forgiven (1:5 – 7). By faith in him, believers also experience a restoration of their broken relationships with one another in the church, the body of Christ. We are made into a "new humanity" that is characterized by the same sort of love, kindness, and compassion for one another that God showed us in Christ (2:15 – 16; 4:32 – 5:1). The effects of sin have been replaced by shalom. So, in the church, there is *one* body, *one* Spirit, *one* Lord, *one* faith, *one* baptism, *one* God and Father of all (4:4 – 6). This unity, this shalom, is the fruit of the Spirit that characterizes the church (4:3) and, when it is visible, will attract like a beacon those who are still far away on a pathless sea of brokenness.

Memory Passage: *Ephesians 2:17*

He came and preached peace to you who were far away and peace to those who were near.

Repairing the brokenness caused by sin cannot be dealt with as easily as gluing a broken coffee mug back together in some garage workshop. No, sin has entered every corpuscle of its human victims so that brokenness becomes woven into the fabric of our lives and is also the effect of our lives. We are incapable of delivering ourselves from its lethal poison. Any repair of the brokenness caused by sin requires a momentous, divine act of complete re-creation prompted by nothing else but God's immense love and mercy (2:8 – 9). And it requires the death of a perfect human being, a divine human being, God's own Son, to accomplish it. We who were far away from any possibility of shalom with God or with one another can only realize both through faith in the one who brings us near at the cost of his own blood (2:13).

The Jesus Lens

Jesus' death on the cross paid the debt of our sin and also drove a stake into the heart of its ability to produce brokenness. Jesus broke the Great Breaker. Jesus broke the back of sin so that it can only exert any of its slithery, divisive influence on us when we choose to go visit it in the hospital. Our strength over sin comes from the strength of the one with whom our faith unites us. Our shalom, our unity, our wholeness, our restoration, and our reconciliation are described in terms of our being the body of Christ (1:22; 3:6), and in terms of our being the building of which he is the chief cornerstone (2:19–22). Paul begins (1:2) and ends (6:23) his letter to the believers in Ephesus with an expression of his desire for them to know shalom, or peace. Much of the rest of his letter is spent explaining to them where that peace comes from.

> For he [Christ] himself is our peace. (Ephesians 2:14)

Christ is our peace. He alone is able to mend the greater-than-Grand-Canyon-size rift between us and God and between us and other human beings. When we come to him in faith, that peace should become more apparent in our lives both to ourselves and to others.

Contemporary Implications

We, as those who have been restored, those who have experienced shalom, have the responsibility to demonstrate that shalom to a broken world filled with broken people. The unity of the church under Christ our head points forward to the day when God, under the headship of Christ, will remove all of sin's disunifying effects in the world (1:10). The second half of Paul's letter to the believers in Ephesus (chaps. 4–6) is full of encouragements to live in a way that makes God's shalom in Jesus Christ obvious to those who still suffer from sin's brokenness.

> Be completely humble and gentle; be patient, bearing with one another in love. Make every effort to keep the unity of the Spirit through the bond of peace. (Ephesians 4:2–3)

This Spirit of this heroic shalom-maker has been sent to indwell every believer. So, in the strength of this Spirit, let us imitate Christ by working toward peace. Let us extend the shalom we enjoy to others by word and example. We have been re-created in Christ for just this purpose (2:10). This won't be easy. Sin is virulent, addictive, and insidious. But God equips us with his own weapons so that we can engage in the battle. No longer are we defenseless against "the flaming arrows of the evil one" (6:16). We have strength "in the Lord and in his mighty power" (6:10) to stand our ground and advance the gospel of peace (6:13, 15).

Hook Questions

- Do you know peace in your life? Why should there be any brokenness at all?
- Do others see peace in your life? How would they be able to see it? What have you done to promote the gospel of peace?
- Where do you look for peace? What is the difference between what unbelievers call "peace" and what you call "peace"? Could you explain the difference to an unbeliever? Have you?

Sometimes it seems that as fast as God puts the jigsaw pieces of our broken lives together, sin is following along behind us and pulling them apart again. But even though our circumstances might be as unpleasant as Paul's when he wrote this letter, nothing can separate us from the love of Christ (Romans 8:38–39). Our great enemy still tries to obscure the church's message of interpersonal shalom by spray-painting over it the ugliness of personal grudges, offenses, inconsiderations, and pride. Let's be aware that the good news that sin's brokenness finds healing in Jesus Christ is threatened by every one of these battles that we lose, and let's take up the weapons of the invincible God and wield them with the strength and confidence he provides so that we lose fewer of them.

PHILIPPIANS

Joy

Paul had a lot to rejoice about. He was experiencing imprisonment in Rome (1:7, 13, 14, 17) when he wrote this letter to the congregation at Philippi—a congregation he had helped to form during his second missionary journey (Acts 16:11–40). And if imprisonment weren't enough to rejoice about, he also was dealing with those who were preaching Christ out of envy, rivalry, or selfish ambition (1:17). And to make his joy complete, Paul had heard that his beloved congregation was suffering persecution (1:27–30), along with the harmful blathering of those who wanted to dilute the gospel by adding to it requirements to obey provisions of the Mosaic law (3:2) or who went to the opposite extreme of promoting a lifestyle of self-gratification (3:18–19). But surprisingly, in the midst of all these things, Paul does indeed find much to rejoice about. And he encourages the believers at Philippi to follow his example and rejoice along with him (2:18).

Theme of the Book

God gives resurrection power and joy in the face of persecution and heresy.

Paul is rejoicing because the place where he finds his joy is unaffected by religious or secular opposition. In fact, those difficult circumstances can blow away the loose surface gravel and expose the bedrock sources of joy underneath. Yes, Paul is imprisoned, but he rejoices that his imprisonment has served to advance the gospel (1:12–14). Yes, some were preaching Christ for entirely wrong motives, but Paul rejoices that for whatever motivation, at least Christ is being preached (1:18)! And even though some were opposing the advance of the gospel, Paul could rejoice that he knew many who were joining him in Christian service. Paul rejoices in the selfless work of Timothy (2:19–23), the life-risking efforts of Epaphroditus (2:25–30), the care for him that the believers in Philippi had shown, and their partnership with him in the gospel (1:3–6; 4:1, 10). But even these things, as joy-inducing as they are, are merely aftershocks of the world-shaking joy Paul finds, and wants every believer to find, in Jesus Christ (3:1; 4:4).

> **Memory Passage:** *Philippians 3:10–11*
>
> I want to know Christ—yes, to know the power of his resurrection and participation in his sufferings, becoming like him in his death, and so, somehow, attaining to the resurrection from the dead.

Paul wanted to know the kind of joy and strength that sustained Jesus in his sufferings. He wanted to know what could propel a human being beyond the bounds of normal endurance on behalf of others. He wanted to know what would motivate someone to die so that others could live. In his words, Paul wanted "to take hold of that for which Christ Jesus took hold of me" (3:12). Paul wanted to "know Christ" not in some purely intellectual or purely emotional way, but in a way that would enable him to realize in his own life aspects of Christ's. Anyone who knows Christ in this way will be able to be "content in any and every situation" (4:11–13), because the source of that contentment and joy always lies ahead and not behind (3:13–14).

Paul wants the Philippian believers to follow him in his pursuit of this kind of joy (3:17; 4:9), as they had already demonstrated they were doing by their faithful Christian service (2:12). The energy that drives such service in the face of the real possibility of suffering and death can only be found in the one who can overpower suffering with joy and death with life.

The Jesus Lens

There was something that drove Jesus forward in his earthly ministry. It was powerful enough to sustain him during the years of opposition and suffering and to keep him moving relentlessly toward the horrible end. We have the first mention of it in the angel's announcement at his birth: "I bring you good news that will cause great joy for all the people" (Luke 2:10). "Joy" appears again when Jesus heard a report that the gospel was finding fertile soil in some hearts (Luke 10:21). Jesus later explained that what he told his disciples was for the purpose of their having his joy in them (John 15:11). And right before he was handed over to be crucified, Jesus prayed to the Father that his disciples would have the full measure of his joy within them (John 17:13). It was joy that propelled Jesus forward, but not an object-less joy. Rather, it was a twofold joy that was defined by *a relationship with the Father*. Jesus had joy in the relationship with the Father that his suffering was bringing about for others, and joy in his relationship with the Father toward which his suffering was leading.

> For the joy set before him he [Christ] endured the cross, scorning
> its shame, and sat down at the right hand of the throne of God.
> (Hebrews 12:2)

In the face of crucifixion, Jesus was sustained by the joy of his relationship with the Father that his suffering would bring about for him and for his followers. That is the joy that Paul wants to realize — joy in his own deepening relationship with the Father through Jesus Christ, and joy in the relationship with the Father through Jesus Christ that his labors are producing for others. That kind of joy has a staying power that can weather wildly changing conditions because it is not at all dependent on those conditions. Paul wants to know that joy more fully, and he wants every other believer to know it too.

Contemporary Implications

Paul discovered that the joy in the Christian life is all about relationship with God. Believers seek to nurture that relationship for themselves, through Jesus Christ, and they seek to be used by God to bring about that relationship for others, through Jesus Christ. But an active expression of that joy requires steady infusions of divine strength in order for us to persevere through the physical, emotional, and spiritual challenges that are sure to come. So the object of our joy and the source of our joy are the same. God strengthens our relationship with him so that we can pursue a stronger relationship with him.

> I can do all this [being content in any situation] through him who gives me strength. (Philippians 4:13)

We can be sure that God will give us strength, and even joy, in the midst of the challenges that will come. And in a curious way, the challenges themselves only serve to make our relationship with God stronger, because they force us to turn away from plastic imitations to the only true source of joy that can never fail us. We can put aside the anxiety and fear that arise from cares and concerns about things that pass away, and instead experience the peace of God—the peace that comes from a sure and life-giving relationship with God through Jesus Christ, the peace that keeps us safely inside the fortress of the true joy he gives (4:6–7).

Hook Questions

- What are the people, things, or circumstances that bring you joy? Why do they do so?
- Can those people, things, or circumstances change? When relationships or circumstances change, what or whom do you turn to in order to find the deep contentment, or even joy, that Paul describes?

Sometimes joy is confused with happiness. If our present experience does not result in happiness, we might feel as if we're somehow missing the boat in our Christian life. But joy is not the same thing as happiness. Joy runs much deeper. Happiness comes and goes, but the joy that is found in relationship with God through Christ endures forever. This is the joy that Paul could still enjoy even when he experienced incredible hardships. This is the joy that Jesus could still enjoy even when the cross loomed large before him. This is the joy Paul wants for the believers in Philippi and for us. And this is the joy that drives us to advance the good news of Jesus Christ, even in the face of huge obstacles, so that others can experience this joy as well.

48 | COLOSSIANS
Exalted Christ

In his letter to the church at Philippi, Paul had encouraged believers to pursue the joy that comes from a deepening and shared relationship with God through Jesus Christ. The believers in Colossae, however, were being told by others that they would find that joy elsewhere. Their spiritual father, Epaphras (1:7), was alarmed at what was being foisted on his congregation, and so he had come to Paul's prison cell in Rome to seek his help in dealing with the problem. In response, Paul writes to the Colossian believers to remind them of the truth of the gospel (1:5), to encourage them to stand fast in that gospel truth (1:23), and to reassure them that the human wisdom and tradition they were being offered by silver-tongued false teachers could not compare with what has already been accomplished for them in Jesus Christ.

Theme of the Book

God has exalted his Christ above all human wisdom and tradition.

Though Paul had never visited Colossae (2:1), he shared the concern of Epaphras for the spiritual health of these believers. They might have been ready for a direct frontal attack by the enemy of truth, but were they prepared for the stealthy infiltrations of his agents, who were wearing the disguise of those who professed to be seeking the truth? These undercover enemies came with deadly personal arsenals that included "fine-sounding arguments" (2:4), philosophies based on supposed spiritual mysteries or human understanding (2:8, 18), and an insistence on a raft of regulations that "have an appearance of wisdom" (2:21–23).

The ultimate goal of such pretenders was deception (2:4), leading to mental captivity (2:8) so that the believers would be spiritually ineffective because they would be afraid to do anything else but live under the constraints of the deception (2:18). Paul unmasks these enemies; he blows their cover. And he encourages the Colossian believers to focus once again on Jesus Christ, the source and strength of their faith.

Memory Passage: *Colossians 1:18*

He is the head of the body, the church; he is the beginning and the firstborn from among the dead, so that in everything he might have the supremacy.

In the swirl of options being thrown at the Colossian believers by teachers both true and false, Paul directs them to set their minds and hearts on things above, where Christ is. Christ is preeminent, supreme, exalted over everything. All things find their meaning and purpose in him. He is before all things, and in him all things hold together (1:17). There is nothing before or beyond him. Focusing on such a source of truth will enable the believers to find their way through the fog of religious malarkey that has rolled over their congregation. If the teaching being presented to the Colossians was not based on Christ and did not ultimately lead to a deeper relationship with Christ, that teaching was worthless and harmful. Christ provides the lens through which both the truth and its cheap imitations come into focus.

The Jesus Lens

When we do focus our attention on Christ, we see that all of the spiritual "extras" being offered by the false teachers in Colossae have already been accomplished in Christ. Do you want to contemplate deep spiritual mysteries? How about contemplating the mystery of Christ (1:26,

27; 2:2; 4:3) revealed to us in the gospel! Do you want to achieve an advanced spiritual wisdom? How about engaging more deeply with Christ, "in whom are hidden all the treasures of wisdom and knowledge" (2:3)! Do you think stricter adherence to certain laws will strengthen your spiritual life? How about trusting in the one to whom those laws all point (2:16–17)! Are you interested in exploring powerful heavenly beings? How about exploring the one who is seated at the right hand of the Father (3:1), victorious over all powers and authorities (2:9–10, 15)!

> God exalted him to his own right hand as Prince and Savior that he might bring Israel to repentance and forgive their sins. (Acts 5:31)

The Father himself has exalted his Son. The fact of the Son's exaltation forms the basis for Paul's instructions to the believers in Colossae in the second half of his letter to them. Spiritual truths have practical implications, and there can be no more fundamental spiritual truth than that life owes its origin, its meaning, and its fulfillment to Jesus Christ (1:16).

🏢 Contemporary Implications

In chapters 3 and 4, Paul describes the implications of Christ's centrality to the life of a believer. These things do not involve some sort of spiritual makeovers of our old lives by reupholstering the shabby furniture and applying new paint on the walls to cover over the water damage. It involves dying to our old lives and growing up into our new lives in Christ (3:1–17). This growing happens not by pursuing some new spiritual direction, but by cultivating our relationship with our exalted Lord (2:19). Through our relationship with Jesus Christ by faith, we have access to the source and the transforming effect of divine power. There is nothing lacking in our relationship with Christ that we have to go elsewhere to find. In fact, it is just the opposite. In Christ we have everything.

> For in Christ all the fullness of the Deity lives in bodily form, and in Christ you have been brought to fullness. He is the head over every power and authority. (Colossians 2:9–10)

This fullness manifests itself in practical ways. Paul explains to the believers in Colossae, and to us, that when we recognize and submit to the deity of Christ and begin to grow in our relationship with him, our lives will show it. These behaviors and attitudes do not earn our relationship with our Lord but rather result from it. They include, unsurprisingly, characteristics of any healthy relationship: behavior that brings honor to the other person, a desire to know the other person better, finding strength in the other person, and expressing gratitude for the other person (1:9–12; 2:6–7).

Hook Questions

- What is the most important thing in your life? Where do you look for fulfillment?
- What would other people say is the most important thing in your life? If someone watched you during the day, what would they say is most important to you?
- In what concrete way have you served the exalted Christ today? Is your relationship with him what you would call healthy?

It is easy to begin assimilating the beliefs of those around us who are seeking fulfillment in other things. We are alert to the dangers of elevating money, careers, possessions, beauty, fame, and personal gratification of one sort or another to a place that is reserved for Christ alone. But we may not be alert to the dangers of those who seem to be offering us what we are seeking — a deeper spiritual experience. Wisdom, deeper spiritual insight, humility, and self-abasement all seem like legitimate avenues to a higher spiritual plane — and they are.

Thankfully, all of these things are found perfectly fulfilled in Jesus Christ. We experience them for ourselves as we pursue our relationship with him. Other paths may promise a lot, but they are like the wrong turns in a maze — it may take us a while before we realize we're headed in the wrong direction. Jesus Christ promises a lot in our relationship with him. It won't take us long with him to realize we're definitely going in the right direction.

49 | 1 & 2 THESSALONIANS
Fruitfulness

After helping to establish the church at Thessalonica on his second missionary journey (Acts 17:1–4), Paul later wrote these two letters to them, only a few months apart, to encourage them and instruct them in a fruitful faith even in the face of opposition. The believers were facing opposition from outside their community—the same opposition that led to Paul's earlier hasty departure (Acts 17:5–10). The believers were also wrestling with theological questions arising from their own midst, questions concerning the status of believers who had died and the time and circumstances surrounding the Lord's return. Paul wrote to guide these fledgling believers into a deeper understanding of how they could live fruitful Christian lives as they awaited the day when the Lord returns and their faith will be rewarded.

> ### Theme of the Book
> *God empowers productive, godly lives as believers wait for the Lord's return.*

Paul gives thanks that his ministry to the believers in Thessalonica is bearing fruit (1 Thessalonians 2:13). Continuing to cultivate the metaphor, he describes the faith of the Thessalonian believers in horticultural terms. Like a plant, their faith is "growing more and more" (2 Thessalonians 1:3). Paul encourages them to continue to produce the fruit of a healthy, growing faith (1 Thessalonians 1:3; 2 Thessalonians 3:13). And like farmers nurturing and tending their precious crop, the believers should encourage one another in their faith, so that their fruitfulness continues (1 Thessalonians 4:18; 5:11, 14; 2 Thessalonians 2:16, 17). Of course, all these stages of their growth in the faith — from original sprouting to initial fruit production to mature fruitful Christians — are ultimately evidences of God's activity in their lives. That is, their fruitfulness is evidence of what God has done in them, what God is doing through them, and what God will do for them.

Memory Passage: *2 Thessalonians 2:13*

We ought always to thank God for you, brothers and sisters loved by the Lord, because God chose you as firstfruits to be saved through the sanctifying work of the Spirit and through belief in the truth.

Firstfruits are the earliest evidences of the productivity of fertile soil. They indicate the larger harvest that is to come. So, if there are "firstfruits," then there should be later fruit as well. Paul encourages the Thessalonian believers to participate in God's work by seeking to enhance the fruitfulness of their own lives and the fruitfulness of the gospel message.

Of course, as every farmer knows, there are a host of potential threats to a healthy crop. Like violent weather, those who oppose the gospel can marshal their forces and rage against the church (1 Thessalonians 2:14–16; 2 Thessalonians 1:4). Of a much smaller order of magnitude, but no less potentially damaging, are those within the church who, like insects, nibble away at the effectiveness of the gospel witness by their words or behaviors (1 Thessalonians 4:3–7; 5:14–15; 2 Thessalonians 3:6–15). Like blight or fungus that sucks the life out of a healthy crop, nagging doubts and fears regarding such theological questions as the status of believers who have died (1 Thessalonians 4:13–18) and the time and circumstances surrounding the Lord's return (1 Thessalonians 5:1–11; 2 Thessalonians 2:1–12) can suck the life and fruitfulness out of a healthy congregation. Paul reminds the Thessalonians that in the midst of these dangers, the one the church waits for is the same one, and the only one, who can ensure its sustained fruitfulness until he arrives. We must stop looking for when and start looking at who.

The Jesus Lens

Paul redirects the perspective of the believers in Thessalonica back to the one who is their life and who enables them to channel that life to others. It is their sure hope in Jesus Christ that produces the fruit of endurance that enables them to withstand the challenges that face them (1 Thessalonians 1:3). He is the one who causes love and strength to grow in the hearts of his people and extend tendrils into the lives of others (1 Thessalonians 3:12–13; 2 Thessalonians 2:16; 3:3–5). When our connection to this source of life is damaged by the rough weather of opposition, by the clumsy work of careless spiritual landscapers, or by well-intentioned but ultimately fatal transplantation of our hopes, then any possibility of fruitful life for ourselves is lost, and we'll also produce nothing of nutritional value for the starving people who surround us.

> Remain in me, as I also remain in you. No branch can bear fruit by itself; it must remain in the vine. Neither can you bear fruit unless you remain in me. (John 15:4)

Jesus Christ is the source of our fruitfulness. Our life comes through faith in him. But it is not like the sickly, feeble existence we experienced before our relationship with him. Instead, this new life is generative. It results in luscious, tasty, and nourishing fruit that contains the seeds for even more new life. And as long as our branch remains in the vine, as long as we "stand firm and hold fast" to the truth (2 Thessalonians 2:15), the fruit will keep coming.

Contemporary Implications

A person can tell what kind of tree a certain fruit comes from by its characteristics. Thus, if we have life through faith in Christ, the fruit of our lives should have something of his characteristics. When by faith we tap into the same divine presence and power that gives us life, we will be able to correct the mistaken, strengthen the weak, and be patient with repeat offenders—relentlessly caring, consistently joyful, always prayerful, and unfailingly thankful (1 Thessalonians 5:14–18). This fruit looks an awful lot like our Lord and is only possible in our lives when we have a healthy relationship with him.

> With this in mind, we constantly pray for you, that our God may make you worthy of his calling, and that by his power he may bring to fruition your every desire for goodness and your every deed prompted by faith. (2 Thessalonians 1:11)

Let us pray that God will cause our efforts in his name to bear fruit for the kingdom. Fruit that has been separated from the vine doesn't stay tasty or attractive for long. Artificial fruit requires no vine at all and stays attractive indefinitely, but it has no life and gives no life. We need to help each other keep focused on the source of our life and strength so that we as individuals and as the people of God together continue to bear life-containing, life-sustaining, and life-propagating fruit.

Hook Questions

- Are you a productive, fruitful Christian? What enables you to be fruitful or what keeps you from being fruitful? What is the ultimate source of your fruitfulness?
- How do you measure fruitfulness? How does Paul describe fruitfulness to the believers in Thessalonica?
- What could you do to become more fruitful? What connection does the health of your relationship with God have on your fruitfulness as a Christian?

Fruitfulness requires attentiveness — attentiveness to our own connection to the source of life, and caring attentiveness to the spiritual growth of our brothers and sisters. So Paul urges the Thessalonians to love, encourage, and build up one another (1 Thessalonians 4:9, 18; 5:11, 14), to avoid life-sapping dangers (1 Thessalonians 4:3–4; 2 Thessalonians 3:6), and never to grow weary of doing good (1 Thessalonians 5:15; 2 Thessalonians 3:13). The ability to do these things, to exercise this attentiveness, comes from the one who gives us life in the first place. He initiates, sustains, and propagates life in and through his people. He is coming again to remove everything that is antagonistic to that life.

Paul reminds the Thessalonians and us that as we, like plants, grow up in the faith, we must be careful that as we look heavenward in excited anticipation for the return of our Lord, we don't forget that he is the one who gives us life right now, a life that should be producing fruit that comes from and looks like him.

1 TIMOTHY

Truth versus Error

A lot had happened in Paul's life since he had written to the believers in Ephesus. He had been imprisoned in Rome for a time, and after his release he had undertaken a journey to visit the places where he had previously ministered. Paul left Timothy, his traveling companion on that journey and his "true son in the faith" (1:2), to tend to affairs in Ephesus while he went on to Macedonia (1:3). It was necessary because a lot had also happened in the Ephesian church over the previous several years, and much of it was not good. The church had been infiltrated by spiritual vandals who were defacing the masterpiece of God's gospel truth. Paul encourages and instructs Timothy in the restoration work that had to take place for the beauty of the truth to shine forth clearly once again from this congregation, and for the error that had obscured that truth to be wiped away and protected against.

Theme of the Book

God encourages the (Ephesian) church in promoting the truth and opposing error.

The beautiful brushstrokes of the good news of salvation in Jesus Christ had been spray-painted over with false doctrines (1:3), myths, endless genealogies, controversial speculations (1:4), and meaningless talk (1:6). This defacement could cause some to miss the truth and wander past it into oblivion (4:1). The restoration of the gospel message to its original beauty was critically needed and long overdue. Paul spends much time describing what this work looks like. It involves pursuing righteousness, godliness, faith, love, endurance, and gentleness (6:11). It involves holding on to the faith (1:18) with diligence and self-discipline (4:7, 15). It involves taking hold of the eternal life that is truly life (6:12, 19). It involves putting our hope in the work of the Master, who "richly provides us with everything for our enjoyment" (6:17). To avoid the damage of spiritual vandals, close guard must be kept on the truth (6:20).

> **Memory Passage:** *1 Timothy 4:16*
>
> Watch your life and doctrine closely. Persevere in them, because if you do, you will save both yourself and your hearers.

Paul reminds Timothy and the Ephesian believers that truth and error can be manifested by the behaviors of believers (life) just as well as by the words they speak (doctrine). So Paul provides instructions for how Christians should behave in the church, "God's household" (3:14–15). Indeed, much of the book describes appropriate Christian behavior: for men and women (2:8–9); for overseers and deacons (3:1–13); for widows, elders, and slaves (5:1–20); for the rich (6:17–19); and for Timothy himself (4:12–16). These behaviors are inextricably linked to the truth of the gospel and both demonstrate and corroborate its message. Those who appraise the work God is doing in and through his people can determine its divine provenance by the degree to which our lives conform to his revealed truth. Paul encourages Timothy to ensure that his own behavior and the behavior of his flock reveal the Master's hand.

The Jesus Lens

Truth finds its source in God. Truth can be seen. Truth can be lived out before other people. The truth of God finds its perfect expression in Jesus Christ, who "came from the Father, full of grace and truth" (John 1:14). Jesus' life communicated in all of its details the same truth his words did. So when John the Baptist sent his disciples to inquire of Jesus whether or not he was the Messiah, Jesus replied, "Go back and report to John what you *hear* and *see*" (Matthew 11:4, emphasis added). Jesus both showed and spoke the truth. His divine provenance was plain for all to see. When anyone looked at his life, they could see God, the one who sent him (John 12:45). He perfectly represented God (Hebrews 1:3). There were no off-color remarks or behaviors, no errors in perspective or lighting, no faults in technique or execution. Jesus is a perfect picture of the Father, and he sends us out as his signed, limited-edition prints.

> Sanctify them by the truth; your word is truth. As you sent me into the world, I have sent them into the world. (John 17:17–18)

Just as Jesus revealed the truth about the Father, he charges and equips his followers to do the same. He shows us what truth looks like in everyday life, and by his Spirit he makes us apprentices who grow in our ability to imitate his expression of the truth in all of its beauty.

Contemporary Implications

Those who color in the truth with tints or shades from their own palette instead of God's don't end up with a picture of life, but rather one characterized by "envy, strife, malicious talk, evil suspicions and constant friction" (6:4–5). God charges his people to promote truth and oppose error because tracing out a life described by his words leads to the contentment he desires for us (6:6). We will know that contentment when we bring every aspect of our lives into conformity with the truth God has revealed to us. And when that happens, our individual and corporate lives become a canvas on which God's truth finds clear illustration.

> Command and teach these things. Don't let anyone look down on you because you are young, but set an example for the believers in speech, in conduct, in love, in faith and in purity. (1 Timothy 4:11–12)

Of course, in order to communicate the truth in all of its rich tones and subtle hues, we must first know it ourselves. We have to read it, study it, reflect on it, and creatively seek to let it find expression in our lives. It is too easy to contradict what we say we believe by the way we live. Then we become like those in the church at Ephesus who were causing so many problems. Instead, let us join together to understand, defend, celebrate, and promote the truth of God, which leads to fuller life for ourselves and for those who are attracted to the artist's work we represent.

Hook Questions

- How do *you* distinguish truth from error?
- Which one do you communicate more clearly with your words and behaviors? Which one does your congregation communicate more clearly with its words and behaviors?
- Are you willing and ready to stand for the truth? How might you undertake restoration work in your own life or that of your congregation?

Museums spend fortunes to keep their treasures secure from forgers and vandals. We have been entrusted with a treasure far more valuable than museum pieces. We have been entrusted with the good news of salvation through faith in Jesus Christ. There are many who would like to obscure the magnificent work of the Master by painting over it the blasphemous graffiti of their own gangs. Others try to pass off their own amateurish work as divine truth. We need to step up our security to make sure these spiritual criminals cannot succeed. We have God's Word, the preaching and teaching of those who read it and live it, and the spiritual fruit of our brothers and sisters in the faith to help us avoid being victimized like the believers in Ephesus. May God help us to be those who paint a beautiful picture of Jesus with our lives.

Loyalty

In his first letter to Timothy, Paul had encouraged his son in the faith to oppose error and promote the truth by his words and his behavior. But the enemy of the truth had stepped up his game. Now it was not only the gospel message that was under attack, but also the gospel messengers! The emperor Nero had launched a full-scale persecution of Christians, and Paul was caught up in its net. He was now chained like an animal in a cold, damp prison cell in Rome. Yet from this desolate place where most who entered abandoned all hope, Paul in confident hope writes to urge Timothy and the wider Christian community to remain loyal to the message, the work, and the focus of the gospel.

Theme of the Book

God appeals to Timothy and the churches to remain loyal to the gospel message in the face of persecution and error.

Paul was in chains, but he was never more free. The prison door was closed behind him, but heaven was open before him. In captivity and physically weak, he describes to Timothy where his true freedom and strength are found. They are not found in his physical comfort, his public esteem, or even his own faithfulness—he knows these are transient at best. Paul's freedom and strength come from nothing less than the power of God realized through faith in Jesus Christ.

Paul describes to Timothy how this limitless resource has sustained him in his suffering in order to encourage Timothy and the church to draw upon it too as they face similar struggles. The Spirit of God has given Paul power instead of weakness, love instead of resentment, and self-discipline instead of self-pity (1:7). Incredibly, Paul does not warn Timothy to seek out an easier and safer line of work; rather, he invites him to join him in his suffering for the gospel (1:8; 2:3). The wonderful redemption and promise revealed by God's truth must be protected from false teachers and proclaimed at any cost by the power of the indwelling Holy Spirit (1:14).

Memory Passage: *2 Timothy 2:15*

Do your best to present yourself to God as one approved, a worker who does not need to be ashamed and who correctly handles the word of truth.

Like nitroglycerin, the gospel needs to be correctly handled. Paul describes what this care involves with imperatives that occur in his letter as rhythmically as the dripping of water in his dank prison cell: *keep* the pattern of sound teaching (1:13); *guard* the good deposit (1:14); *be strong* in the grace of Christ (2:1); *remember* Jesus Christ (2:8); *keep reminding* God's people; *continue* in what you have learned (3:14); *preach, correct, rebuke,* and *encourage* (4:2). This loyalty to the hard work of the gospel, however, was (and always is) under ferocious attack. Anyone who has ever glued something together knows that the strength of the bond is only obvious when someone tries to pull it apart. There were many strong and persistent forces trying to pull the church away from its bond with the truth. False teachers were yanking at it from the inside (2:16–18; 3:1–9), and government-sponsored persecution was yanking at it from the outside. But the focus of the gospel truth, Jesus Christ, has made such a separation impossible.

The Jesus Lens

The bond between believers and the Father that Jesus has established cannot be broken (Romans 8:35–39). His obedience to the requirements of the covenant relationship was perfect. And his payment for our violations of those requirements was complete. Consequently, by our faith in Jesus Christ, our relationship with the Father is just as secure as the Father's relationship with the Son. So, even if we are faithless, "he remains faithful, for he cannot disown himself" (2 Timothy 2:13). As our representative by faith, Jesus has cemented forever our relationship with the Father.

The incredible security and strength that this truth gives to us is good news in the extreme. It must be safeguarded from anything that might dilute its potency. It is a bombshell that must be lobbed into every stronghold of the enemy. No matter what attacks the enemies of the truth might launch against us—whether Roman persecutions, infiltrating false teachers, or surreptitiously injected doubts about our own worthiness—we must stand firm in the truth that our deliverance has already been accomplished by Jesus' loyalty to the Father.

> I have come down from heaven not to do my will but to do the will of him who sent me. (John 6:38)

In the face of persecution and error, Jesus remained unwaveringly faithful to the will of the Father. So there is nothing more that needs to be, or that can be, done to secure our relationship with the Father. As the Spirit of Jesus, who perfectly does the will of the Father, transforms us into the likeness of Christ, our lives will begin to conform to the will of the Father as well—even when we, like Christ, encounter stiff opposition to doing so.

Contemporary Implications

Paul writes to remind his beloved Timothy of the precious and powerful truth that God has revealed in Jesus Christ. In the face of the death and hardship that are all around us and that were staring Paul in the face, we have life and immortality in the gospel (1:10). This is the message God has entrusted to us and the message to which Paul encourages Timothy to remain loyal. We have the Spirit of the only human being who was ever perfectly loyal dwelling within us to give us the strength to carry out this task.

> What you have heard from me, keep as the pattern of sound teaching, with faith and love in Christ Jesus. Guard the good

deposit that was entrusted to you—guard it with the help of the
Holy Spirit who lives in us. (2 Timothy 1:13–14)

By that help of the indwelling Holy Spirit, let us express our loyalty
to Christ and the gospel message by learning and doing the will of the
Father. Let us resist falsehood (2:25), nurture our faith (2:22), and learn
the Scriptures (3:14–17). And let us make it obvious to everyone with
our words and behaviors that our loyalty now and forever lies with God,
and let us invite them into that loyal fellowship as well.

Hook Questions

- What truths are you willing to die for? Why would you be willing to make such a stand? Are you driven more by a desire to
  preserve your own reputation, status, or influence or by a desire
  to advance the gospel's reputation, status, or influence?
- What truths are you willing to live for? What if living for the
  truth means ridicule by others, marginalization by society,
  imprisonment, or worse? How can a person live such a life?

One rarely hears about loyalty today except in references to bygone
Victorian-era days, movies about the mob, or discount programs offered
by businesses to steady customers. But Paul shows Timothy that the
Christian life is all about loyalty. The loyalty of Jesus to the will of the
Father makes eternal life possible for those who unite with him by faith.
As those who put our faith in him, we remain loyal to this message of
good news in the face of all who try to distort or compromise it—and
today, as always, there are quite a few. And as those who alone know the
way to eternal life, we loyally persevere in communicating this truth to
others, even when it could cost us comfort, respect, or even our lives.
God has given us his own Spirit to give us the power to do these things.
So, ultimately, our loyalty to God is only possible because of his loyalty
to us. His loyalty will never fail. By his power and grace and our own
disciplined effort, may our loyalty to the focus, the message, and the
work of the gospel fail less and less.

Paul knew Titus well. They had worked together closely on Paul's third missionary journey (2 Corinthians 7:6, 13, 14; 8:6, 16, 17, 23). After Paul was released from his first imprisonment in Rome, he had gone right back to his evangelistic work, and he brought Titus along with him to the island of Crete. Paul went on ahead, but he left Titus behind to "put in order what was left unfinished and appoint elders in every town" (Titus 1:5). This was a lot harder than it sounded. Crete wasn't known for its cultural sophistication. Quite the opposite. Paul describes the people in the words of one of their own poets: "Cretans are always liars, evil brutes, lazy gluttons" (1:12) — not exactly shining jewels of moral rectitude! How in the world would poor Titus organize congregations from people like this? How could such people ever manifest the new life in Christ for all to see? Paul knows Titus is going to need some guidance, and he writes this letter to give it to him.

Theme of the Book

God provides instruction to a young church leader regarding defending, speaking, and living out the truth.

As usual, it doesn't take Paul long to get to the point. He describes for Titus what the qualifications are for the elders he has commissioned him to appoint. Perhaps surprisingly, the lengthy list of attributes is almost entirely behavioral (1:6 – 8). Only at the end of the list does Paul get around to mentioning the ability to encourage believers and refute error "by sound doctrine" (1:9). Evidently, holding firmly to this sound doctrine is primarily manifested by corroborating behavior. You are what you eat. When you eat the truth of God, it begins to show up in your complexion. However, those whose diets are "full of meaningless talk and deception" (1:10) show by their unhealthy actions that they have been feeding too long at the greasy spoon of falsehood. Paul describes such people as "unfit for doing anything good" (1:16). He charges Titus to serve up a healthier menu.

❤ Memory Passage: *Titus 2:1*

You, however, must teach what is appropriate to sound doctrine.

What is appropriate for sound doctrine is behavior that corresponds to it. Doctrine that remains imprisoned without parole in theology books soon atrophies and dies. It is only when that doctrine is furloughed regularly in actual life situations that its truth is experienced and manifested. Paul describes for Titus what sound doctrine should look like in the behavior of older men (2:2), older women (2:2–3), younger women (2:4), young men (2:6), and even slaves (2:9–10). The doctrine of "the grace of God ... offers salvation to all people" and "teaches us ... to live self-controlled, upright and godly lives" (2:11–12). When people respond to the verbally and behaviorally proclaimed gospel truth with repentance and faith, the Spirit who comes to dwell within us begins a wonderful work of transformation in us from the inside out. Instead of being characterized as "liars, evil brutes, lazy gluttons," we become communicators of truth, doers of good, and those who energetically attend to the spiritual and physical hunger of others. Jesus shows us exactly what this kind of truth-conforming life looks like.

◯ The Jesus Lens

Jesus displays for us what a life given wholly over to the Father looks like. He came from the Father "full of grace and truth" (John 1:14).

His meaning and purpose in life was to do the will of the Father (John 4:34; 6:38). He sought to please the Father (John 5:30) and experience uninterrupted fellowship with him (John 15:10). His life was nothing less than lived-out truth. In fact, his life was so perfectly in conformity to the word of truth that Jesus is even called "the Word" (John 1:1).

Those who observed Jesus' life knew that it was motivated by and directed toward something different from and better than theirs. And Jesus holds this life out for others to enjoy. It is available simply by believing that he is and that he accomplishes exactly what he says. When anyone (whether cultural sophisticate or Cretan schlub) responds to the good news of salvation in Jesus Christ, there is new life and there is the gift of the Holy Spirit to lead us into a fuller realization of that new life.

> The words I have spoken to you—they are full of the Spirit and life. (John 6:63)

The words of Jesus are true words of life. And his own Spirit, the "Spirit of truth" (John 14:17; 15:26; 16:13), accompanies his words and makes them powerfully transformative in the life of everyone who believes. The Spirit testifies to the believer about life in Christ, and testifies to others about that life *through* the transforming life of the believer (John 15:26). In other words, the life that transformative truth produces is unfailingly observable, and also reproductive.

 ## Contemporary Implications

Because the words of the gospel radiate life, the enemy of life will direct his fire squarely at its center. If he can get us to relax our grip on the truth, he can not only make our own spiritual lives anemic, but he can significantly reduce the candlepower of our regenerated and generative life for those who are still groping about for light in the darkness of death. We relax our grip simply by failing to live out the truth that indwells us. Paul describes this living out the truth simply as "doing good" (3:1, 8, 14). Leaders of the church teach sound doctrine best by setting an example of how to live it out (2:7).

> [An overseer] must hold firmly to the trustworthy message as it has been taught, so that he can encourage others by sound doctrine and refute those who oppose it. (Titus 1:9)

Both teacher and learner must hold firmly to the truth so that we can be equipped to defend and promote the precious message of life. Imagine how clearly the church in Crete would stand out as they lived the words they spoke before those struggling with meaning, purpose, direction, and significance in life. Imagine how clearly the church in our culture would stand out if we did the same.

Hook Questions

- Where does one find truth? Have you done any digging for it there lately?
- How does one effectively communicate truth in a world where falsehood has been made to appear more attractive? What makes lies attractive? What can make the truth unattractive?
- How does one defend the truth today when doing so is viewed as narrow-minded? Which is more restricted, those to whom the gospel appeal should be made or those for whom the gospel is appealing?

It was hard for the Christians in Crete to break free from their culturally conditioned behaviors. It is hard for us to do so too. Thankfully, we don't need to rely on our own strength to do this. We have nothing less than the Spirit of Almighty God within us — the Spirit of the source of all life, who will guide us deeper into an experience of that rich, vibrant life. This is the life that gives us meaning and energy, that sparks out from us like electricity, that gives visual expression to the words of truth we speak. This is the life that communicates the transformative truth about Jesus Christ, the living Word, by lived-out words of truth.

Things aren't always what they seem. Paul was under house arrest in Rome, but his spirit was free. Onesimus, Philemon's runaway slave, had come to know freedom from the power and penalty of sin by faith in Christ. People as diverse as a former Jewish rabbi, a Gentile slave-owner, and a fugitive slave could all be brothers in Christ. This is what this brief letter communicates to us by means of a specific situation arising between brothers in Christ that places the new reality of the brotherhood of believers against a particular cultural institution at odds with it. Onesimus had run away from Philemon and had ended up in the service of another Master, whom Philemon also served. Onesimus, who, according to the social reality of his day, was considered useless, had become, according to the social reality of the new humanity headed by Jesus Christ, what his name meant in Greek: "useful" (v. 11). From house arrest in Rome, Paul writes with great tact and affection to Philemon in Colossae, encouraging him to regard Onesimus no longer as a slave, but as a Christian brother.

Theme of the Book

God shows Philemon how his slave, Onesimus, has become a Christian brother.

In his short letter, Paul masterfully uses clever turns of phrase to communicate the reality of brotherhood in Christ. He subtly rebalances the scales of interpersonal relations by referring to both Philemon and Onesimus as "brother" (vv. 7, 20, 16). He delicately reminds Philemon that Onesimus is regarded as his equal in the family of God by suggesting that Onesimus "could take your place" in helping him (v. 13). Paul even places himself on the same level as Onesimus by asking Philemon to "welcome him as you would welcome me" (v. 17).

Paul is aware that it is going to be difficult for Philemon to regard Onesimus as something other than a slave. It will be even more difficult not to treat him as the culture expected *escaped* slaves to be treated. So Paul appeals to Philemon's heart — especially his demonstrated heart for others. Paul thanks Philemon for refreshing the hearts of the Lord's people (v. 7), then asks that Philemon refresh his heart (v. 20), and finishes off his verbal tour de force by explaining that such heart refreshment would come to Paul through Philemon's good treatment of Onesimus, who is Paul's "very heart" (v. 12).

Memory Passage: *Philemon 16*

He is very dear to me but even dearer to you, both as a fellow man and as a brother in the Lord.

Nothing could present a stronger challenge to the notion of the brotherhood of believers in Christ than the societal institution of slavery. If a Christian slave-owner could regard a Christian slave — and not just any kind of slave, but the worst kind there was, a fugitive slave — as a Christian brother, then there was indeed something powerfully different about this new community of believers. In Paul's letter to Titus, we saw how difficult it can be for believers to pull away from harmful cultural influences. But in this letter, we are confronted with a specific cultural phenomenon affecting specific people.

It was amazing that Onesimus would be willing to go back to his master, Philemon. The threat of death was real. But his humble willingness to make things right with his master-turned-brother in the face of such personal danger evidences an amazing transformation toward Christlikeness. Paul hopes for similar evidence of amazing transformation on the part of Philemon. What makes possible these amazing transformations from owner and owned to brothers is something even more amazing: God himself has become a human being in Jesus Christ in order to become *our* brother.

The Jesus Lens

There can be no greater disparity in status than the one that exists between God and human beings. Yet, because of God's great love for us, he spanned that huge divide and became human. And he went even further. He lowered himself to become a servant, like Onesimus. In fact, the word used in Philippians 2:7 to describe what kind of human being Jesus became is the same word used to describe Onesimus in Philemon 16: servant/slave. The one who makes possible our new brotherly relationship with all fellow believers is the one who has already done this himself. Paul is appealing to Philemon to regard Onesimus as a brother, just as Paul regarded Philemon (vv. 8–9), and just as Jesus regards us. When we have our vision corrected by the Jesus lens, we begin to see one another in an entirely new way, the way Jesus does.

> Both the one who makes people holy and those who are made holy are of the same family. So Jesus is not ashamed to call them brothers and sisters. (Hebrews 2:11)

The Son of God himself calls us his brothers and sisters. And if the almighty Creator of heaven and earth is willing to become our brother in Jesus Christ, then surely we must be willing to regard each other as brothers and sisters as well — even when doing so goes against everything our culture has insisted upon.

Contemporary Implications

When we become brothers and sisters in Christ, we transform from being competitors in life, jockeying for advantage over one another, to being partners in the service of our Lord. In fact, Paul uses the word "partner" (v. 17) or "partnership" (v. 6) in his appeal to Philemon. Instead of desperately grasping for glory, we begin to display characteristics of Christ, who set aside his divine glory for our sakes. We willingly participate in the lives of one another out of love for each other and concern for the honor of our Lord.

> I pray that your partnership with us in the faith may be effective in deepening your understanding of every good thing we share for the sake of Christ. (Philemon 6)

Our partnership in the faith should lead us to love one another as brothers and sisters. As we deepen in our "understanding of every good thing we share," we will begin to see that the family into which we have been adopted as brothers and sisters of our Lord makes us heirs of a royal inheritance (Ephesians 1:18; Colossians 1:12). Whatever cultural conventions or social distinctions we have been trained to seek as status symbols are embarrassingly petty by comparison.

Hook Questions

- Do you regard *all* believers as your brothers and sisters? What if they are different from you? Are you willing to become caringly involved in the lives of those people society describes as beneath you? Does your congregation welcome such people? What if God regarded us the way we regard others?
- What are you willing to risk to bring brothers and sisters together? Christ was willing to endure slander, humiliation, ridicule, mistreatment, and torture; are we up for that? Are we willing to risk *anything*?

All of our lives have baggage. Onesimus had to square things away with Philemon. Philemon had to wrestle with the contradiction that was his Christian slave, Onesimus. Usually without our being aware, society has trained us to regard ourselves and others as positioned on a continuum of cultural value. The new reality of our brotherhood in Jesus Christ is that we are all of inestimable value to God — so much so that he was willing for his Son to die for us. Paul wanted Philemon to look at Onesimus from this new perspective. God wants all of his children to regard each other the same way that he does. He wants us to begin to help each other with our baggage as we move into our new family.

In the book of Titus, we see how it can be hard for new Christians to pull away from the harmful influence of their culture. In the book of Philemon, we see how it can be even harder for a Christian to pull away from a particular cultural phenomenon. In the book of Hebrews, the stakes are raised even further. What if the cultural influence on the new believer is not easily recognizable as harmful? What if it is religious?

We don't know who wrote the book of Hebrews, but we do know what it is about. It is written to Jewish converts to Christianity who are feeling the magnetic pull of their old religious tradition. There is comfort in the familiar, especially when the going gets rough. These Jewish Christians need to be reassured that their faith in Jesus is properly placed. They need to be shown that Jesus has brought to fulfillment everything Judaism was pointing toward. They need to be encouraged to press on in their faith.

Theme of the Book

Christ is the ultimate revelation and mediator of God's gracious new relationship with his people.

The author presents these wavering Jewish Christians with a big-screen, high-definition, feature-length documentary of the epicenter of their new relationship with God — Jesus Christ. He begins by pointing out that the revelation of God's redemptive plan is far clearer in Jesus than it was in the Old Testament, simply because the whole Old Testament was pointing toward him (1:1–3). And though Moses and Joshua factor prominently in leading God's people to the land of rest, the rest into which we enter through faith in Christ is far superior because it is unconditional, comprehensive, and everlasting (3:1–4:13). And even though these Jewish Christians might be tempted to look back to the sacrificial system with its comforting, rhythmic, and incessant regularity, the author of Hebrews describes the futility of this when the ultimate sacrifice, Jesus Christ, has secured the new relationship between God and his people once and for all (4:14–10:18). And although angels are significant heavenly beings, and during his earthly life Jesus allowed himself to be outshone by them, his present glory far eclipses theirs precisely because of his self-sacrifice (1:4–2:18).

Memory Passage: *Hebrews 2:9*

We do see Jesus, who was made lower than the angels for a little while, now crowned with glory and honor because he suffered death, so that by the grace of God he might taste death for everyone.

Going back to the trappings of the old relationship after the new relationship has been established is like trying to fish with the catalogue picture of a rod and reel after the actual items have been purchased. The author of Hebrews describes the difference between the old and new covenants in similar terms. The old relationship involved "copies of the heavenly things" while the new relationship involves "the heavenly things themselves" (9:23). The old traditions and requirements proving to be so attractive to these Jewish Christians were merely "a shadow of the good things" that were coming and "not the realities themselves" (10:1). They were being hypnotized by an "obsolete and outdated" relationship (8:13) so that it was becoming difficult for them to see the "new and living way" (10:20) stretching out ahead of them. Everything was looking fuzzy because they had misplaced their glasses. They needed to have everything brought back into focus by the corrective lens of Jesus Christ (12:2).

The Jesus Lens

The author of Hebrews reminds Jewish believers that the one in whom they have placed their faith is far better than what they trusted in before. In fact, he uses the word "better" to describe the hope that is guaranteed for us by Christ (7:19, 22), the promises that Christ fulfills for us (8:6), the ultimate purifying sacrifice Christ has made with his own body (9:23), and the country into which Christ escorts us (11:16). What makes this new relationship better is the fact that it is eternal. Jesus is a high priest forever (6:20; 7:3, 17, 21, 24), whose sacrifice is "once for all" (7:27; 9:12, 26; 10:10). By his perfect sacrifice, he has secured for those who trust in him an *eternal* salvation (5:9), an *eternal* redemption (9:12), an *eternal* inheritance (9:15), and an *eternal* relationship with God (13:20).

> For this reason Christ is the mediator of a new covenant, that those who are called may receive the promised eternal inheritance. (Hebrews 9:15)

Jesus is one who mediates to us the grace of our new relationship with God. He is the one foreshadowed by the shadows of the past — the laws, the sacrifices, and the priesthood. But when the light comes, the shadows disappear. And the relationship he secures for us with the Father is just as perfect, eternal, and life-giving as he is. Through hope in Jesus, he is our "anchor for the soul, firm and secure" (6:19).

Contemporary Implications

Jesus is therefore a better motivation for faith and perseverance. We can hold firmly to our confidence and hope in Christ (3:6; 6:18; 10:23). We can hang on to our conviction that he is our redemption (3:14). We can "hold unswervingly to the hope we profess, for he who promised is faithful" (10:23). And we can give thanks to God that in place of a religious system that was provisional and preparatory, we are receiving an everlasting kingdom "that cannot be shaken" (12:28).

> Let us throw off everything that hinders and the sin that so easily entangles. And let us run with perseverance the race marked out

for us, fixing our eyes on Jesus, the pioneer and perfecter of faith.
(Hebrews 12:1–2)

We may not wrestle with Judaism, but we may be wrestling with the allure of the promised comfort of those things that we used to look to for security. It is easy to fall back into the old patterns. The book of Hebrews is a call to hang on, to keep focused, to keep looking upward rather than backward (3:1; 12:2). God himself will equip us with the ability to do so (13:20–21).

Hook Questions

- Why does *Jesus* need to be our mediator? Don't all religions lead to God? If they do, was the death of Christ necessary? If the death of Christ was unnecessary, does his resurrection have any significance?
- What is *new* about the new covenant? How does this new quality give us a stronger confidence?
- What are some practical ways for us to keep from getting distracted or discouraged and to keep our focus on Christ instead?

As we motor along in our journey of faith, we are prone to fall victim to the same problems that faced the Jewish Christians in the book of Hebrews. We can grow fatigued from the effort and fall asleep at the wheel or pull off into a rest area. We can be dangerously distracted by all sorts of fascinating things along the road. If we don't pay attention, we could even end up going in the wrong direction!

The author of this letter is our good friend in the front seat, encouraging us to pay careful attention (2:1), hold a steady course (10:23), and not turn off the path (3:12; 12:25) or grow weary (12:3). He reminds us again about what is at the end of our journey and who built the road we're traveling on. He supplies us with the caffeine of reenergized faith and a reappreciation for our relationship with God through our mediator, Jesus Christ, so that we remain wide awake until we arrive at the glorious destination God has prepared for us.

JAMES

Working Faith

James, the half brother of Jesus and a leader in the Jerusalem church, writes to Jewish Christians who have been "scattered among the nations" (1:1) to encourage them to give a good account of their faith by the way they live. The problem he is addressing seems to be at the other end of the spectrum from those tempted to look to their good works as somehow able to earn salvation. Instead, James writes to those who are tempted to look to their salvation by grace through faith in Jesus Christ as a pass to do no good works at all. He makes it clear that such an attitude is about as compatible with true faith as a porcupine in a petting zoo. If the Spirit of the one who lived to please the Father (John 8:29) is living in us, it is inescapable that we will begin to live to please the Father as well by doing those things that bring him honor.

Theme of the Book

God enables a life of good works that flow from a genuine faith.

James wastes no time getting to the point. After a one-verse greeting, he spends the rest of the letter describing what a working faith looks like. Our faith shows up in the way we deal with trials (1:2–18; 5:7–11). It betrays its presence in the way we humbly receive instruction (1:19–20). James insists that our faith is evidenced just as much by the way we dispense words (1:26; 3:1–12; 5:12) as by the way we dispense help to the needy (1:27). A life of faith shows no favoritism (2:1–13) and in humility demands none for itself (3:13–17). In faith, we are to rely on the Lord in prayer (5:13–18) and seek the spiritual welfare of our brothers and sisters (5:19–20). In short, James demands that believers send their couch-potato faith to the gym for some exercise.

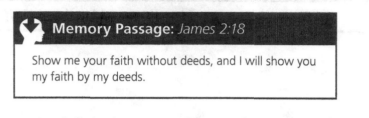

Memory Passage: *James 2:18*

Show me your faith without deeds, and I will show you my faith by my deeds.

Amid all the descriptions of the specific ways a true faith is manifested, James tucks in a couple of passages that drive the point home (1:22–25; 2:14–26): there is no such thing as faith in Jesus Christ that does not show up in a life that begins to look like his. In insisting on a working faith, James is doing no more than Jesus did, who charged his followers to "let your light shine before others, that *they may see your good deeds* and glorify your Father in heaven" (Matthew 5:16, emphasis added).

The Jesus Lens

Jesus communicated the good news through his words *and* his actions. His divine acts were another channel through which he communicated the truth of his redemptive message. For example, once when Jesus announced to a paralytic that his sins were forgiven, the crowd became upset that Jesus would say something that was a prerogative of God alone. To corroborate his message of good news, so that everyone would "know that the Son of Man has authority on earth to forgive sins" Jesus added to the spiritual healing a physical one as well (Matthew 9:1–8). When John the Baptist sent his disciples to ask Jesus whether he was indeed the Messiah, Jesus told them, "Go back and report to John what you *hear and see*" (Matthew 11:2–6, emphasis added). That Jesus was who he said he was could be seen by his actions.

Jesus answered, "I did tell you, but you do not believe. The works I do in my Father's name testify about me." (John 10:25)

Jesus demonstrated the truth of his words by his works. His words announced a gracious, divine undoing of the effects of sin. He often demonstrated that sin had more than met its match by undoing the physical effects of sin. Those who want to be his disciples must similarly demonstrate the truth of their words by their works.

Contemporary Implications

The behavioral aspect of our Christian witness is not some sort of welcome but unnecessary factory option. It is essential and complementary to our verbal witness, giving visible expression to our faith. One of the biggest obstacles to the faith for unbelievers is the hypocrisy they often encounter among believers. When people look at an individual Christian or a congregation and see no evidence of the grace of God at work within them — no compassion, no kindness, no gentleness, no justice, no love — then for them there is no good news evident. All they see is more of what they already know and experience every day.

> Do not merely listen to the word, and so deceive yourselves. Do what it says (James 1:22)

We must demonstrate the truth of our testimony about Christ by means of a corroborating life. If our lives do not correspond to what we say, it is not only other people we are trying to fool, but ourselves as well. It is impossible for those indwelt by the Spirit of a compassionate, giving, and self-sacrificial God not to give evidence of compassion, giving, and self-sacrifice. James calls on believers to haul their faith off the couch and put it to good work.

Hook Questions

- What does your faith look like? Does it have a visible aspect?
- What could faith look like in *your* particular circumstances? How could someone see that you are a follower of Jesus Christ?
- What are you going to *do* about your faith?

Many of us have been rightly trained by our faith traditions not to look to our good works for our salvation. Unfortunately, many of us seem to have not quite finished the sentence. We put a period after "good works" and go on our way. However, anyone can say the right words. Only those who really believe those words will do the right things.

The apostle Paul encourages believers to *conduct themselves* "in a manner worthy of the gospel of Christ" (Philippians 1:27). He describes for Titus those in the church who talk a good line, but whose compromised lives are shouting down their words. "They claim to know God, but by their actions they deny him" (Titus 1:16). Faith is not to be compartmentalized into a broom closet in our minds that is only inhabited by other politically correct words; it is to be given the run of the house. And God does not leave us to our own resources in our efforts to live out our faith. He gives us wisdom to know how to put our faith to work in any situation (James 1:2; 3:17) in order that we might begin to bear some resemblance in our behavior to the one who has given us faith in the first place (1:17–18).

1 PETER

Standing Firm

It is one thing to express our faith through good works, as James has encouraged us to do, when our lives are sailing along fairly steadily. It is quite another thing to stand firm when enormous waves of trials come crashing against our faith and threaten to overwhelm us. If there was anyone who knew firsthand the difficulties of standing firm in threatening situations, it was the apostle Peter. When push came to shove, three times he had denied that he even knew the Lord (Mark 14.66–72). Now, when he is older and much more seasoned in his faith, he writes to encourage believers who are experiencing persecution by the Roman authorities. He counsels them to stand firm in the midst of their trials by finding their strength in the same place he found his when he had been beaten and imprisoned for his faith (Acts 5:40; 12:1–5)—in the grace and strength of God that come through faith in Jesus Christ.

Theme of the Book

God equips struggling believers to stand firm in his grace as they live holy lives.

Peter's encouragement to stand firm in the grace of God is not just a sweet platitude that he tosses to struggling believers like some life preserver made of cotton candy. He gives his words divine substance and force. Believers can stand firm in the tempests, and our hope can have life just as surely as Christ rose from death to life (1:3–5). When the waves crash against us, we can hang on securely to our Lord, "the living Stone" (2:4 – 10). We follow the course charted for us by Christ, obeying his orders as we submit to him and one another (2:11 – 3:7). We are foreigners here (1:17; 2:11), and as we navigate through these foreign waters, we can expect to hit some rocks of hardship and suffering along the way (1:6 – 7; 4:12 – 19). But our course ultimately leads to a glorious destination — an inheritance kept in heaven for us (1:4).

> **Memory Passage:** *1 Peter 5:10*
>
> And the God of all grace, who called you to his eternal glory in Christ, after you have suffered a little while, will himself restore you and make you strong, firm and steadfast.

Peter explains that believers can stand firm on the sure promises of God that are ours through faith in Jesus Christ, our living hope (1:3 – 4, 21, 23; 5:12). We take our stand against the devil and his schemes by being alert and counteractive (5:8). He gets in his blows through the struggles and persecutions he orchestrates for believers. But Christians have a twofold defense. The first line of defense is the community of believers. We encourage, support, and help each other reload (1:22; 3:8; 4:8 – 10) as we stand side-by-side in the fight. But our final and impregnable defense against the enemy's attacks is the power and promise of God. Nothing can rob us of our inheritance in Jesus Christ because we are safeguarded by God himself (1:5).

By the strength of God (4:10), we are able not only to withstand the enemy's attacks, but also to launch our own relentless counteroffensive by discharging continual salvos of good deeds that burst like star flares behind enemy lines, flooding his darkness with the light of Christ. When believers take on the enemy in this way, as Peter encourages us to do, we show that we are loyal troops of our commanding officer, Jesus Christ.

The Jesus Lens

No one ever suffered more unjustly than Jesus. The enemy went out of his way to derail his mission, but he only accomplished the fulfillment of it. While Satan launched attack after attack, Jesus responded by doing good — bringing life and healing to those who believed in him. He was deprived of justice and led like a sheep to the slaughter (Acts 8:32–33). Though the enemy thought he had won, he had only contributed to bringing about through the suffering of Christ the salvation that God had planned all along. Wickedness was defeated by raw goodness and relentless grace. Jesus showed us how the battle is to be fought (2:21). As he did with our Lord, the enemy attacks us with temptations and trials. But our risen Lord is right there with us to help us stand firm in the faith.

> Because he himself suffered when he was tempted, he is able to help those who are being tempted. (Hebrews 2:18)

Jesus shared in our humanity to free us from the power of sin so that by his strength we can stand firm in the face of trials and temptations. Are we facing the internal assaults of temptations? He has experienced them. Are we facing the external attacks of persecution? He experienced those as well. He knows our weaknesses and has promised to be with us always to help us (Matthew 28:20). And our Lord "is faithful, and he will strengthen you and protect you from the evil one" (2 Thessalonians 3:3).

🏢 Contemporary Implications

We have the example of our Lord, who stood firm in the face of temptations and trials. And we have the promise of our Lord that he will give us strength to do the same. All that remains is for us to trust him and boldly follow his example (2:21). It is not easy to do good things when we don't feel like it, are struggling with our own issues, or are being mistreated. But this is exactly what Jesus did, and it is exactly what God, through his servant Peter, is pushing us to do. It's not easy for us, but it is for God. We can commit our lives to God and trust that somehow he will make our feeble efforts significant.

> So then, those who suffer according to God's will should commit themselves to their faithful Creator and continue to do good. (1 Peter 4:19)

Of course, "continuing" to do good implies that we have been actively doing so in the first place. As Christians, we're always on call.

Our only purpose is to communicate by our words and our behaviors the new life God has made available in Jesus Christ. For our lives to communicate God's love and compassion truthfully, we need to behave in ways that express that love and compassion. Even when we don't feel like it. Even when it could cost us personally. The ability to live such a life comes from the one who gives us that life in the first place. We must stand firm in the grace God gives us in order to lead a holy life (1:15; 5:12).

Hook Questions

- Is your Christian life on shaky ground? What is the foundation of your life? What keeps your feet from slipping?
- Where are you looking for help? Where are you giving help?
- Have you ever suffered for doing good? Do you regard good works as optional or essential? Have you pushed yourself to do good things when you didn't feel like it?

Standing firm in God's grace and strength that come to us through faith in Jesus Christ is not a passive activity. It isn't accomplished by means of the clenched jaw and jutting chin of a fortress mentality. It doesn't come about by withdrawing into comfortable bunkers of slogans and choruses. It is accomplished by going forth alert and circumspect (4:7; 5:8) in faith and hope in God (1:21), armed with the same attitude as Christ (4:1), and caringly supporting one another. It is accomplished by living such good lives before others that they end up praising God (2:12). It is accomplished by doing these things even when it seems as if no one except God himself appreciates them.

Holding on to Truth

Enemy operatives had infiltrated the church! They were skillfully using disinformation to weaken the resolve and effectiveness of believers — those charged with safeguarding the truth and broadcasting it across enemy lines. By their words and behaviors, these spiritual con artists were denying some of the basic truths of the faith and were having some measure of success in leading believers astray. They were scoffing at, casting doubt on, or outright denying the source of truth, the life engendered by truth, and the sure hope that truth promises. The apostle Peter, near the end of his life (1:14), writes again to believers who are under attack from enemy moles within their ranks in order to encourage them to hold on to truth — God's "very great and precious promises" (1:4) — so that they can remain grounded and effective in their divine mission as they confidently look toward Christ's return.

Theme of the Book

God encourages believers in the security and grace of divine truth as they patiently await the Lord's return.

Peter has his work cut out for him. These enemy agents were very, very good at their job. They secretly introduced destructive heresies (2:1) and fabricated stories (2:3), while distorting the actual truth of Scripture (3:16). With a dismissive wave and condescending chuckle, they scoffed at human and divine authority, even denying the authority of Christ

(2:1, 10), and instead led their dupes to follow their own destructive desires (3:3). With silken words, they seduced (2:14), appealed, enticed, and promised (2:18) the unguarded into believing their lies. For those who yet hesitated, they led by example. They did whatever they chose, unguided by any moral compass (2:2, 13, 18–19).

Peter writes to blow the cover of these enemy infiltrators. He does this by holding up before believers divine truth—the only standard by which human error is fully exposed. He "reminds" them of it (1:12; 3:1), "refreshes" their memory of it (1:13), and makes every effort to get them "to remember" (1:15) and "recall" it (3:2). Because only with this divine truth always before them will the lies of the enemy be revealed for what they are.

> **Memory Passage:** *2 Peter 3:17–18*
>
> Be on your guard so that you may not be carried away by the error of the lawless and fall from your secure position. But grow in the grace and knowledge of our Lord and Savior Jesus Christ.

That knowledge of our Lord, writes Peter, comes from eyewitness accounts (1:16) and the "completely reliable" testimony of Scripture, the divine truth that originates and is directed by the will of God himself (1:19–21). Peter encourages believers to "make every effort" to use this divine truth to gain confidence in their own salvation (1:10); to "make every effort" to use this divine truth as a catalyst for further spiritual growth (1:5); and to "make every effort" to use this divine truth as a goal for their lives as they look forward to Christ's return (3:14). In other words, the Word of God should inform the origin, the conduct, and the objective of our Christian lives. What this should look like in practical terms could never be displayed more clearly than by the life of the one who lived in such total conformity to God's Word that he is even called "the Word" (John 1:1).

The Jesus Lens

The Word was a flesh-and-blood manifestation of divine truth. He was truth that was a perfect integration of proposition and action, of fact and feat. When the devil tempted him in the wilderness with some of his most effective enticements, Jesus denied him entry at every point by exposing his forged passport under the penetrating light of divine truth (Matthew 4:1 – 11). Pointing out the fallacies of the devil's silver-tongued spiel, Jesus held forth the scriptural truth that true life, safety, and contentment are not found in anything the tempter could provide, but rather in what God alone can provide. The enemy has no defenses against such a life rooted and guided by God's Word.

> Jesus answered, "It is written: 'Man shall not live on bread alone, but on every word that comes from the mouth of God.'" (Matthew 4:4)

Jesus himself resisted the devil's temptations by means of the Word of God, and so can those who are his followers. Those who hold on to that truth are kept safe and also begin to know more fully the same life that energized and radiates from Jesus, the Word of God.

Contemporary Implications

We often pay about as much attention to divine truth as we do to our health. We only begin to give it some serious consideration when things go wrong. And, unfortunately, for both our physical and spiritual health, too often things have been going wrong for quite a while before they come to our attention. We need to develop a healthy lifestyle that can prevent many of the problems that come from neglect. A regular diet of the Word of God and attentiveness to its metabolization into a godly life are fine preventative measures against susceptibility to the viruses of error and their life-sapping effects on our spiritual health and witness. God's Word, fortified with divine power, provides us with everything we need to grow in our spiritual life.

> His divine power has given us everything we need for a godly life through our knowledge of him who called us by his own glory and goodness. Through these he has given us his very great and precious promises, so that through them you may participate in the divine nature, having escaped the corruption in the world caused by evil desires. (2 Peter 1:3 – 4)

Let us make every effort to know the truth so that we may be protected from error and grow in the grace that such knowledge brings.

Not only can we parry the enemy's advances with the sword of the Spirit, the Word of God (Ephesians 6:17), but that same Word of God feeds our souls with confidence, energy, and endurance so that we can do a little advancing of our own. Maybe it's time we gave it some regular attention.

 ## Hook Questions

- Can you explain the basic truths of your faith to someone else? Can you explain them to yourself? Does your life display them?
- Can you defend those basic truths against attack? Are you even aware that the truth is under attack?
- Do *you* question those basic truths? What might you be regarding as truer than Scripture? Why?

Truth is life-giving; lies are debilitating. Lies slowly drain us of health and vitality. Of course, the most dangerous lies are those that aren't obvious but gradually incapacitate us like an undetected carbon monoxide gas leak until we slip into unconsciousness. It is only when the truth rushes in, throws open the windows and doors, and drags us to safety that we begin to return to our senses and feel our strength coming back. If only we would hang on to the truth in the first place, we would never end up in such threatening situations. In fact, just the opposite would be the case. We would be continually on guard, armed and ready for anything with the confidence and spiritual stamina that sustained our Lord and his followers in the most challenging situations. The truth is living, active, eternal, and powerful (Matthew 24:35; Hebrews 1:3; 4:12), and this precious gift has been given to us. Peter appeals to us to hold on to it with all the strength God provides.

1 JOHN

Christlikeness

The apostle John is getting on in years, but he still has work to do. In a fatherly, deeply caring letter, he gives his "dear children" in the faith the benefit of his decades of reflection on the fundamental truths regarding life in Christ. His letter is prompted by the blather of some in the churches who thought they knew more than the apostles, or even Jesus himself. These misguided souls maintained that Jesus wasn't really human *and* divine. John's response to this attempted dagger to the heart of the gospel is both passionate and profound. He asserts that God's relentless, redemptive love for us requires Jesus to be both human and divine, and that this love of God, displayed in Jesus Christ, should be displayed in all those in whom his Spirit dwells.

Theme of the Book

God calls those who believe in the divinity of the incarnate Christ to become like him.

If Jesus were only divine, he would have had nothing in common with human beings and could hardly be our representative before the Father. If Jesus were only human, he would have had to bear the penalty for the sin all human beings have inherited from Adam. But because he was conceived by the Holy Spirit (Matthew 1:20), he is — mysteriously — both human *and* divine. He can truly represent us before the Father and pay the price for the human sin for which he bears no guilt. John is concerned that believers stand firm on this gospel truth. He is also concerned that the implications of this gospel truth are fully realized. When we experience the salvation that comes through faith in Jesus Christ, the God-man, the Holy Spirit indwells us and begins his work within us, assuring us of our fellowship with the Father and Son (1 John 3:24; 4:13) and transforming us into the likeness of the one whose spiritual DNA we now share.

> ### ♦ Memory Passage: *1 John 2:29*
>
> If you know that he is righteous, you know that everyone who does what is right has been born of him.

Some people who were *not* doing what was right were circulating among the believers. They were holding themselves up as teachers of the truth but were actually presenting believers with lies that called into question the very truth that gives life, the truth they had heard "from the beginning" (1:1; 2:7, 24; 3:11). John makes believers aware of the divine watermark that certifies the authenticity of any message alleged to be from God. Such a message, if genuine, will acknowledge that Jesus Christ has come in the flesh (4:1 – 2). When held up to the light, the love for the Father and the love for his children will be visible (5:1). This is the authenticating watermark that enables us to discern truth from error. Teaching that purports to lead us into a life of closer fellowship with God must focus our attention on the divine human being, Jesus Christ, who showed us perfectly what love for the Father and love for his children look like.

○ The Jesus Lens

Because Jesus fulfilled the law of God (Romans 10:4), it is not surprising that John describes a life like that of Jesus as one that is characterized by the summary of the law: "'Love the Lord your God with all your heart and with all your soul and with all your strength and with all your mind'; and, 'Love your neighbor as yourself'" (Luke 10:27). John holds up the presence of these two loves as the definitive spiritual genetic test for those who claim divine paternity. Those who really are children of

God by faith in Jesus Christ will exhibit a love for fellow believers and a love for God that is manifested in obedience to his commands. The fact that we are brothers and sisters of Jesus should be obvious by our family resemblance to him.

> For those God foreknew he also predestined to be conformed to the image of his Son, that he might be the firstborn among many brothers and sisters. (Romans 8:29)

Jesus is the perfect human to whom all believers are being divinely conformed. Jesus is the focus of every believer's transformation by the power of the Spirit. God is love (1 John 4:16), and he has demonstrated that love by sending his own Son as an atoning sacrifice for our sins (4:10). So Jesus is the physical, human expression of God's love. Those who have the Spirit of Christ within them will begin to express that love for God and fellow believers as well.

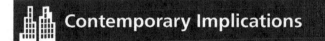

Contemporary Implications

For John, the deep truths of the faith must always be exegeted by Christian behavior. Life *from* Christ should exhibit characteristics of the life *of* Christ. Jesus is exhibit A of God's love for his children. A Christian's love for fellow believers, then, should be exhibit B. Jesus gave his life in obedience to the Father. Those who take on his name should display at least a bit of that loving obedience as well.

> This is how we know we are in him: Whoever claims to live in him must live as Jesus did. (1 John 2:5–6)

Whoever claims to have life in Christ should begin to behave like him. Instead of selfishness, there should be selflessness. Instead of greed, there should be generosity. Instead of pride, there should be humility. Instead of sin, there should be love for God and fellow believers. Instead of seeking a name for ourselves, we should seek to represent well the name of Christ, in the strength of the Holy Spirit.

Hook Questions

- Why does Jesus need to be human?
- Why does Jesus need to be divine?
- Whom do you try to model your life after? Why?

In the face of the dangerous talk of those who were making wild and problematic statements about Jesus Christ, John directs the focus of his spiritual children back to the basic truths of the gospel. Christ has overcome sin and death by exercising his love. His humanity makes his suffering ours. His divinity makes his victory ours. His Spirit makes his life ours. The error of those who don't have life in Christ will be obvious because there will be no evidence of a life being transformed to his by the power of the Spirit. Those who do have life in Christ can be identified by their increasing resemblance to him. John encourages us to rest assured that our faith in Jesus Christ means eternal life for us. And John challenges us to find in the mirror of our everyday lives clearer reflections of Jesus and to disregard the teachings of those who, like vampires, have no reflection at all and seek to suck the life from those who do.

In this second installment of John's letter-writing campaign, he continues to encourage believers to hang on to the truth, especially in the face of those who are trying to get them to turn away from it and buy into worthless substitutes. John follows up here the big and complex ideas of his first letter with a specific application. Teachers of the truth, as well as teachers of error, traveled around from place to place, relying on the hospitality of the local inhabitants for their food and lodging. Providing this kind of hospitality to these teachers was a way for people to participate in their work and help to advance their ideas. John strongly warns against providing such hospitality to those promoting teachings contrary to the gospel of Jesus Christ.

Theme of the Book

God warns against showing hospitality to those who promote error.

A quick scan of this short letter makes the emphasis of John obvious. Before one finishes reading four verses, John has written the word "truth" five times. He uses this word almost as a synonym for Jesus Christ, who is the truth (John 14:6). Believers know the truth (2 John 1) because they know Christ; they are indwelt by the truth (v. 1) because they are indwelt by the Spirit of Christ; grace, mercy, and peace are communicated to them by the truth (v. 3) because these are found in Christ; and they walk in the truth (v. 4) because they are followers of

Christ. So, those opposed to the truth are opposed to Christ; or, to use John's word, are antichrists (v. 7). Those who are Christ's should give no quarter in their minds or lives to anything opposed to the truth because lies, like pathogens, spread their poison to everything they touch. Similarly, believers should not give assistance to people opposed to the truth of Jesus Christ because their error is likewise opposed to life.

> **♦ Memory Passage:** *2 John 10*
>
> If anyone comes to you and does not bring this teaching, do not take them into your house or welcome them.

Another repeated phrase in John's letter is "[this] teaching." John encourages believers to "continue in the teaching of Christ" (v. 9) and not assist those who do not bring "this teaching" (v. 10). It is bad enough to be deceived into believing lies; it is quite another thing to be promoting those lies so that others are deceived as well. John calls for a spiritual quarantine of the disease carriers so that the deadly virus of error can be arrested. This may sound harsh to us today, but any health professional knows that there are two sides to fitness: doing those things that promote wellness and turning away from those things that promote illness. Continuing in the teaching of Jesus Christ and turning away from deceivers, "who do not acknowledge Jesus Christ as coming in the flesh" (v. 7), promotes a spiritually healthy life, because Jesus is our life.

◎ The Jesus Lens

There were even those who rejected the truth when it walked among them, preferring instead the sugar rush of lies. Jesus used some strong words to describe these people. He called them "hypocrites," "blind guides," "whitewashed tombs," "snakes," and worse (see, for example, Matthew 23:13 – 36). These supposed teachers of the truth were, in fact, slamming the door of the kingdom of heaven shut in people's faces (Matthew 23:13). The apostle John urges believers instead to slam the door shut in the deceivers' faces. Jesus describes the deadly effect of the poison peddled by these spiritual hucksters as yeast (Matthew 16:6), which, if given a place in the dough, will soon extend its influence throughout. The remedy, of course, is to ban it from the kitchen in the first place.

Jesus said to them, "Watch out that no one deceives you." (Mark 13:5)

As the truth itself, Jesus warned his followers about those who promoted error. We cannot be hospitable to truth and error at the same time. There is no place for the shadows of falsehood when the light of truth is shining brightly in our lives.

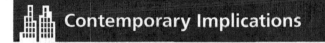

Contemporary Implications

If we insist on giving hospitality to the shadows of falsehood, we will have to dim the light of Christ. To the degree we do that, however, is the degree to which the rich life of fellowship with Christ is attenuated. Of course, we wouldn't allow this to happen all at once. We would only even consider it at all if it started out very small. Maybe just a questionable television show now and then. Maybe just an Internet site that makes us feel a twinge of guilt. But in for an inch, in for a mile. John warns believers against cracking the door even an inch.

Watch out that you do not lose what we have worked for, but that you may be rewarded fully. (2 John 8)

By our words and by our lives we must promote truth and oppose error. This will take diligence, alertness, and proactivity. Like identity thieves, deceivers are looking for any opportunity to take over our lives and rob us of everything we have worked for. It's time for us to upgrade our security system. It's time for us to make sure that we are "walking in the truth" (v. 4) and "continu[ing] in the teaching of Christ" (v. 9). That teaching is an impregnable firewall for any spiritual hacker.

Hook Questions

• What about your words or behavior promotes the truth for yourself and others? How do you contribute toward the advance of the gospel of life?

- What about your words or behavior promotes error for yourself and others? How have you been contributing, perhaps unconsciously, toward undermining the good news of life in Jesus Christ? Do you need to upgrade your security system?

John wants us to keep the cockroaches out of our houses. We must examine everything we bring inside to make sure that there are no unwanted stowaways slipping in. When we aren't careful and error slips into the truth, we provide a breeding ground for that error to grow and multiply. We also have to be careful not to provide aid and assistance to enemies of the truth by thoughtlessly engaging in the behaviors and/or entertaining the perspectives that promote their cause. When we know the truth and live it, we will be protected from suffering or even from unconsciously promoting any error, and instead the "grace, mercy and peace from God the Father and from Jesus Christ, the Father's Son, will be with us in truth and love" (v. 3). The light of God's truth in Jesus Christ will send the cockroaches of deceit running for the exits.

John continues his theme of hospitality from 2 John but this time applies the principle to specific individuals. He names names. The letter is formally addressed to Gaius (v. 1), a believer who had taken to heart the advice in John's second letter. He was "walking in the truth" (vv. 3–4) and was providing hospitality and support for Christian missionaries passing through his city (vv. 5–8). Diotrephes, by contrast, was refusing hospitality to the wrong people! Instead of turning away false teachers and helping those who promoted the truth, Diotrephes was turning away those who promoted the truth and was himself "spreading malicious nonsense" (v. 10). The body of Christ had sustained some body blows and John needed to address the problem.

Theme of the Book

God inspires John to praise Gaius for his hospitality toward John's messengers and to condemn Diotrephes for his inhospitality toward them.

John provides two specific examples that give a face to the two possible responses to his warning to exercise wise hospitality. The first, positive, example is Gaius, who knows the truth and therefore recognizes the truth in the brothers and sisters who come to him (vv. 3–5). Consequently, he opens the door of hospitality to them and so participates with them in advancing that truth (vv. 6–8). The second, negative, example is Diotrephes, a leader in the church who had previously let in the error of spiritual pride (v. 9). Consequently, when the truth shows up, he does not or will not recognize it. He leaves it standing at the door, and he even advances his error by demanding that others follow his lead (v. 10). John encourages believers to imitate instead those who join forces in promoting the truth.

> ### ♥ Memory Passage: *3 John 8*
>
> We ought therefore to show hospitality to such people so that we may work together for the truth.

John wants believers to imitate "such people" as Gaius, not Diotrephes. Of course, one can only make the distinction between what is good and what is evil if one has an unfailingly accurate standard of truth. As John has described it in his previous letters, this standard of truth is that God has provided salvation in his Son, Jesus Christ, and that fellowship with the Father and the Son will result in a life that begins to resemble our Savior's. That life, though it may include great suffering now, is nevertheless rich, vibrant, and headed for certain glory, the likes of which we can only imagine (Romans 8:18; 1 Corinthians 2:9).

That is why John has "no greater joy" than to hear that his spiritual children are "walking in the truth" (v. 4). Having rejected the truth, Diotrephes is left with only the faulty guide of his pride-driven judgment. He wants nothing to do with anyone who could take the spotlight off of him. But it is the believers he leaves standing at the door whose lives look like Christ's, because Jesus experienced the same thing.

◯ The Jesus Lens

Jesus came from the Father, "full of grace and truth" (John 1:14). But when he came to his own, "his own did not receive him" (John 1:11). Jesus even went to those who were spiritual leaders, like Diotrephes, with the wonderful news of redemption from the penalty and power of sin and of new life in him. But most did not recognize that the truth itself was speaking to them. They rallied opposition to him and removed him from their midst. The obstacle to their faith was their pride, their refusal to humble themselves by admitting their error and submitting to the truth of God. Jesus reminded them that "those who exalt themselves will be humbled, and those who humble themselves will be exalted" (Matthew 23:12). The doors to their hearts were closed. But whoever embraces the truth and continues to pursue it will always give it a warm welcome.

> Here I am! I stand at the door and knock. If anyone hears my voice and opens the door, I will come in and eat with that person, and they with me. (Revelation 3:20)

Our response to Jesus is nothing less than our response to the truth. Just as we opened up to the truth at the beginning of our Christian lives, so John urges us to continue opening up to it as we live in fellowship with Christ.

Contemporary Implications

When we respond to Jesus' invitation by embracing the truth, we are adopted into the family of God. We are part of a new community, the body of Christ. Each of us needs everyone else for the body to function well. We encourage and support one another as we work side by side to advance the fantastic news of new life in Christ. There is no room for individualism or pride (1 Corinthians 12:15–26). Instead, we are to imitate Jesus himself, who gave himself for us all by humbling himself to the point of death on a cross.

> Dear friend, do not imitate what is evil but what is good. Anyone who does what is good is from God. Anyone who does what is evil has not seen God. (3 John 11)

In our lives, we should be hospitable to the good and inhospitable to evil. Diotrephes had forgotten that his only boast should have been that he had fellowship with the Lord (1 Corinthians 1:31). He had forgotten that he had been made part of a body in which each member belongs to all the others (Romans 12:5). He had forgotten that he should not put any stumbling block or obstacle in the path of a brother or sister (Romans 14:13), but instead should be doing what he could to build up the brothers and sisters (Romans 15:1–3). He had taken his eyes off of Christ. Gaius had kept his focus. Let's press forward with Gaius.

Hook Questions

- How do you choose your friends? What does every believer have in common with every other believer? Can unbelievers see that commonality? Do you regard agreeing with you as the same thing as agreeing with the truth? Do you still welcome the truth?
- What would cause you *not* to associate with someone else? Do you regard any brother or sister in Christ as an enemy?

Before we were Christians, we defined ourselves by our possessions, our careers, our authority—anything by which we could make a name for ourselves. That was our only hope for significance. Now that we have fellowship with the Father and the Son, our significance comes from the one whose name is above every name (Philippians 2:9). It is easy, if we're not careful, to slip back into old patterns, even in the church. But John reminds us to keep pressing forward on the way of truth—to keep knocking on doors. And he also reminds us to do what we can to help our brothers and sisters along that way as we "work together for the truth" (3 John 8).

Secure in Love

It seems that every few months or so we are warned about a new computer virus that we must guard against. The virus passes itself off as a legitimate website or email attachment, but when we access it, our files are compromised and our computers crash. Jude, the half brother of Jesus (Matthew 13:35), writes to warn believers of a similar virus. It passes itself off as legitimate biblical truth, but if it is accepted, our faith will be compromised and our effective witness to Christ will crash. This letter is an alert regarding this new danger, as well as guidance for successful virus protection.

Theme of the Book

God warns his people against those who encourage them to view his grace as a license to sin.

The virus Jude warns against gains access to believers' hard drives by appealing to a genuine truth: God is gracious and forgives sin. The destructive effect of this virus is realized in the devious and immoral way this truth is applied. It was being claimed by those seeking to inflict spiritual harm to unwary believers that since God graciously forgives sin, we are free to sin with impunity as much as and however we want (v. 4).

Of course, the fatal omission in this logic is the lack of any mention of Jesus Christ. Those who receive God's gracious forgiveness of sin do so by their faith in the atoning sacrifice of Jesus Christ—an amazing demonstration of God's love (Romans 5:8). These true believers are then led by the indwelling Spirit of Christ to become like him (v. 19). True believers seek, by the power of the Spirit, to reciprocate God's love for them by their loving service to him. The lifestyle promoted by those who have introduced their faith-damaging virus only highlights the absence of the Holy Spirit in their lives.

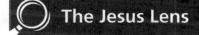

Memory Passage: *Jude 19*

> These are the people who divide you, who follow mere natural instincts and do not have the Spirit.

The antivirus protection that Jude urges believers to activate against these troublemakers is seen in the first and last verses that bracket this letter. In the first verse, Jude describes believers as those "loved in God the Father and *kept* for Jesus Christ." In the last two verses, Jude gives glory to God, through Jesus Christ our Lord, who is able *to keep* believers from being victimized by faith-viruses. The key words in these verses are "keep/kept," "God," and "Jesus Christ." By these words Jude reminds believers whose faith is under attack that they are kept secure by the love of God himself through their faith in Jesus Christ. Christians are reminded once again to keep their lives focused on Jesus Christ, the source, protector, and object of their faith.

The Jesus Lens

The loving care and security that Jesus provides for those who put their faith in him he describes with the image of a shepherd who lays down his life for his sheep, to protect them from thieves and robbers who come intending "to steal and kill and destroy" (John 10:8, 10–11). This image is in stark contrast to the kind of shepherds Jude describes, for whom death and darkness had been reserved, and who are trying to lead believers to the same deadly place (Jude 12–13). Those in Jesus' flock rest secure in his protective, pastoral care. They recognize his voice and follow his leading, directly into eternal life.

> My sheep listen to my voice; I know them, and they follow me. I give them eternal life, and they shall never perish; no one will snatch them out of my hand. (John 10:27–28)

Jesus is the good shepherd, who guards his sheep from those who try to steal them away. It might be a little unnerving to realize that there are those who are trying to snatch us out of God's hand. But God's hand is an almighty hand. We are kept secure in God's love by the power of God himself.

Contemporary Implications

In the midst of all the radio chatter and static of those who "reject authority and heap abuse on celestial beings" (v. 8), "slander whatever they do not understand" (v. 10), grumble, find fault, boast, and flatter (v. 16), it may be difficult for us to tune into God's voice. Yet we have his voice available to us in the written Word, and we can avoid many problems if we pay more attention to it (2 Peter 1:19). And we respond to that voice with our own words and behavior. As we come to know God better by dialoguing with him in this way, our defenses against potential viruses will be built up. This is what Jude encourages believers to do in order to keep themselves in God's love.

> But you, dear friends, by building yourselves up in your most holy faith and praying in the Holy Spirit, keep yourselves in God's love as you wait for the mercy of our Lord Jesus Christ to bring you to eternal life. (Jude 20–21)

We keep ourselves in God's love when we jump into the deep end of the full, vibrant, energizing life he desires for us and has provided through Jesus Christ. When we embrace that life through faith in our Lord and by our Spirit-empowered imitation of him, we will come to know more fully the desperate, relentless love that led God to give his own Son for our salvation and to secure our relationship with him forever.

Hook Questions

- What do you do when your faith is threatened? Does your faith ultimately depend on you or on God? How do we access the security of God's love in the midst of faith-threatening circumstances?

- How do you know when your faith is being threatened? How would you know if your faith has been compromised by a theological virus? How do you gauge the strength of your relationship with God?

We sometimes forget that Jesus leads us on the way of life in the security of his care and protection (John 14:6). As believers, we can be grateful that we are not left to find our way through the confusing streets and back roads of life by our own understanding. Along the way there will be many thieves and robbers who claim to have the directions we need. But their advice will only lead us to dead-end alleys, where muggers are waiting. Jude reminds us that we have a good shepherd who guides us, and we recognize his voice. It's the same voice we responded to at the beginning of our Christian lives. As we continue to trust in him and listen to his voice, he will guide our steps and keep us secure in his love. If we occasionally get a little lost along the way, it's okay to ask him for directions. We'll find that he has been guiding and guarding our progress the whole time.

Once again God's people are under attack. With faith-wearying regularity, punctuated only occasionally by periods of peace, throughout its history the forces of opposition have crashed against the walls of the church. One might begin to wonder how long the walls can withstand such a battering. It would appear to be much easier for believers if they would simply make greater efforts to blend into the culture by compromising their faith.

The apostle John ends the New Testament with his fifth inspired composition—an encouragement to believers to hold on tight to their faith during the storm of persecution intensifying against them. John himself has experienced that persecution and writes this letter to them from exile on the island of Patmos (1:9), a Roman penal colony off the coast of Asia Minor. He reminds believers that though evil may seem to be winning the day, God is still in control, and the ultimate victory over sin and its cancerous consequences belongs to Jesus Christ, the Lamb of God, and to all those who put their faith in him.

 Theme of the Book

God enables his people to stand fast against Satan and his forces until God brings about the ultimate and sure victory.

The book of Revelation describes the ultimate triumphant outcome for all who put their faith in Jesus Christ, as well as the disastrous outcome for all who oppose God and his people. Perhaps to protect believers in case this writing came to the attention of their oppressors, John describes these outcomes in highly symbolic language. It is this often enigmatic symbolism that has been the cause of so much disagreement among interpreters and theologians. What, exactly, do all the symbols mean? When will these things happen, and in what order?

Though these specifics are hotly debated among Christians and probably will continue to be so as long as at least two Christians exist, there can be no question about the double-edged message of the book: (1) God will completely destroy everything opposed to him and his people (17:1 – 18:24), and (2) God will bring about complete victory for Jesus Christ and those who trust in him (19:1 – 21). This end will be ultimately realized when Jesus comes again, this time in unmistakable divine power and glory. These truths provide great comfort and encouragement for Christians at any time in history, but especially during times of persecution.

Memory Passage: *Revelation 21:6 – 7*

It is done. I am the Alpha and the Omega, the Beginning and the End. To the thirsty I will give water without cost from the spring of the water of life. Those who are victorious will inherit all this, and I will be their God and they will be my children.

The Bible opens with the removal of humanity from Eden as a consequence of the infestation of sin in God's good creation, and it ends with the repatriation of humanity into a new Eden as a consequence of the eradication of sin from God's good creation. Because there will then be no relationship-impeding sin, believers of all nations will live in closest fellowship with the Lord (21:3; 22:4). And because the corrosive effects of sin will be removed from creation itself (Romans 8:19 – 21), there will be no more death or mourning or crying or pain (Revelation 21:4). All things will be renewed in a new heaven and a new earth scrubbed sparkling clean of every stain, healed of every scar, and rid of every shadow by the light of the glory of God (21:1, 23). Flowing from the throne of God and the Lamb in the center of this new creation will be the river of the water of life (22:1 – 2). With this image, John draws the attention of believers back to the one who provides this life even now.

It is the same image used by Jesus to refer to himself when he discussed eternal life with a Samaritan woman by Jacob's well (John 4:4–26).

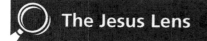

The Jesus Lens

In John's vision, it is the Lamb who accomplishes salvation. He is the one who gives the water of life to those who are thirsty for it (21:6; 22:17). He is the one who by his blood has "purchased for God persons from every tribe and language and people and nation" (5:9). The New Testament leaves no doubt that this Lamb is Jesus Christ (John 1:36; 1 Corinthians 5:7; 1 Peter 1:19), who brings near the "kingdom of heaven" (Matthew 3:2; 10:7).

Though Jesus was seemingly overpowered by evil, God was still in control, accomplishing his redemptive purposes by the exercise of his divine power. In an unambiguous demonstration of that divine power, Jesus rose victorious over sin and death and now reigns forever (11:15). Those who, by the power of the Holy Spirit, follow him faithfully into suffering will continue to follow him into victory over sin and death and will reign together with him forever (5:10; 22:5) when he establishes his rule in all its grand fullness over the entire earth (11:15).

> For he [Christ] must reign until he has put all his enemies under his feet. (1 Corinthians 15:25)

The persecuted believers throughout the ages have asked the same question: "How long, Sovereign Lord" (6:10)? All we are told is that he will come to enforce his rule when the gospel of the kingdom has been preached in the whole world (Matthew 24:14), and that it will be sooner rather than later (1:1; 2:16; 3:11; 6:11; 22:6, 7, 10, 12, 20). All those who are trusting in Christ will not be disappointed (Romans 5:5) but will share in his victory (21:7).

Contemporary Implications

There is an already/not yet character to the victory of the Lamb. He is now at the right hand of the Father, "far above all rule and authority, power and dominion, and every name that is invoked, not only in the present age but also in the one to come" (Ephesians 1:21). And those who put their faith in him are more than conquerors through him (Romans 8:37). Yet we often don't feel much like conquerors. Our victory is *already* secured forever through our risen Lord, but it is *not yet* fully realized. We still live with the ruinous effects of sin. But just as surely as the Lamb who was slain is worthy to reign, so shall all of us who put our faith in him.

> You are worthy to take the scroll
>   and to open its seals,
> because you were slain,
>   and with your blood you purchased for God
>   persons from every tribe and language and people and nation.
> You have made them to be a kingdom and priests to serve our God,
>   and they will reign on the earth. (Revelation 5:9–10)

Consequently, though we may in fact still mourn the consequences of sin in our own lives and in the lives of others, we don't do so as those who have no hope (1 Thessalonians 4:13). Jesus Christ is our hope (Colossians 1:27; 1 Timothy 1:1), and he is a living hope (1 Peter 1:3). And "if we hope for what we do not yet have, we wait for it patiently" (Romans 8:25). In the meantime, John's words to the seven churches should guide our lives (2:1–3:22). We should persevere and not grow weary, be faithful even to the point of death, and keep the fire of our faith well stoked.

Hook Questions

- What gives you strength when evil seems overwhelming?
- What might God say in a letter to *your* congregation?
- Are you thirsty for the Lord's return? Or are you fairly content with the way things are now?

We don't like delays. It is hard enough to wait for something better when there is nothing going wrong. It is extremely difficult to wait for it when lots of things are going wrong. We know God was in control at the beginning of history, and we trust that he will be in control at the end of history. After all, he is the Alpha and the Omega, the Beginning and the End (1:8; 21:6; 22:13). We have a harder time with the middle.

But God is in control of the middle too, even when everything suggests otherwise. He is the Almighty, "who is, and who was, and who is to come" (1:8). Jesus reigns now, and he has already begun the transformation from sin and death to the health and life that will characterize the new heavens and the new earth under his rule. The transformation has already occurred in every believer. All of creation is next.

FROM BIBLICAL BOOK TO CONTEMPORARY HOOK

BIBLICAL BOOK	THEME	CHRIST-FOCUS	IMPLICATIONS	HOOK
Genesis *Separation for Blessing*	*God separates out one through whom he would bless all nations.*	Christ is the one through whom God would bless the nations (Acts 4:12).	As Christ's ambassadors, we are "separated out" with the task of blessing others with the good news of God's salvation in Jesus Christ (2 Corinthians 5:18–20).	In what ways has God equipped you to be a blessing to other people? Are Christians a blessing to you? What can you do to make yourself a clearer message of the good news of Jesus Christ to those around you?
Exodus *Deliverance into Presence*	*God delivers his people from slavery into his presence.*	In Christ, God delivers his people from slavery to sin into fellowship with him (Romans 7:21–25).	We can trust in God's saving power to deliver us from sin's grip and into his saving presence (Romans 5:9–10).	Does the fact that you are a Christian feel like a burden (something to be delivered from) or deliverance? Do you feel like you're in the grip of God, or of sin?
Leviticus *Life in God's Presence*	*God instructs his people how to live in his presence.*	The holiness of Christ admits us into God's holy presence (Hebrews 7:27).	We must grow in the grace and knowledge of our Lord and Savior Jesus Christ as we live in God's presence (2 Peter 3:11–18).	Are you cultivating a life of holiness? What does such a life look like today?
Numbers *Promised Rest*	*God chastens his disobedient people but reaffirms his intent to bring them into the Promised Land.*	Because Christ bore the penalty for our sin, we may enter into God's promised rest (Hebrews 4:3).	We must let God's discipline guide us to the peace and rest he intends for us (Hebrews 12:5–11).	In what ways have you already begun to know God's rest? What is keeping you from knowing God's rest more fully?
Deuteronomy *Instruction*	*God gives Moses instructions for the second generation of Israel regarding faithful living in the Promised Land.*	Christ perfectly fulfills the law, and so secures our relationship with God (Matthew 5:17).	We may now serve God confidently in the power of the Spirit of the one who fulfills the law, without fear of the penalty of the law (Romans 7:4–6).	What drives your relationship with God, fear or gratitude? Whose effort secures your relationship with God?

BIBLICAL BOOK	THEME	CHRIST-FOCUS	IMPLICATIONS	HOOK
Joshua *Victorious Rest*	God uses Joshua to lead his people to victorious rest in the Promised Land.	Christ brings his people victory over the challenges of this life (John 16:33).	We are able to realize victorious rest even now in the face of the challenges of this life through the power of him who loves us (1 Peter 1:3–5).	What battles are you fighting today? Where do you look for strength? What counts as victory?
Judges *Rebellion and Rescue*	God raises up judges to rescue his errant people from the consequences of their rebellion.	God raised up Christ, the ultimate judge, to rescue us from our sin and its consequences (1 Corinthians 15:55–57).	By the power of the Spirit of Christ, we may count ourselves dead to sin but alive to God in Christ Jesus (Romans 6:11–14).	Are you overcoming the world, or do you feel as if it is overcoming you? In what areas are you most in need of divine rescue?
Ruth *Empty to Full*	God uses Ruth and Boaz to fill Naomi's emptiness by providing her with food and a son.	God became flesh in order to be our guardian-redeemer and provide us with fullness of life (John 10:10).	We can embrace the fullness of life in Christ (Ephesians 3:14–21).	Are the things you are relying on for fulfillment only leaving you empty instead? Is your Christ-card maxed out?
1 & 2 Samuel *Exalted and Humbled*	God exalts the weak and humbles the proud.	God has exalted the humbled Christ (Philippians 2:5–11).	We should serve God in humility while we await our exaltation in Christ (James 4:10; 1 Peter 5:6).	What have you bragged about lately? Does the source of your pride focus on God, or on yourself?
1 & 2 Kings *Turning Away*	God expels Israel and Judah from his presence in the Promised Land when their kings turn away from Torah.	God turns away from Jesus on the cross as judgment against those who have turned away from him (Romans 3:10–12; Matthew 27:45–46).	We need to rely on God's strength and the encouragement of each other to keep from turning away from the path of life (Hebrews 3:12–13).	What is your "rule of life"? What are you more likely to do; what you know is right or what you want to do at the time? What are you doing to guard against turning away from God?
1 & 2 Chronicles *Encouragement*	God encourages postexilic Israel by means of an account of Davidic kings who acknowledge the Lord's rule.	God encourages us by means of an account of Jesus, in the line of David, who has perfectly done all that the Father has commanded (Revelation 5:5).	Be encouraged by the fact that Christ has perfectly kept the covenant and accomplished our salvation (Romans 10:4).	Are you good enough for heaven? How do you acknowledge the Lord's rule in your own circumstances?

BIBLICAL BOOK	THEME	CHRIST-FOCUS	IMPLICATIONS	HOOK
Ezra *Temple Restoration*	*God brings the exiles back to Jerusalem and directs that his temple be rebuilt.*	Through Christ, God is building a living temple (Ephesians 2:19–22).	Let us join God's construction crew (1 Corinthians 3:10–17).	What are you building with your life? What kind of life does this building demand?
Nehemiah *Distinctions*	*God moves the returned exiles to rebuild the wall of Jerusalem.*	Christ's true home (and that of his disciples) is not of this world (John 17:14–15).	Let the world see what it means to be distinctively Christian (2 Corinthians 6:14–7:1).	What difference does your relationship with Christ make in your marriage, friendships, career, student life, or entertainment choices? Is there a visible distinction between your life and that of an unbeliever?
Esther *Providential Deliverance*	*God providentially provides Esther and Mordecai to bring Israel deliverance from her enemies.*	The Father provides Christ to deliver his people "when the set time had fully come" (Galatians 4:4–5).	As Christ's ambassadors, we have been providentially provided to proclaim deliverance through him to those who are perishing (2 Corinthians 5:20).	What does it mean to be Christ's ambassador? How could you be an agent of God's deliverance in the place where he has put you?
Job *God and Suffering*	*God is active in areas and realms beyond our understanding.*	Christ gives us the ultimate picture of the righteous sufferer as he accomplishes God's saving purposes (1 Peter 3:18).	We can believe that God is with us even during the hard times, just as he was with his own Son (1 Peter 4:12–19).	Where is God when it hurts? When things go the way you want, does that mean God is blessing you?
Psalms *Lament and Praise*	*God the Great King provides the words of lament and praise that are appropriate responses to him.*	Christ is the embodiment and means for our appropriate response to the Great King (Colossians 1:15–18).	We can talk to God about everything as we grow in the unbreakable relationship with the Father that Jesus has secured for us (Philippians 4:6–7).	Is your faith strong enough for you to be honest with God? Is there room in your faith community for you to express these feelings? What is your motivation for prayer?
Proverbs *Wise Order*	*God has placed an order in creation to which we should pay attention in order to live wisely.*	Christ shows us what it means to live wisely (1 Corinthians 1:30).	We become wise when we let our lives be transformed by Christ's Spirit (Romans 12:2).	How do we go about developing the wisdom that finds its fulfillment in Christ? Is it foolish to live according to biblical guidelines in today's world?

BIBLICAL BOOK	THEME	CHRIST-FOCUS	IMPLICATIONS	HOOK
Ecclesiastes *Life Purpose*	*God prompts the Teacher to question the purpose of life.*	In Christ alone is found meaning, purpose, and direction in life (John 14:6).	Let us look for life's purpose in the eternal truths that God has revealed in Christ (Colossians 2:2–3).	Why should we bother drawing in another breath? Where can we go to find out about the true life revealed in Jesus Christ?
Song of Songs *Love*	*God depicts intimate human love as a gift and also as a key to understanding his own love for his people.*	Christ demonstrates what God's love looks like (Romans 5:8).	Let others see Christ's love by our love for one another (John 13:34–35).	Does our love for God or for each other look anything like God's sacrificial love for us? How would an unbeliever recognize the love of God in you?
Isaiah *Divine Presence*	*The Holy One of Israel challenges his people to respond appropriately to his presence among them.*	Jesus is Immanuel, God's presence with us (Matthew 1:23).	The Spirit of Christ is present within us and enables us to respond to our King with grateful service (Hebrews 9:14).	Do our lives of service to God challenge people around us with his presence? Is God served and are people spiritually challenged by your Facebook page?
Jeremiah *New Covenant*	*God promises his people a new covenant beyond the necessary exile.*	Jesus accomplishes the new covenant at the cost of his blood (Luke 22:20).	Our new covenant relationship with God is unbreakable in Christ (Romans 8:32–39).	Is God's love for you conditional? Are you more demanding than God is of yourself or others?
Lamentations *Comfort in Cataclysm*	*God's loving compassion and faithfulness are present even during the cataclysmic destruction of Jerusalem.*	The faithful presence of the Spirit of Christ comforts us in any trouble (John 14:26–27).	The comfort we receive from God enables us to comfort others (2 Corinthians 1:3–5).	Where do you find your security and comfort in life? Are you as compassionate with others as God has been with you?
Ezekiel *Life from God*	*God's presence is the key to life.*	Life is found in Jesus Christ (John 1:4).	Let us keep our eyes focused on Christ, who is our life (Colossians 3:1–4).	Does your focus enrich your life or deplete it? Does your life point others toward the source of life?
Daniel *Cosmic Authority*	*God asserts his authority over human kingdoms.*	Jesus has divine authority over all things in heaven and on earth (Matthew 28:18).	Our kingdom service flows from, and is strengthened by, the limitless power and authority of God (1 Peter 4:11).	Are you embarrassed to speak the truth? Do you trust your source?

BIBLICAL BOOK	THEME	CHRIST-FOCUS	IMPLICATIONS	HOOK
Hosea *Divine Faithfulness*	*A faithful God contends with his unfaithful people.*	Jesus' faithfulness makes the church a faithful bride (Revelation 19:7–8).	We may take comfort in knowing that the faithfulness of Christ is counted as our own (1 Thessalonians 5:23–24).	Are any of us faithful? Is our Lord ever unfaithful? Are we trying to become more like our faithful Lord, with the strength he himself provides by his Spirit?
Joel *Day of the Lord*	*The day of the Lord is coming and brings judgment before restoration.*	Jesus will return to judge the living and the dead (Matthew 25:31–32, 46).	We may look forward to the day of Christ's return with confidence that he has paid the price for our sin (1 Thessalonians 5:1–11).	Why should a righteous judge not find us guilty? Do you regard painful experiences in your own life as divine judgment?
Amos *God's Justice*	*God judges his people for their social injustice.*	Jesus demonstrates God's compassion, mercy, and justice (Matthew 9:35–36).	As those called to Christ-likeness, our behavior should communicate truth about God's compassion, mercy, and justice (Matthew 25:31–46.	How do others see God's compassion, mercy, and justice by your behavior? Have you given false testimony? Do you regard social justice as what you must do, or how you must be?
Obadiah *God's Vengeance*	*God will avenge Edom's mistreatment of Israel.*	Jesus, the true Israel, did not take matters into his own hands when he was mistreated, but rather waited patiently for God to avenge the injustice (1 Peter 2:21–23).	Entrust your life to Christ and his justice (Romans 12:17–21).	Whom do you trust more to judge fairly, yourself or God? What is the problem with taking matters into your own hands?

BIBLICAL BOOK	THEME	CHRIST-FOCUS	IMPLICATIONS	HOOK
Jonah *Extended Compassion*	*The Sovereign Lord's compassion extends beyond Israel.*	Jesus is the good shepherd, who gathers his sheep near and far (John 10:14–17).	Let us clothe ourselves with the compassion of Christ as we spread his good news to those near and far (Colossians 3:12–17).	What does your life say about God's compassion? What should God's compassion look like in your circumstances? Do you push yourself to extend to those who are different from you (perhaps even hostile to you) the good news of the compassion of God in Jesus Christ?
Micah *Justice and Mercy*	*God will punish his rebellious people, but promises future salvation.*	Jesus bears our judgment so that we can experience God's mercy (1 Peter 3:18).	Christ died for us so that by his Spirit we may live for him, practicing justice and mercy (2 Corinthians 5:15).	Are you carrying around a load of guilt? What is the motivation for your life, fear or gratitude?
Nahum *Judge of All*	*The Lord is sovereign over all and will judge Nineveh.*	God has raised up Jesus to be the righteous Judge of the living and the dead (Acts 10:42).	The righteous Judge bore our judgment himself, so that we are free to serve him without fear (1 Thessalonians 1:9–10).	Why should God not judge us for our offenses against him? Who ultimately calls the shots in our lives?
Habakkuk *Comfort in God*	*God is my only comfort in life and in death in a world of seemingly unchecked evil.*	Jesus offers true comfort and rest to those who come to him (Matthew 11:28).	In any trouble, we may find comfort in God and in his care for us (1 Peter 5:7).	When things go wrong, where do you turn for comfort? Do you really believe that God knows what he is doing?
Zephaniah *Coming Judgment*	*God announces to Judah the approaching day of the Lord.*	The Son of Man is coming to judge (Acts 17:31).	Let's encourage one another to live in the light of Christ's imminent return (1 John 2:28).	Do you look forward to the Lord's return, or fear it? In what will you take confidence in the coming day of judgment?

BIBLICAL BOOK	THEME	CHRIST-FOCUS	IMPLICATIONS	HOOK
Haggai *Priority of God*	*God directs his people to give priority to him and his house, and so to be blessed.*	Jesus' food was to do God's will and finish his work (John 4:34).	We can be confident that we will be blessed if we seek to serve God as our first priority (Matthew 6:33).	If you had only one day to live, what would you do? How would someone else see that God is the first priority in your life? What specific changes could you make in your life to be more actively engaged in building the Lord's house?
Zechariah *Temple Building*	*God uses apocalyptic, eschatological imagery to encourage his people to complete the rebuilding of the temple.*	Jesus is the ultimate temple in which God's presence dwells with his people (John 1:14; 2:19).	We join in the building of God's new temple as we seek to expand the church by the Spirit's power (1 Corinthians 3:16).	In the building of God's new temple, are you a craftsman builder or a construction-site gofer? What kind of building materials should we use for this new temple? Where do we get them?
Malachi *Honor God*	*When he comes to judge, God will spare those who honor him.*	The Father honors Jesus, who honored him with faithful service (Hebrews 3:2–6).	By the power of the Spirit of Christ, we must strive to honor God with our lives (John 12:26; 1 Corinthians 6:19–20).	Does your life bring honor to God? What have you consciously done today to bring honor to God?
Matthew *Torah Fulfillment*	*Jesus is the new Moses who reinterprets Torah.*	Jesus fulfills the Torah of Moses (Matthew 5:17–20).	Our faith in Christ satisfies the demands of Torah (Romans 10:4–13).	Are you a good person? How good is good enough? Is there any use for the law of God in a Christian's life today?
Mark *Suffering Servant*	*Jesus is the suffering Son of Man.*	God became flesh in Christ to suffer for our sakes (Acts 26:22–23).	We should be ready to suffer as a consequence of our faith in Jesus Christ and our service to him (Philippians 1:29).	Do hard times cause you to question your faith? How does suffering fit with your understanding of salvation and service?
Luke *Costly Saving*	*The Son of Man came to seek and to save what was lost.*	Jesus came to give life to sinners (Luke 22:19–20).	With the strength God provides, we must be ready to endure hardship to bring the gospel to the lost (2 Timothy 2:1–10).	How much would you pay for your salvation? Has your faith cost you anything? How much would you be willing to pay for someone else's salvation?

BIBLICAL BOOK	THEME	CHRIST-FOCUS	IMPLICATIONS	HOOK
John *Union with God*	*Jesus, the Word, is God.*	Jesus and the Father are one (John 10:30).	We have union with the Father through Jesus Christ (John 17:20–23).	How close do you feel to God? How closely do people associate you with God? How does your union with God affect your behavior?
Acts *Witness*	*God expands and empowers his church through his Spirit.*	The Spirit of the risen Christ empowers witness about him (Mark 1:17).	Let the Spirit of the risen Christ empower our witness to the gospel (2 Timothy 1:7–8).	When was the last time you told someone the good news of salvation in Christ? Is the effectiveness of your witness of Christ ultimately up to you?
Romans *Death to Life*	*Through Christ, God brings his chosen ones from death to life.*	Jesus died to sin and lives for the glory of God (Romans 6:10).	We have died to sin through the death of Christ, and through the resurrection of Christ we live for God's glory (Romans 6:11).	What harmful habits are you having a hard time kicking? What is standing in your way to a more fulfilling life?
1 Corinthians *Maturing*	*God gives guidance to the spiritually gifted but immature Corinthian church.*	Jesus shows us that Christian maturity is other-focused, not self-focused (Ephesians 4:11–13).	Let us grow in spiritual maturity by using our divinely bestowed gifts to build up the body of Christ (1 Corinthians 14:12).	Are you a mature Christian? How do you measure maturity?
2 Corinthians *Self-Giving*	*God directs Paul to explain and vindicate his apostolic authority while encouraging the generosity of the Corinthians church.*	Jesus gave himself completely for the welfare of his people (2 Corinthians 8:9).	God will provide for our needs as we give ourselves to others (2 Corinthians 9:6–11).	Is it really better to give than to receive? Is it possible for you to give any more than you have already received?
Galatians *Grace verses Legalism*	*God calls for rejecting the legalistic demands of the Judaizers and embracing the gospel of his grace.*	Christ redeemed us from the curse of the law so that by faith we could participate in the blessing given to Abraham (Galatians 3:13–14).	Let us live and serve in the joy of our freedom in Christ and not as slaves to the law (Galatians 5:1).	Do you think of yourself more as a human being or a human doing? If faithfulness to God in the New Covenant is not measured by obedience to the law, how is it measured?

BIBLICAL BOOK	THEME	CHRIST-FOCUS	IMPLICATIONS	HOOK
Ephesians *Shalom*	*God establishes the church as the firstfruits of his shalom.*	Christ is our peace (Ephesians 2:14).	In the strength of the Spirit, let us imitate Christ by working toward peace (Ephesians 4:2–3).	Do you know peace in your life? Do others see peace in your life? Where do you look for peace?
Philippians *Joy*	*God gives resurrection power and joy in the face of persecution and heresy.*	In the face of crucifixion, Jesus was sustained by the joy set before him (Hebrews 12:2).	We can be sure that God will give us strength, and even joy, in the midst of the challenges that will come (Philippians 4:13).	What are the people, things, or circumstances that bring you joy? Can those people, things, or circumstances change?
Colossians *Exalted Christ*	*God has exalted his Christ above all human wisdom and tradition.*	The Father himself has exalted his Son (Acts 5:31).	In the power and authority of the exalted Christ, let us serve him with gratitude and confidence (Colossians 2:9–10).	What is the most important thing in your life? What would other people say is the most important thing in your life? In what concrete way have you served the exalted Christ today?
1 & 2 Thessalonians *Fruitfulness*	*God empowers productive, godly lives as believers wait for the Lord's return.*	Jesus is the source of our fruitfulness (John 15:4).	Let us pray that God will cause our efforts in his name to bear fruit for the kingdom (2 Thessalonians 1:11).	Are you a productive, fruitful Christian? How do you measure fruitfulness? What could you do to become more fruitful?
1 Timothy *Truth verses Error*	*God encourages the (Ephesian) church in promoting the truth and opposing error.*	Just as Jesus revealed the truth about the Father, he charges and equips his followers to do the same (John 17:6–8, 17–18).	Let both our words and our actions promote truth and refute error (1 Timothy 4:11–12).	How do you distinguish truth from error? Which one does your life communicate more clearly? Which one does your congregation communicate more clearly? Are you willing and ready to stand for the truth?
2 Timothy *Loyalty*	*God appeals to Timothy and the churches to remain loyal to the gospel message in the face of persecution and error.*	In the face of persecution and error, Jesus remained faithful to the will of the Father (John 6:38).	Let us express our loyalty to Christ and the gospel message by learning and doing the will of the Father with the strength the Spirit provides (2 Timothy 1:13–14).	What truths are you willing to die for? What truths are you willing to live for?

BIBLICAL BOOK	THEME	CHRIST-FOCUS	IMPLICATIONS	HOOK
Titus *Transformational Truth*	*God provides instruction to a young church leader regarding defending, speaking, and living out the truth.*	The words of Jesus are true words of life (John 6:63).	Let us hold firmly to the truth so that we are equipped to defend and promote the message of life (Titus 1:9).	Where does one find truth? How does one effectively communicate truth in a world where falsehood has been made to appear more attractive?
Philemon *Brotherhood*	*God shows Philemon how his slave, Onesimus, has become a Christian brother.*	The Son of God himself calls us his brothers and sisters (Hebrews 2:11).	Our partnership in the faith should lead us to love one another as brothers and sisters (Philemon 6).	Do you regard all believers as your brothers and sisters? What if they're different than you? What are you willing to risk to bring brothers and sisters together?
Hebrews *Mediator*	*Christ is the ultimate revelation and mediator of God's gracious new relationship with his people.*	Jesus is the one who mediates to us the grace of our new relationship with God (Hebrews 9:15).	As we live in the grace of our new relationship with God, let us keep our eyes on Jesus, the one who mediates it to us (Hebrews 12:1–2).	Why does Jesus need to be our mediator? What is new about the new covenant? What are some practical ways to keep our focus on Christ?
James *Working Faith*	*God enables a life of good works that flow from a genuine faith.*	Jesus demonstrated the truth of his words by his works (John 10:25).	We must demonstrate the truth of our testimony about Christ by means of a corroborating life (James 1:22–25).	What does your faith look like? What could faith look like in your particular circumstances? What are you going to do about your faith?
1 Peter *Standing Firm*	*God equips struggling believers to stand firm in his grace as they live holy lives.*	Jesus shared in our humanity to free us from the power of sin so that by his strength we can stand firm in the face of trials and temptations (Hebrews 2:18).	We must stand firm in the grace God gives us to lead a holy life (1 Peter 4:19).	Is your Christian life on shaky ground? Where are you looking for help? Have you ever suffered for doing good?

BIBLICAL BOOK	THEME	CHRIST-FOCUS	IMPLICATIONS	HOOK
2 Peter *Holding on to Truth*	*God encourages believers in the security and grace of divine truth as they patiently await the Lord's return.*	Jesus himself resisted the devil's temptations by means of the word of God (Matthew 4:1–11).	Let us make every effort to know the truth so that we may be protected from error and grow in the grace that such knowledge brings (2 Peter 1:3–4).	Can you explain the basic truths of your faith to someone else? Can you defend those basic truths against attack? Do you question those basic truths?
1 John *Christlikeness*	*God calls those who believe in the divinity of the incarnate Christ to become like him.*	Jesus is the perfect human to whom all believers are being divinely conformed (Romans 8:29).	Whoever claims to have life in Christ should begin to behave like him (1 John 2:5–6).	Why does Jesus need to be human? Why does Jesus need to be divine? Whom do you try to model your life after? Why?
2 John *Opposing Error*	*God warns against showing hospitality to those who promote error.*	As the truth itself, Jesus warned his followers about those who promoted error (Mark 13:5).	By our words and our lives we must promote truth and oppose error (2 John 8).	What about your words or behavior promotes truth? What about your words or behavior promotes error?
3 John *Wise Hospitality*	*God inspires John to praise Gaius for his hospitality toward John's messengers and to condemn Diotrephes for his inhospitality toward them.*	Jesus invites those who recognize their need for him, not the self-righteous (Revelation 3:20).	In our lives, we should be hospitable to the good and inhospitable to evil (3 John 11).	How do you choose your friends? What would cause you not to associate with someone else?
Jude *Secure in Love*	*God warns his people against those who encourage them to view his grace as a license to sin.*	Jesus is the good shepherd, who guards his sheep from those who try to steal them away (John 10:26–30).	By God's love we are kept secure in the faith (Jude 20–21).	What do you do when your faith is threatened? How do you know when your faith is being threatened?
Revelation *Ultimate Victory*	*God enables his people to stand fast against Satan and his forces until God brings about the ultimate and sure victory.*	The crucified Christ rose victorious over sin and death, and will destroy all dominion, authority, and power other than God's (1 Corinthians 15:20–28).	We are able to stand firm in God's strength until he brings about the ultimate victory for us through Jesus Christ (Revelation 5:9–10).	What gives you strength when evil seems overwhelming? What might God say in a letter to your congregation? Are you thirsty for the Lord's return?